BIRDS OF PREY

Terrifying Talons

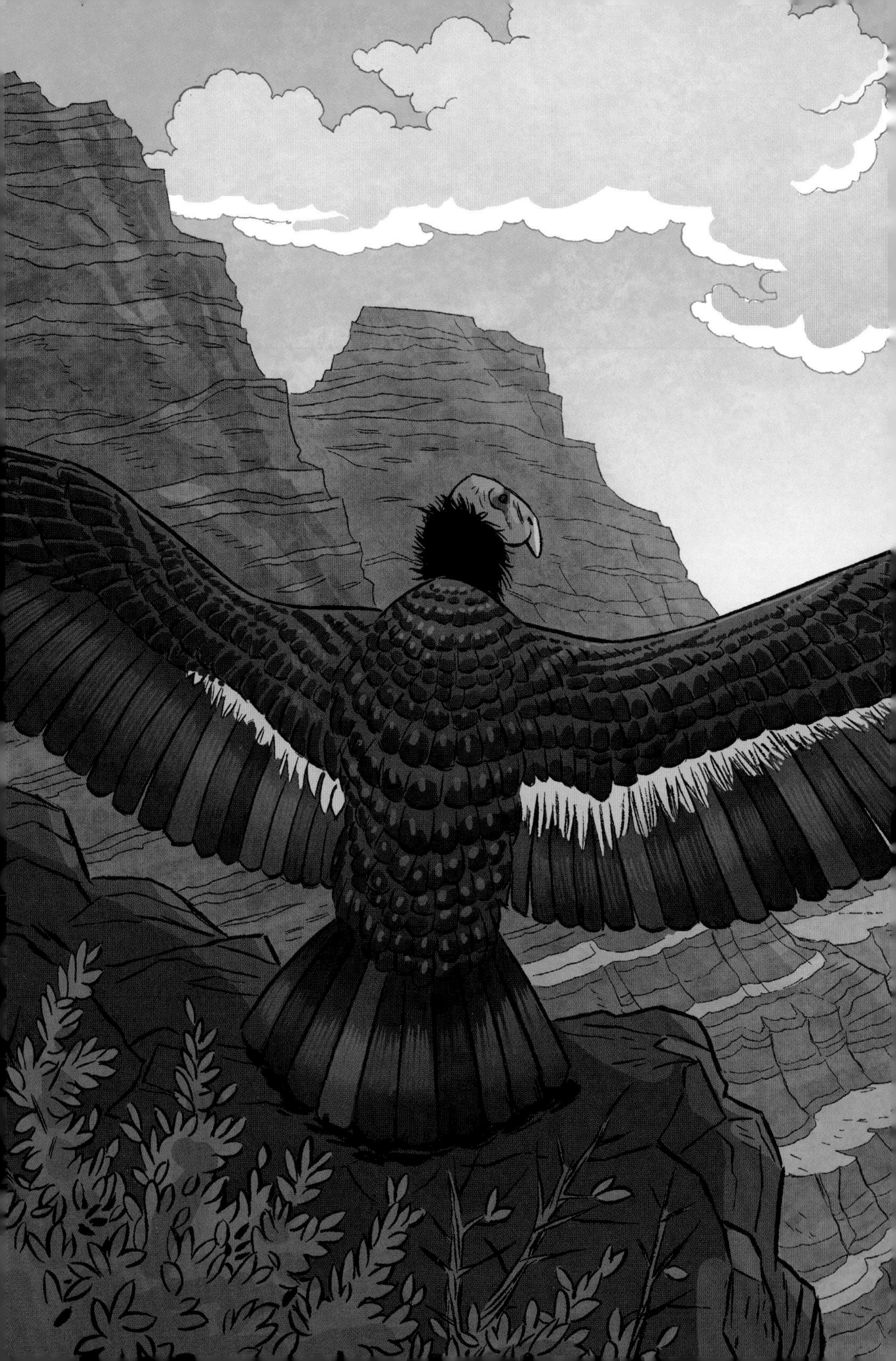

BIRDS OF PREY

Terrifying Talons

Joe Flood

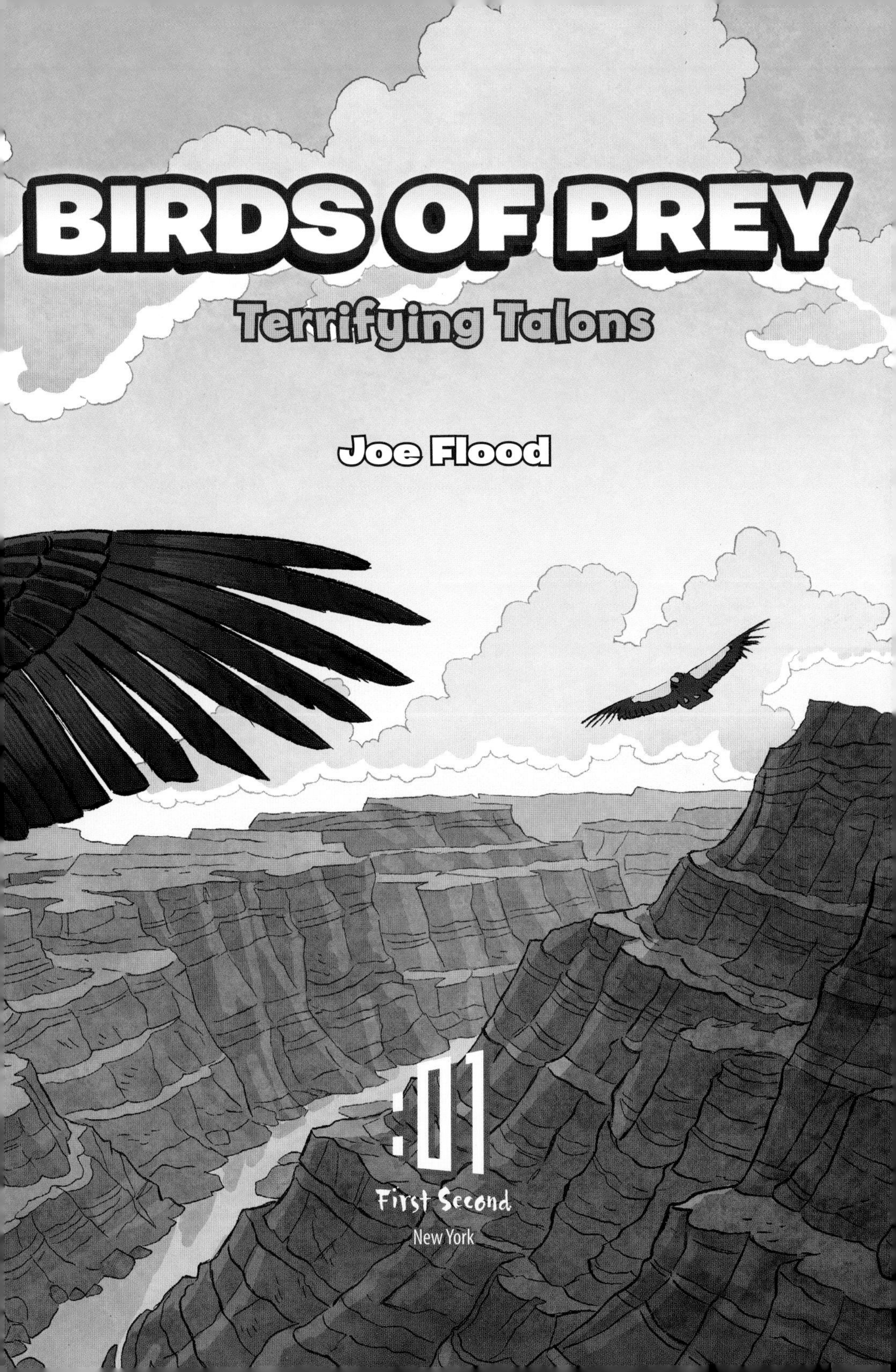

First Second
New York

Special thanks to David Spillo, wildlife caretaker at Green Chimneys in Brewster, NY, and master falconer James Eyring. You both care for some amazing raptors—thank you for letting me meet them and draw them in person.

—JF

First Second

Published by First Second
First Second is an imprint of Roaring Brook Press,
a division of Holtzbrinck Publishing Holdings Limited Partnership
120 Broadway, New York, NY 10271
firstsecondbooks.com
mackids.com

Library of Congress Control Number: 2021941449

Our books may be purchased in bulk for promotional, educational, or business use. Please contact your local bookseller or the Macmillan Corporate and Premium Sales Department at (800) 221-7945 ext. 5442 or by email at MacmillanSpecialMarkets@macmillan.com.

First edition, 2022
Edited by Dave Roman
Cover design by Kirk Benshoff and Sunny Lee
Interior book design by Sunny Lee and Madeline Morales
Birds of prey consultant: David Bird

Drawn on two-ply vellum Strathmore 500 Series Bristol with blue color pencil lead in a Rotring 600 .07 mm mechanical pencil. Inked with Dr. Ph. Martin's Bombay India Ink using a Raphael 8408 size 1 sable brush and Nikko Maru pen nib. Colored digitally with a Wacom Cintiq and Adobe Photoshop.

Printed in March 2022 in China by Toppan Leefung Printing Ltd., Dongguan City, Guangdong Province

ISBN 978-1-250-26948-5 (paperback)
10 9 8 7 6 5 4 3 2 1

ISBN 978-1-250-26947-8 (hardcover)
10 9 8 7 6 5 4 3 2 1

Don't miss your next favorite book from First Second! For the latest updates go to firstsecondnewsletter.com and sign up for our enewsletter.

I saw my first bald eagle on an eighth-grade field trip to Maine. I have a memento of that sighting: a grainy black-and-white photograph of an out-of-focus speck. You can't tell it's a bird, much less an eagle! Seeing a bald eagle in 1977 was exciting because their populations were just beginning to rebound from DDT, an insecticide used worldwide that consequentially ended up poisoning birds. DDT caused birds to lay thin-shelled eggs that broke under the weight of the incubating parents, which led to a catastrophic population decline. The banning of DDT in 1972 heralded the return of raptors. Little did I know as a fourteen-year-old awestruck by an eagle that I would devote a career to studying these regal birds.

Raptors inhabit every continent except Antarctica, and my studies have taken me from the tundra of the North Pole to tropical seashores. Raptors come in a variety of sizes and shapes as they have adapted to different environments. In this book, you will learn about raptor anatomy and how sharp talons, strong beaks, and keen eyesight make them formidable predators. I have seen falcons catch ducks on the wing, found the remains of fawns in eagle nests, and watched ospreys submerge while diving for fish. To hunt, some raptors soar on broad wingspans wider than you are tall, while others flap vigorously on narrow, pointed wings no longer than the length of a shoe.

Those same wings carry raptors thousands of miles each year during spring and autumn migrations, thereby linking our planet's Northern and Southern Hemispheres. Each autumn, the peregrine falcons I studied in Greenland would travel down the east coast of Canada and the US. Arriving at the Gulf of Mexico, they would either fly partway across the Caribbean Sea to winter on islands like Cuba, or they would keep going, some all the way to Argentina. They would complete this 7,000-mile journey in just a few weeks. Then, a few months later, they would repeat the trip by heading north to breed on cliffs overlooking the tundra. Talk about frequent fliers! Peregrine falcons got their name from the long migrations they undertake. In some European languages, their common name translates as "wandering falcon."

How did we learn about the peregrinations of peregrines? We backpacked across the tundra wilderness for weeks to find nesting cliffs. Then we rappelled to the nests. Hanging on a rope hundreds of feet above the ground or over a fjord, with shrieking parents swooping by at lightning speed to protect their young, was a breathtaking thrill. Once safely at the aerie ledge, we attached a small aluminum band around each leg of the young falcons. A band bore a unique identifier, just like your Social Security number. If a banded peregrine was seen or found dead during migration, the band number and other information that had been stored in a national database would reveal its origin.

Each year, migrating raptors face countless challenges as they travel thousands of miles, and you are probably curious about how long they live. Longevity varies from only a few years for falcons to decades for condors. Researchers record the date and age of the raptors they band, so if a banded raptor is found years later, its life span is known. That's how I learned that two banded ospreys I encountered in Montana had reached the ripe old ages of fifteen and eighteen years old. The average life span of ospreys is half that, and what was truly remarkable about those two birds was that they were siblings! The long-lived sister and brother duo had the right stuff.

My first bald-eagle sighting was a rarity, but now hardly a day goes by when I don't see one soaring on thermals or perching on a shoreline tree. No matter where you live—in a city or in the country—you, too, can see raptors as they go about their lives, hunting, nesting, and migrating. The peregrine falcons I studied in the Arctic nested miles from the nearest village, but did you know that peregrines also nest on skyscrapers in major cities? Think about it; skyscrapers resemble cliffs near a rich source of prey: the hundreds of pigeons loitering around every city park. Harris's hawks are just as flexible—they nest in the outback of the southwestern desert and within cities like Tucson, Arizona. Ospreys and bald eagles nest and hunt along waterways across North America, often in proximity to humans. The list goes on . . . Raptors thrive if you and I give them a chance.

Keep reading and learning about raptors, and then grab a pair of binoculars and get outside! You might spy your first bald eagle, and if you're lucky, you will snap a quality photo with your smartphone. Who knows, perhaps a raptor research career that takes you up and down and around the world is in your future!

—Marco Restani
Professor Emeritus of Wildlife Ecology
St. Cloud State University

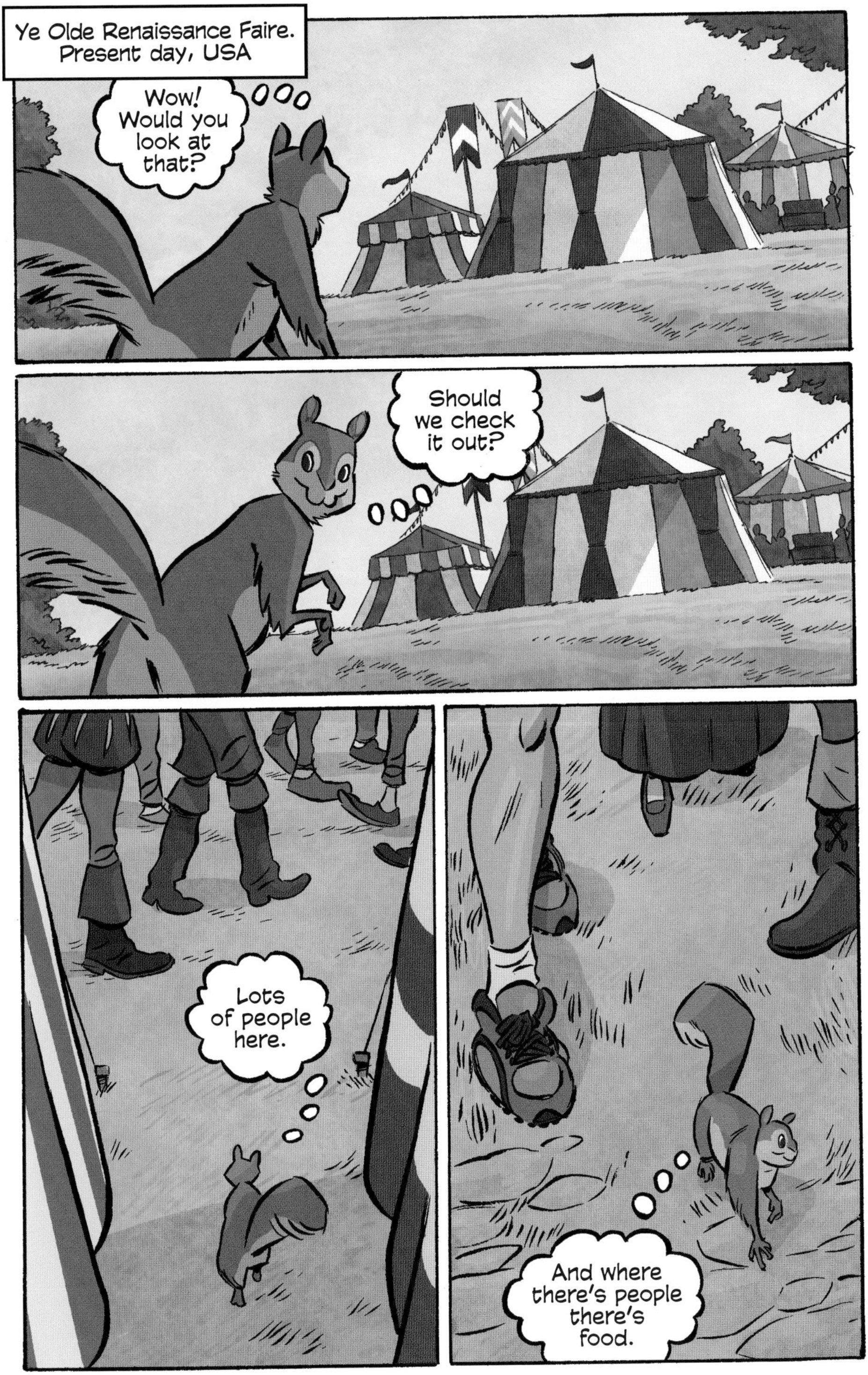
Ye Olde Renaissance Faire. Present day, USA
Wow! Would you look at that?
Should we check it out?
Lots of people here.
And where there's people there's food.

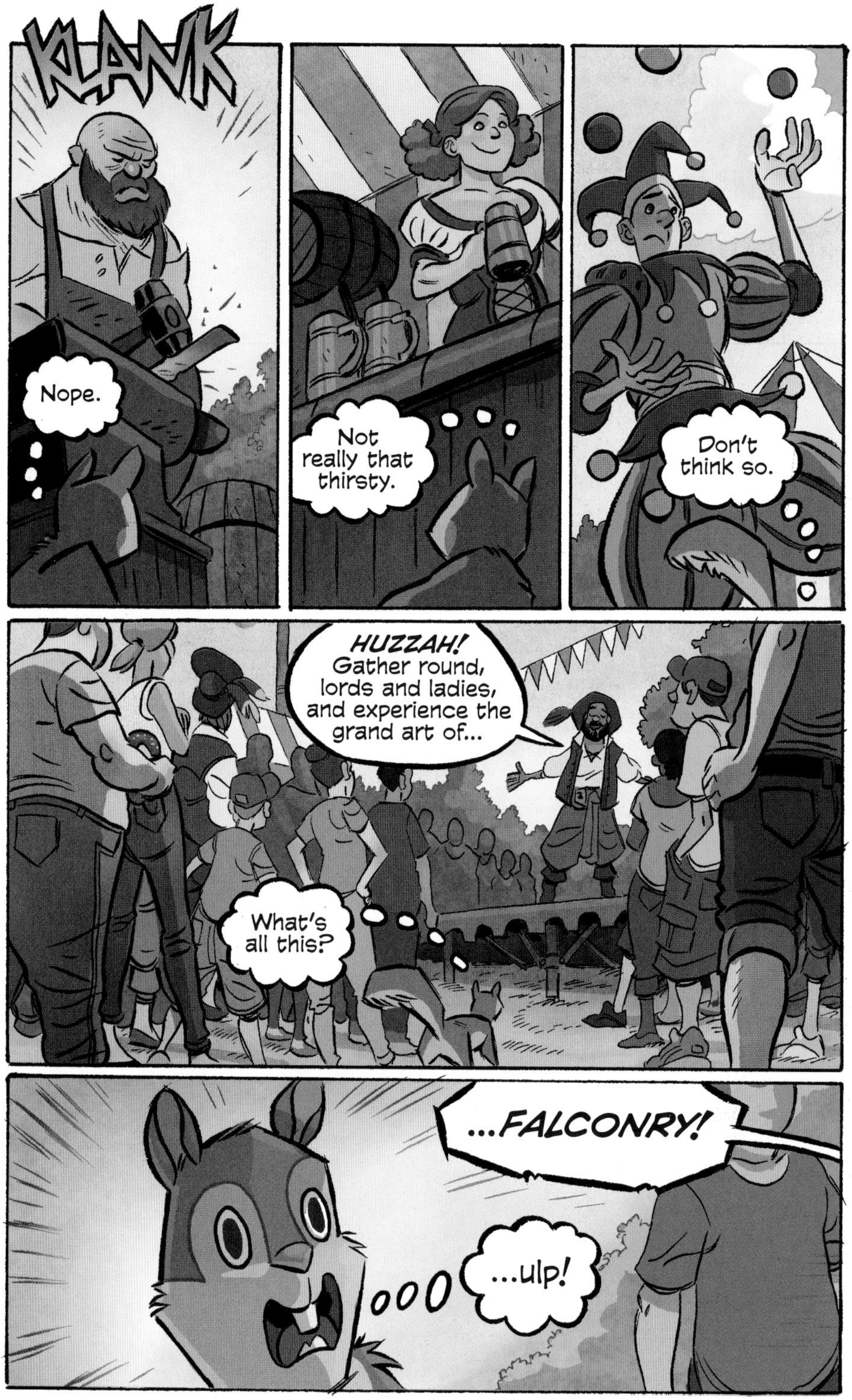
KLANK
Nope.
Not really that thirsty.
Don't think so.
HUZZAH! Gather round, lords and ladies, and experience the grand art of...
What's all this?
...FALCONRY!
...ulp!

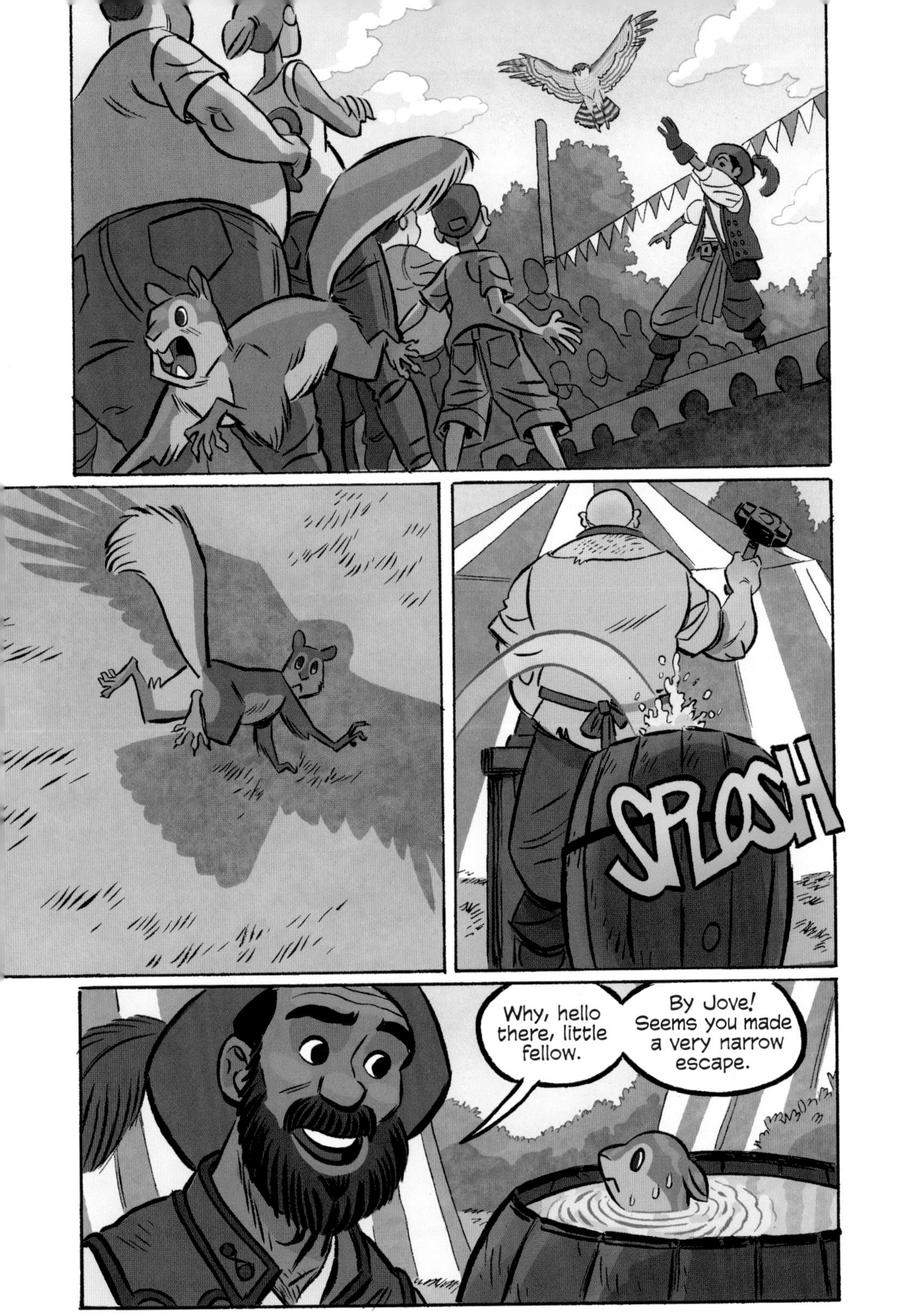
SPLOSH
Why, hello there, little fellow.
By Jove! Seems you made a very narrow escape.

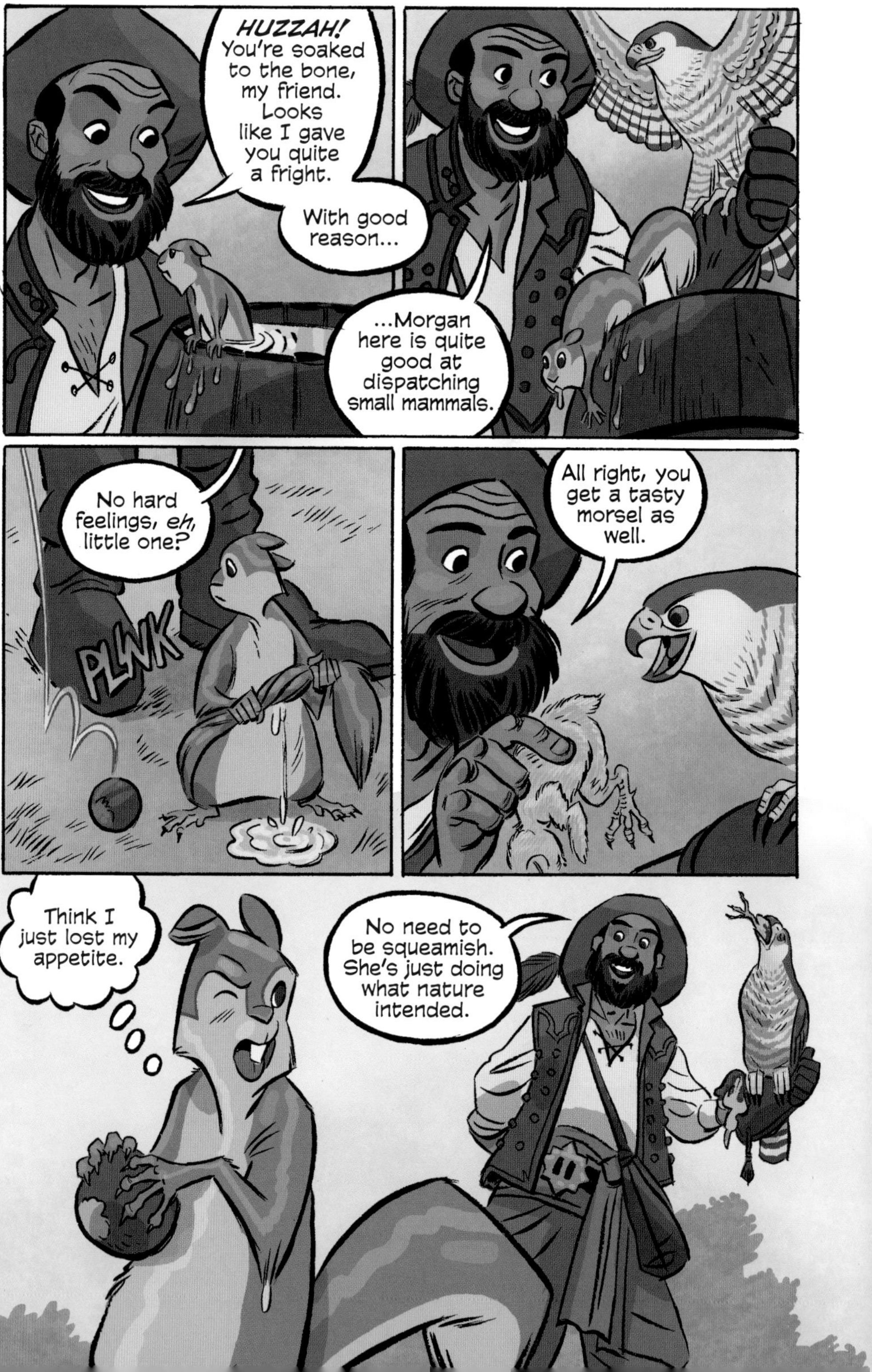
HUZZAH! You're soaked to the bone, my friend. Looks like I gave you quite a fright.
With good reason...
...Morgan here is quite good at dispatching small mammals.
No hard feelings, eh, little one?
PLNK
All right, you get a tasty morsel as well.
Think I just lost my appetite.
No need to be squeamish. She's just doing what nature intended.

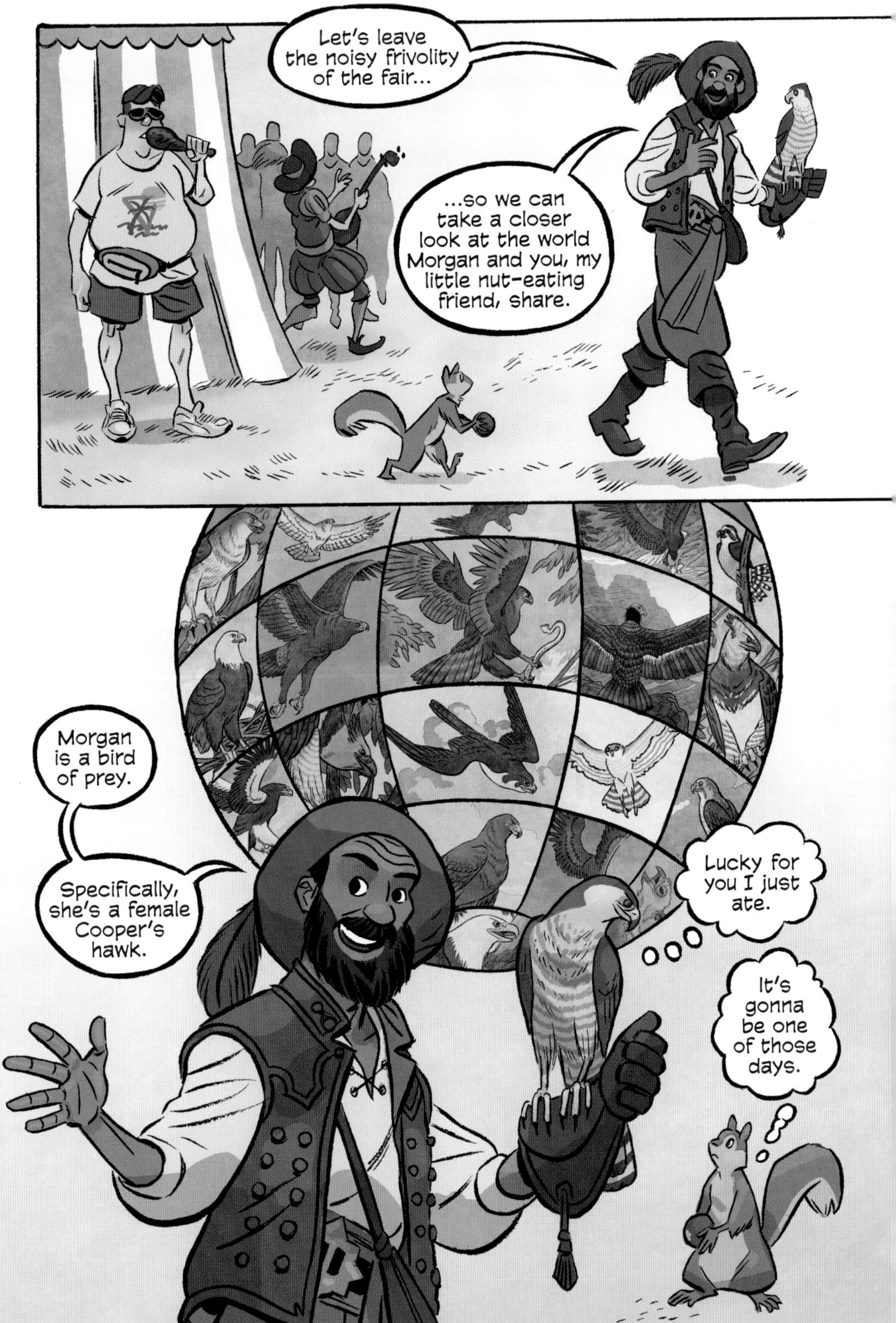
Let's leave the noisy frivolity of the fair...
...so we can take a closer look at the world Morgan and you, my little nut-eating friend, share.
Morgan is a bird of prey.
Specifically, she's a female Cooper's hawk.
Lucky for you I just ate.
It's gonna be one of those days.

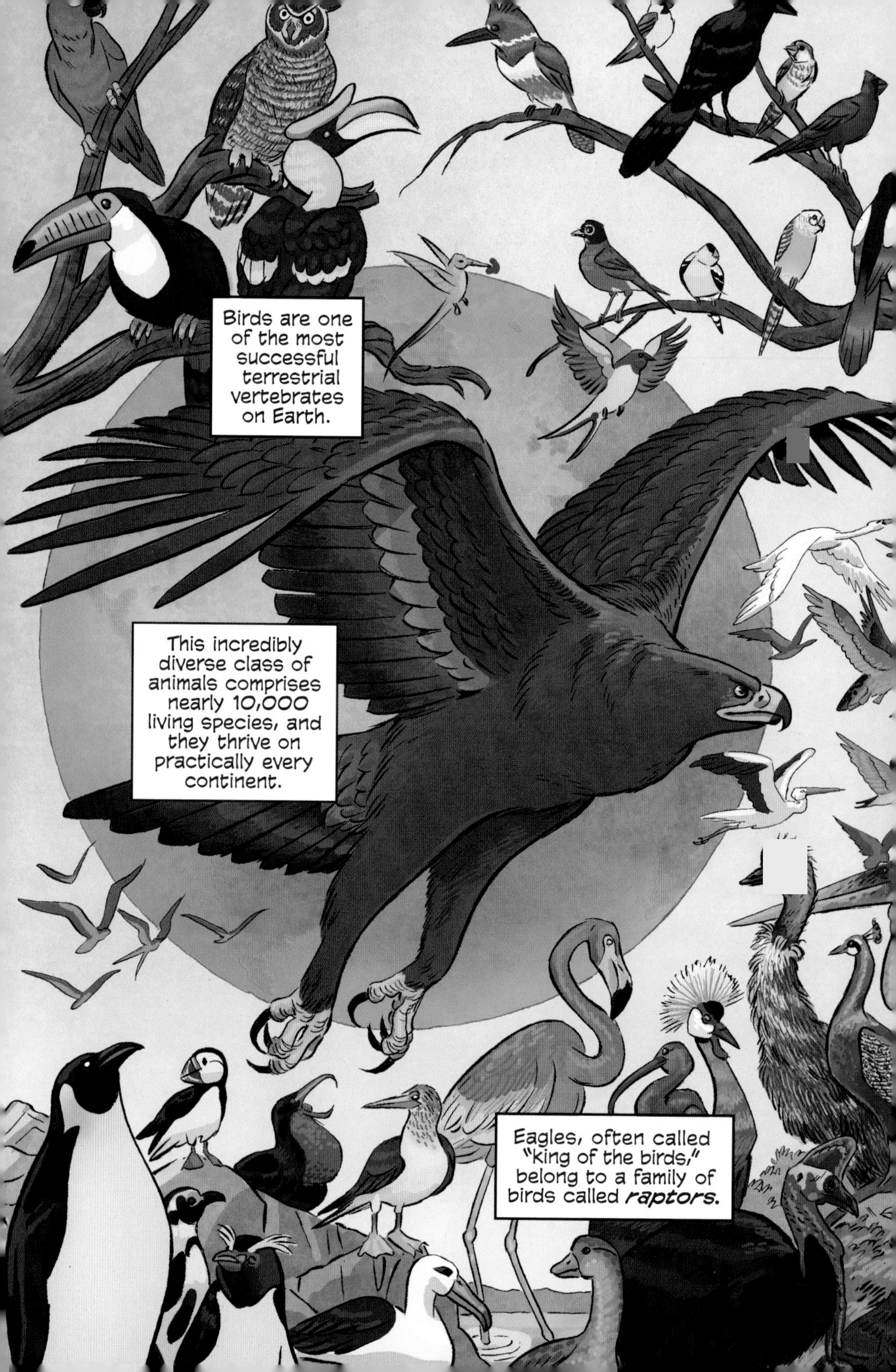
Birds are one of the most successful terrestrial vertebrates on Earth.
This incredibly diverse class of animals comprises nearly 10,000 living species, and they thrive on practically every continent.
Eagles, often called "king of the birds," belong to a family of birds called *raptors*.

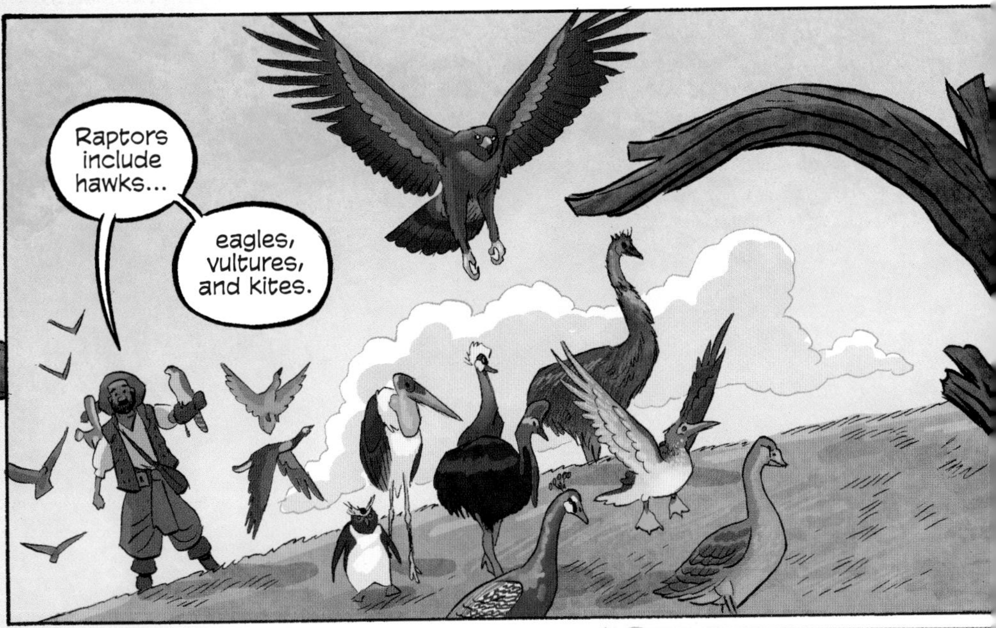

Raptors include hawks...
eagles, vultures, and kites.

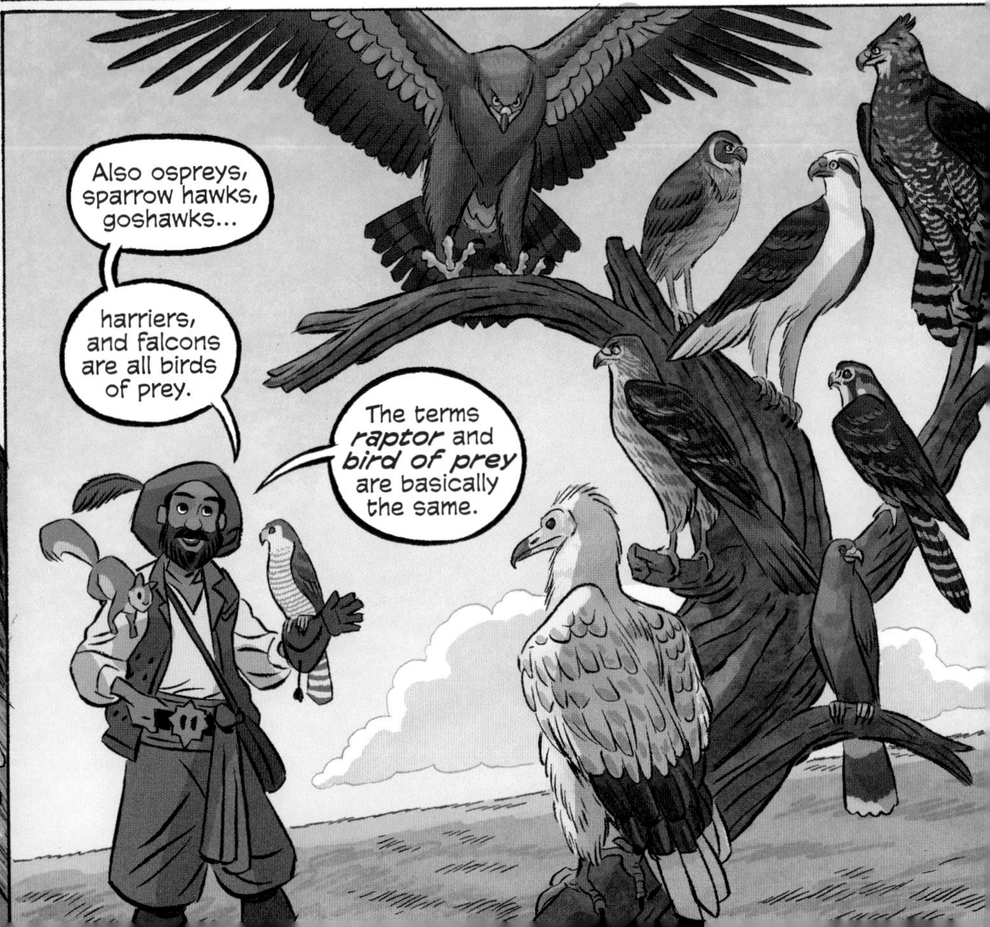

Also ospreys, sparrow hawks, goshawks...
harriers, and falcons are all birds of prey.
The terms ***raptor*** and ***bird of prey*** are basically the same.

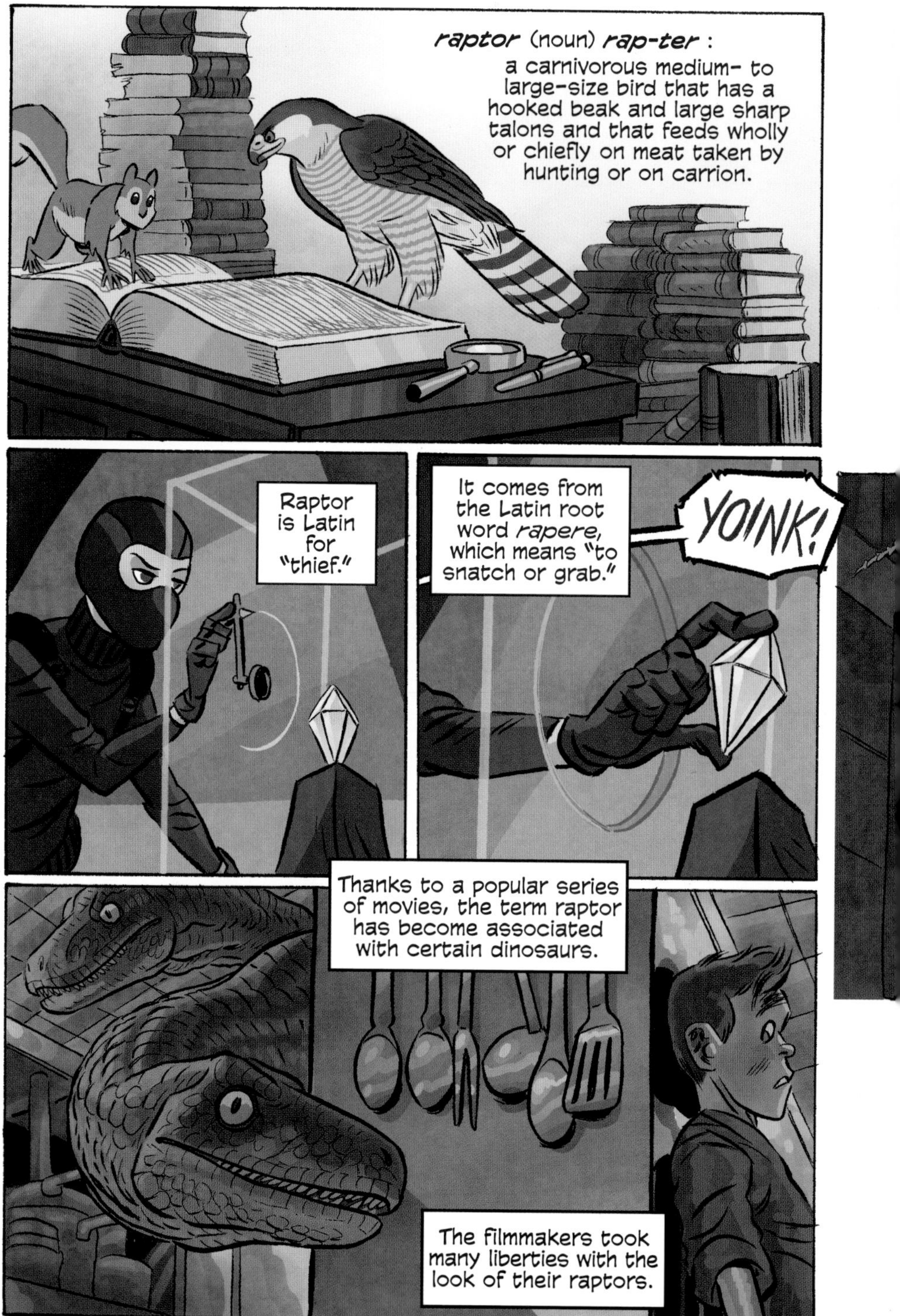
raptor (noun) *rap-ter* :
a carnivorous medium- to large-size bird that has a hooked beak and large sharp talons and that feeds wholly or chiefly on meat taken by hunting or on carrion.
Raptor is Latin for "thief."
It comes from the Latin root word *rapere*, which means "to snatch or grab."
YOINK!
Thanks to a popular series of movies, the term raptor has become associated with certain dinosaurs.
The filmmakers took many liberties with the look of their raptors.

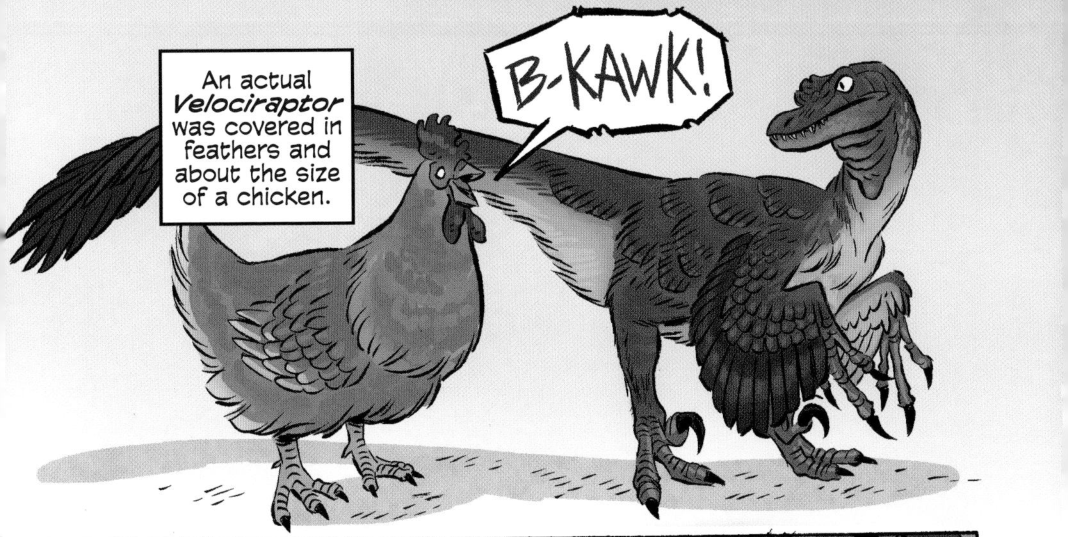
An actual *Velociraptor* was covered in feathers and about the size of a chicken.
B-KAWK!

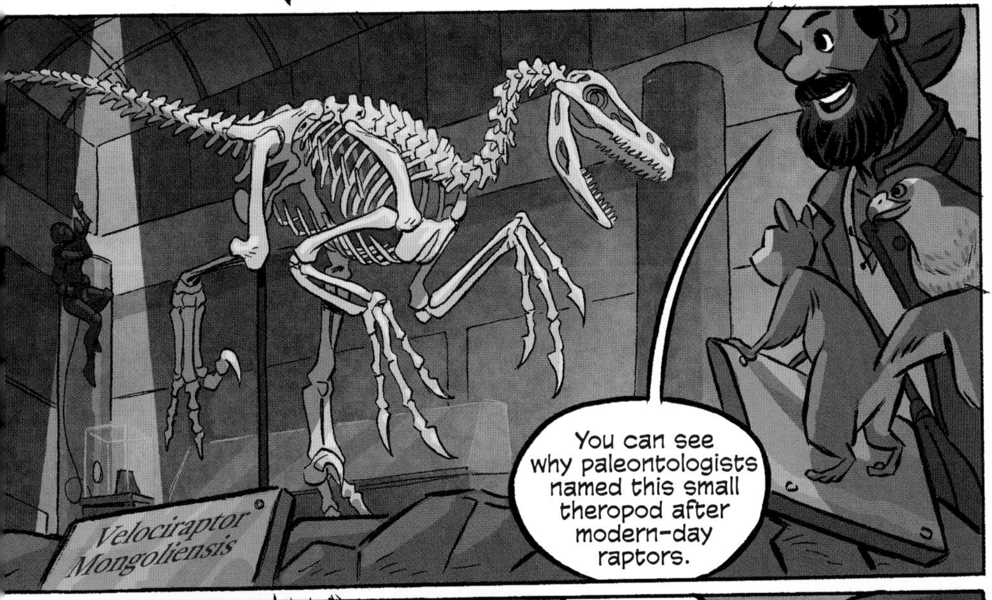
Velociraptor Mongoliensis
You can see why paleontologists named this small theropod after modern-day raptors.

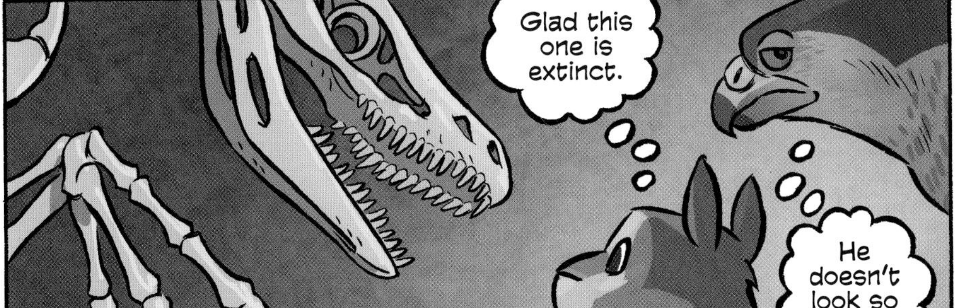
Glad this one is extinct.
He doesn't look so tough.

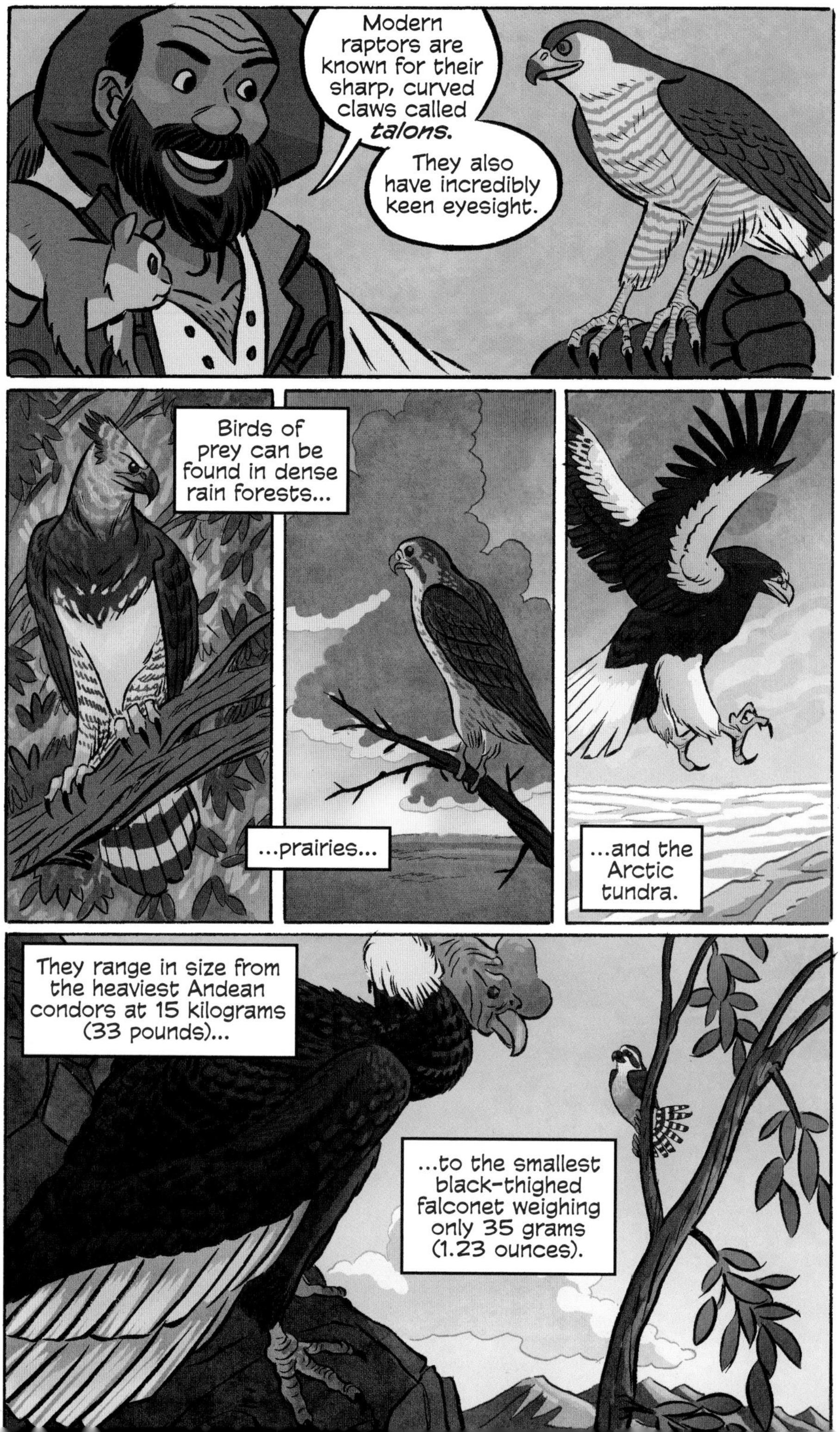
Modern raptors are known for their sharp, curved claws called *talons.*
They also have incredibly keen eyesight.
Birds of prey can be found in dense rain forests...
...prairies...
...and the Arctic tundra.
They range in size from the heaviest Andean condors at 15 kilograms (33 pounds)...
...to the smallest black-thighed falconet weighing only 35 grams (1.23 ounces).

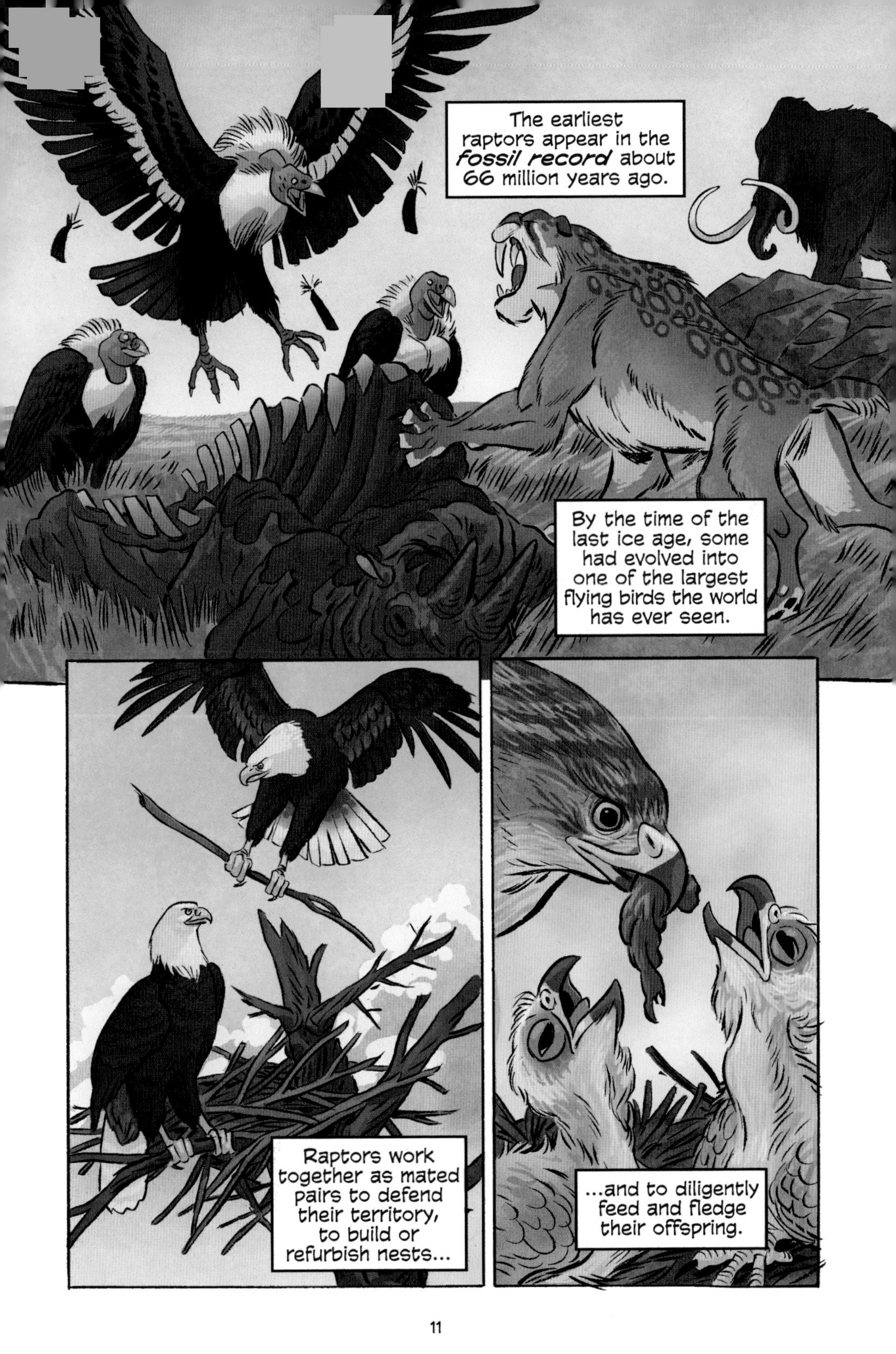
The earliest raptors appear in the *fossil record* about 66 million years ago.
By the time of the last ice age, some had evolved into one of the largest flying birds the world has ever seen.
Raptors work together as mated pairs to defend their territory, to build or refurbish nests...
...and to diligently feed and fledge their offspring.

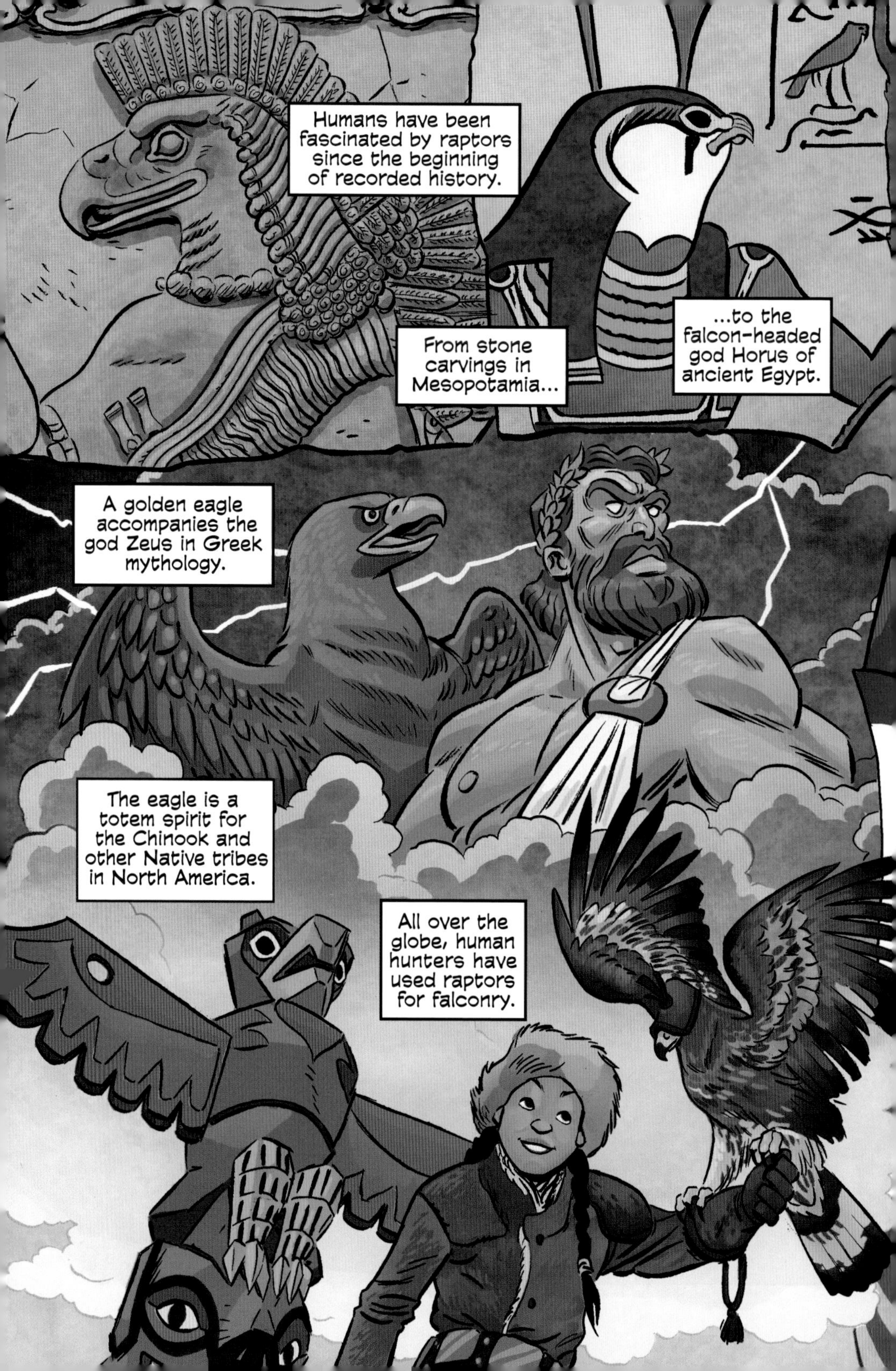
Humans have been fascinated by raptors since the beginning of recorded history.
From stone carvings in Mesopotamia...
...to the falcon-headed god Horus of ancient Egypt.
A golden eagle accompanies the god Zeus in Greek mythology.
The eagle is a totem spirit for the Chinook and other Native tribes in North America.
All over the globe, human hunters have used raptors for falconry.

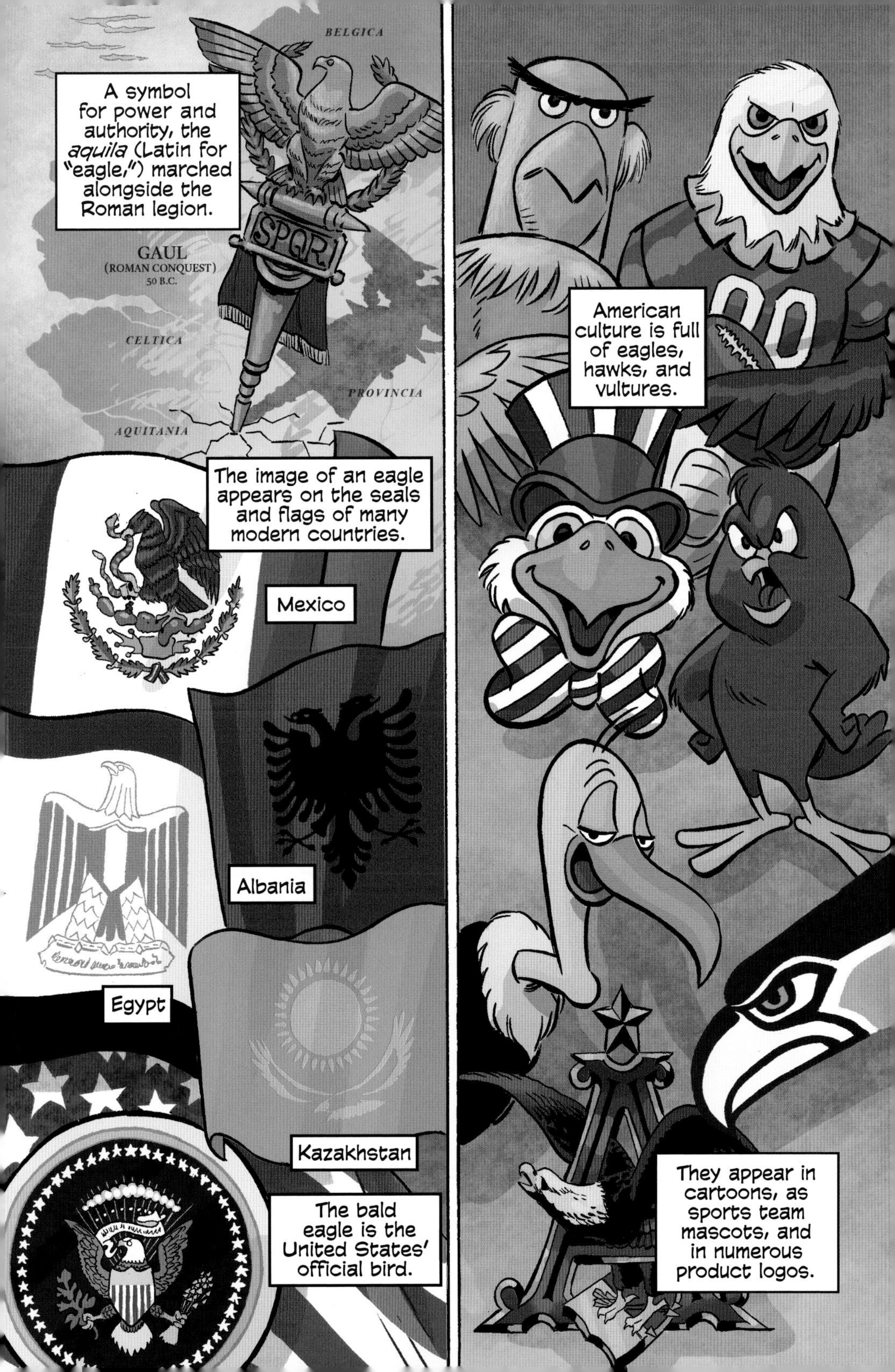
BELGICA
A symbol for power and authority, the *aquila* (Latin for "eagle,") marched alongside the Roman legion.
SPQR
GAUL
(ROMAN CONQUEST)
50 B.C.
CELTICA
PROVINCIA
AQUITANIA
The image of an eagle appears on the seals and flags of many modern countries.
Mexico
Albania
Egypt
Kazakhstan
The bald eagle is the United States' official bird.
American culture is full of eagles, hawks, and vultures.
00
They appear in cartoons, as sports team mascots, and in numerous product logos.

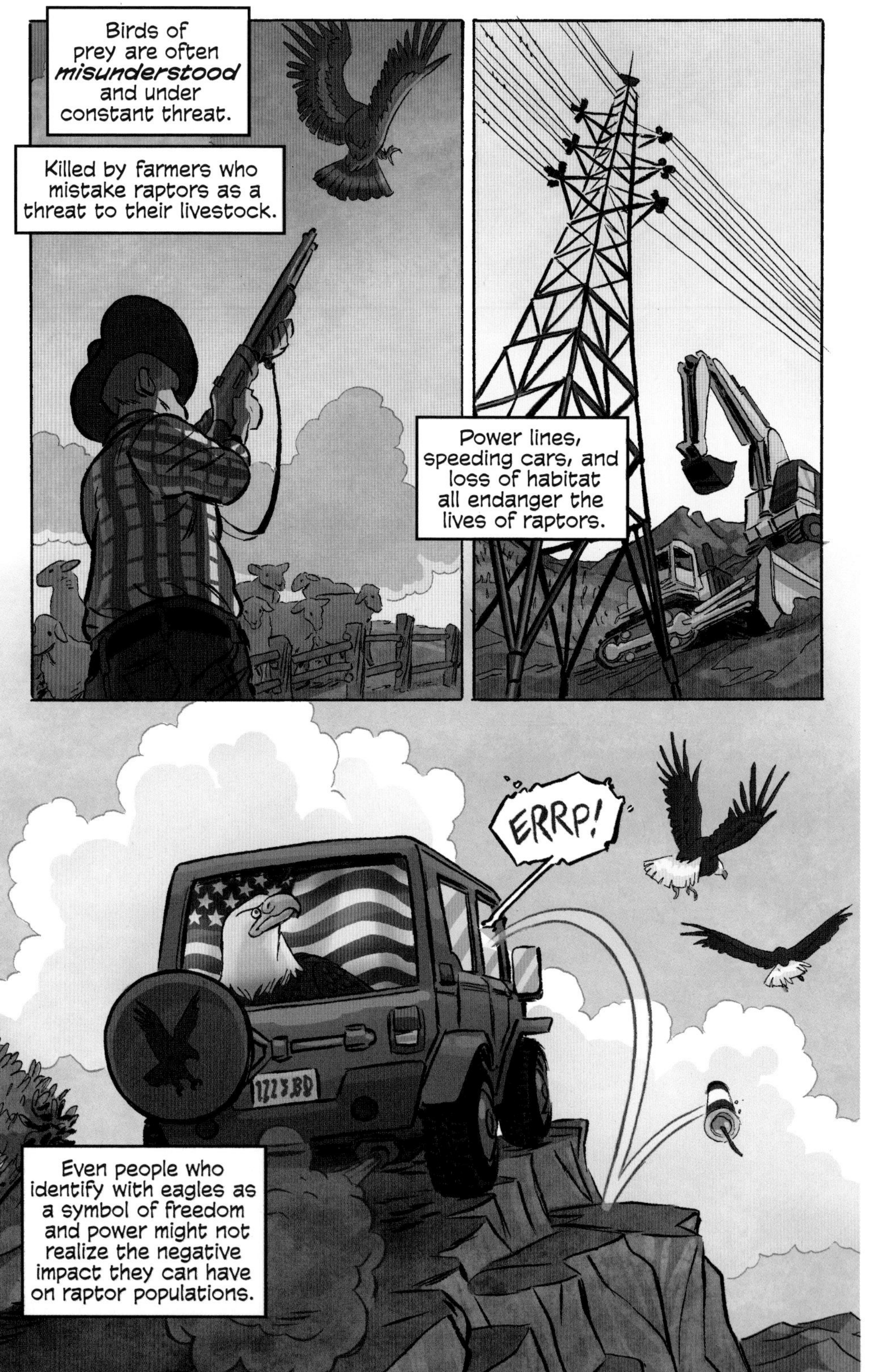
Birds of prey are often misunderstood and under constant threat.
Killed by farmers who mistake raptors as a threat to their livestock.
Power lines, speeding cars, and loss of habitat all endanger the lives of raptors.
ERRP!
Even people who identify with eagles as a symbol of freedom and power might not realize the negative impact they can have on raptor populations.

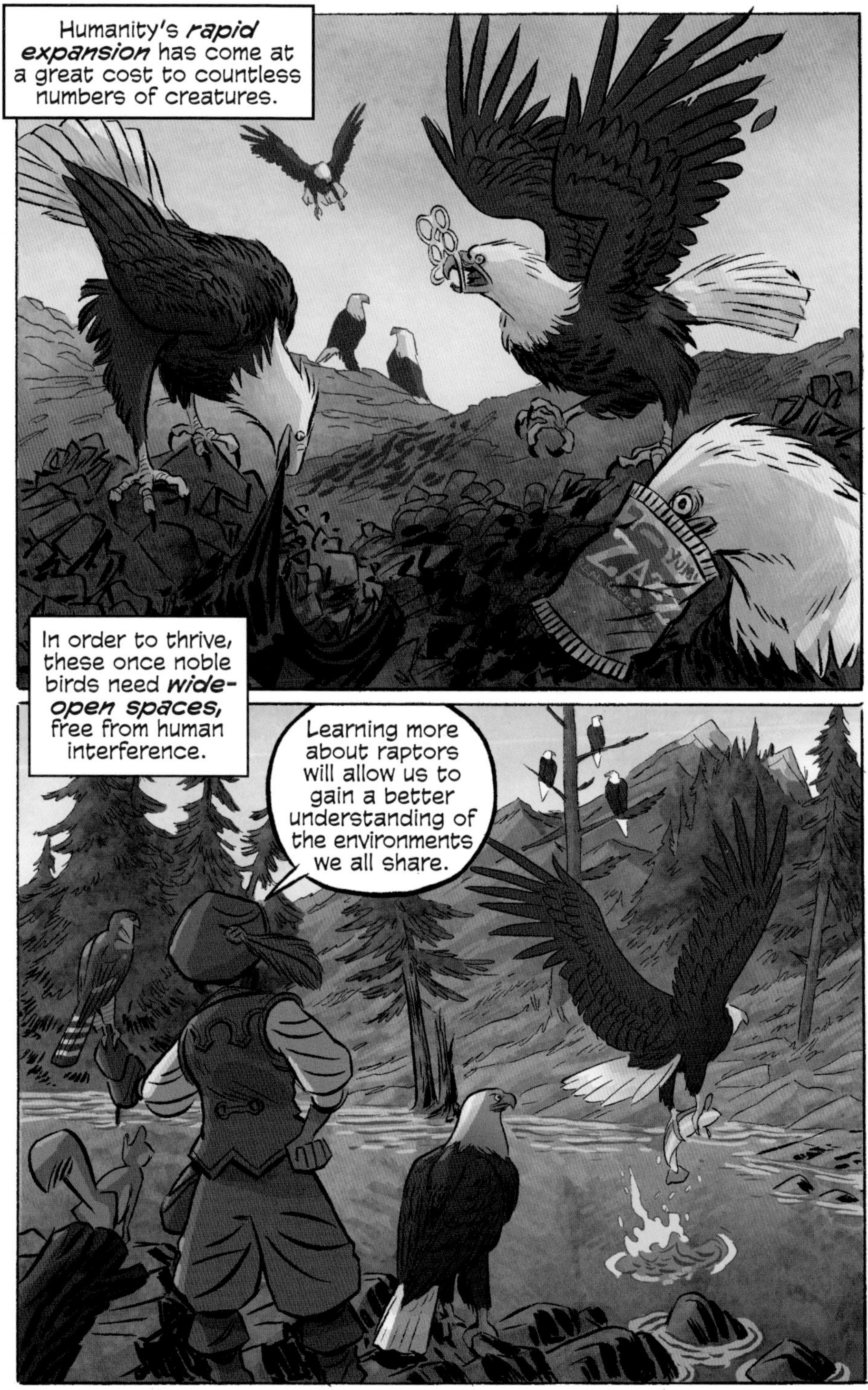
Humanity's *rapid expansion* has come at a great cost to countless numbers of creatures.
In order to thrive, these once noble birds need *wide-open spaces,* free from human interference.
Learning more about raptors will allow us to gain a better understanding of the environments we all share.

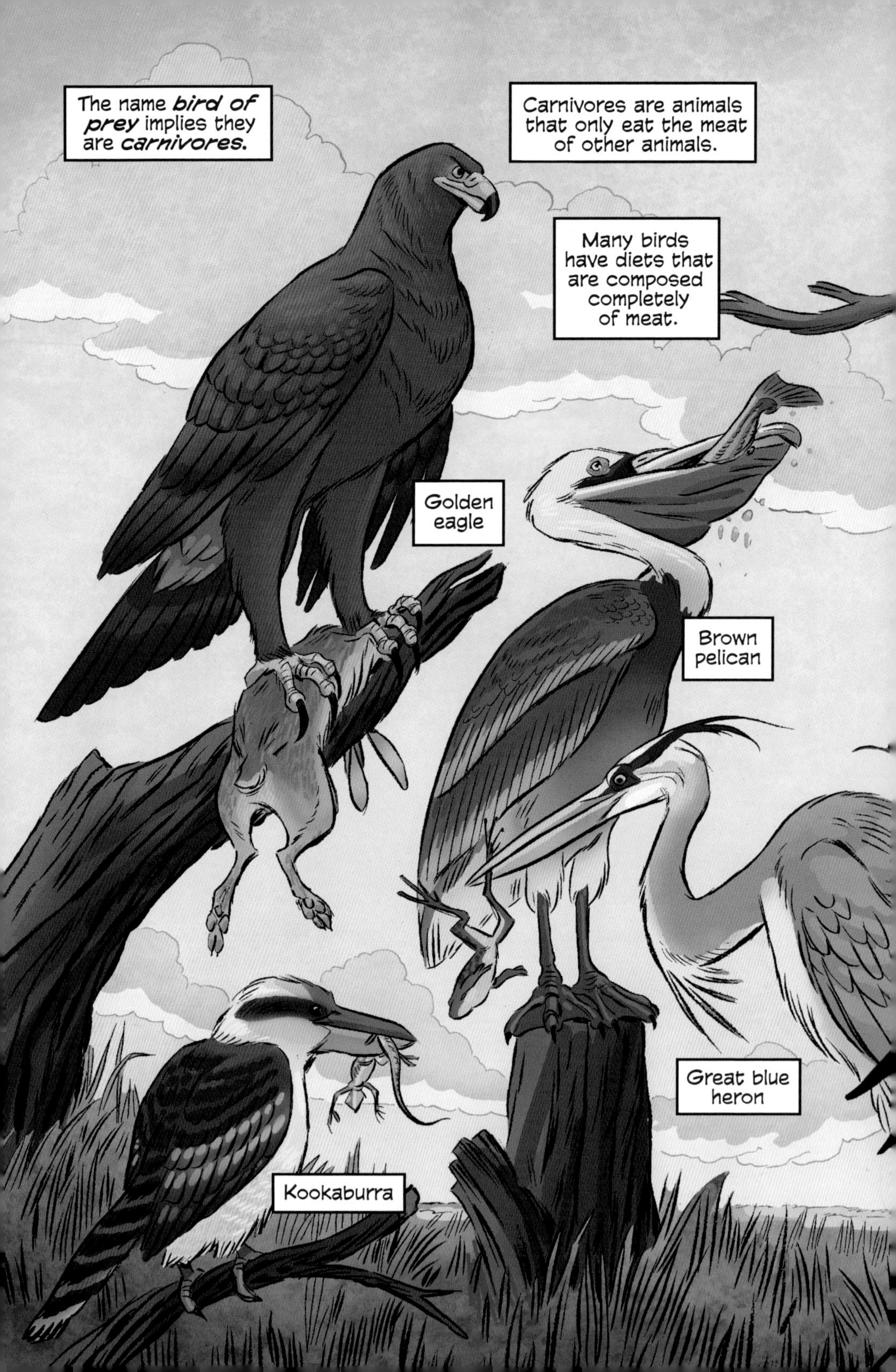
The name *bird of prey* implies they are *carnivores.*
Carnivores are animals that only eat the meat of other animals.
Many birds have diets that are composed completely of meat.
Golden eagle
Brown pelican
Great blue heron
Kookaburra

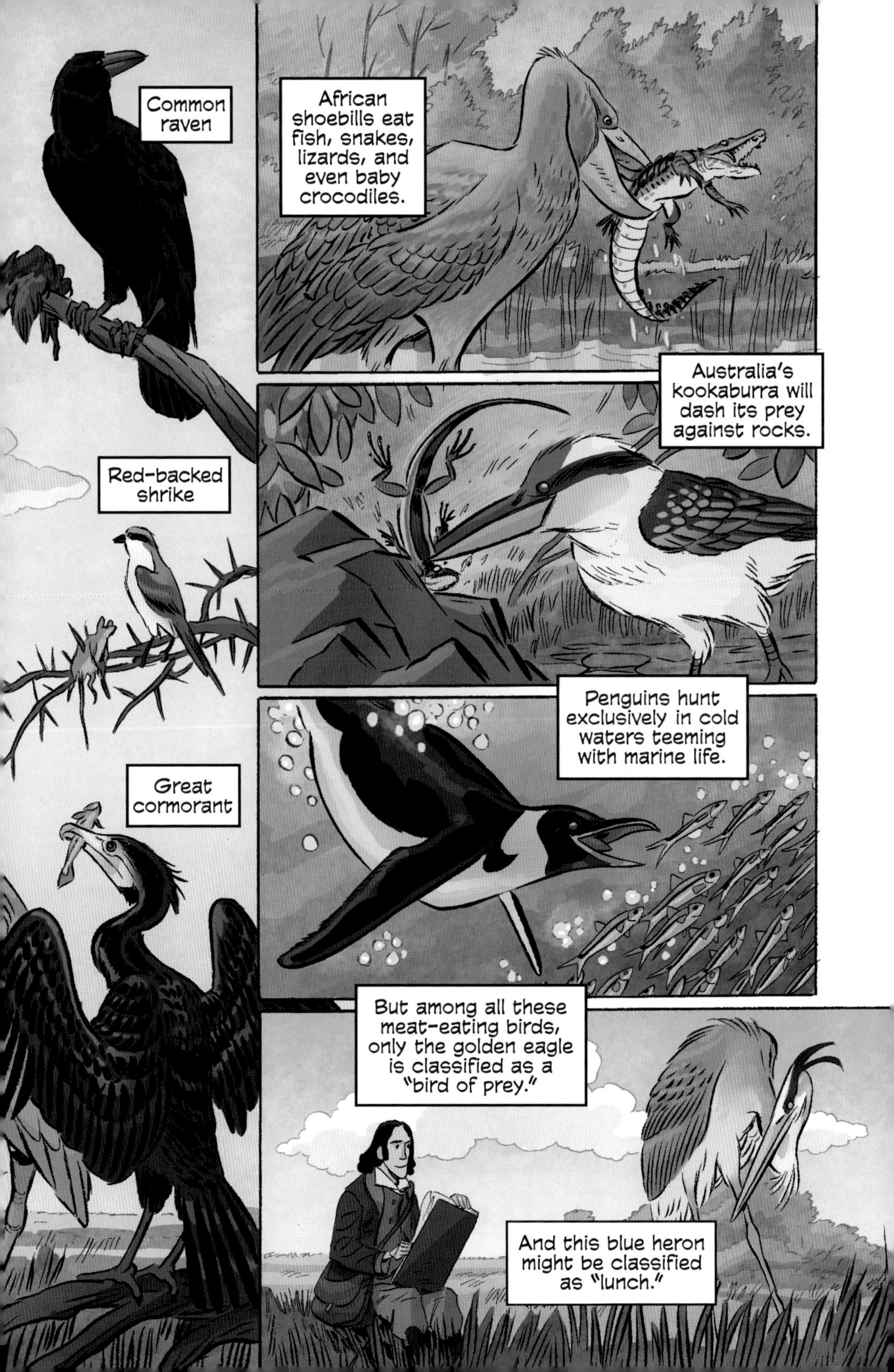
Common raven
African shoebills eat fish, snakes, lizards, and even baby crocodiles.
Red-backed shrike
Australia's kookaburra will dash its prey against rocks.
Great cormorant
Penguins hunt exclusively in cold waters teeming with marine life.
But among all these meat-eating birds, only the golden eagle is classified as a "bird of prey."
And this blue heron might be classified as "lunch."

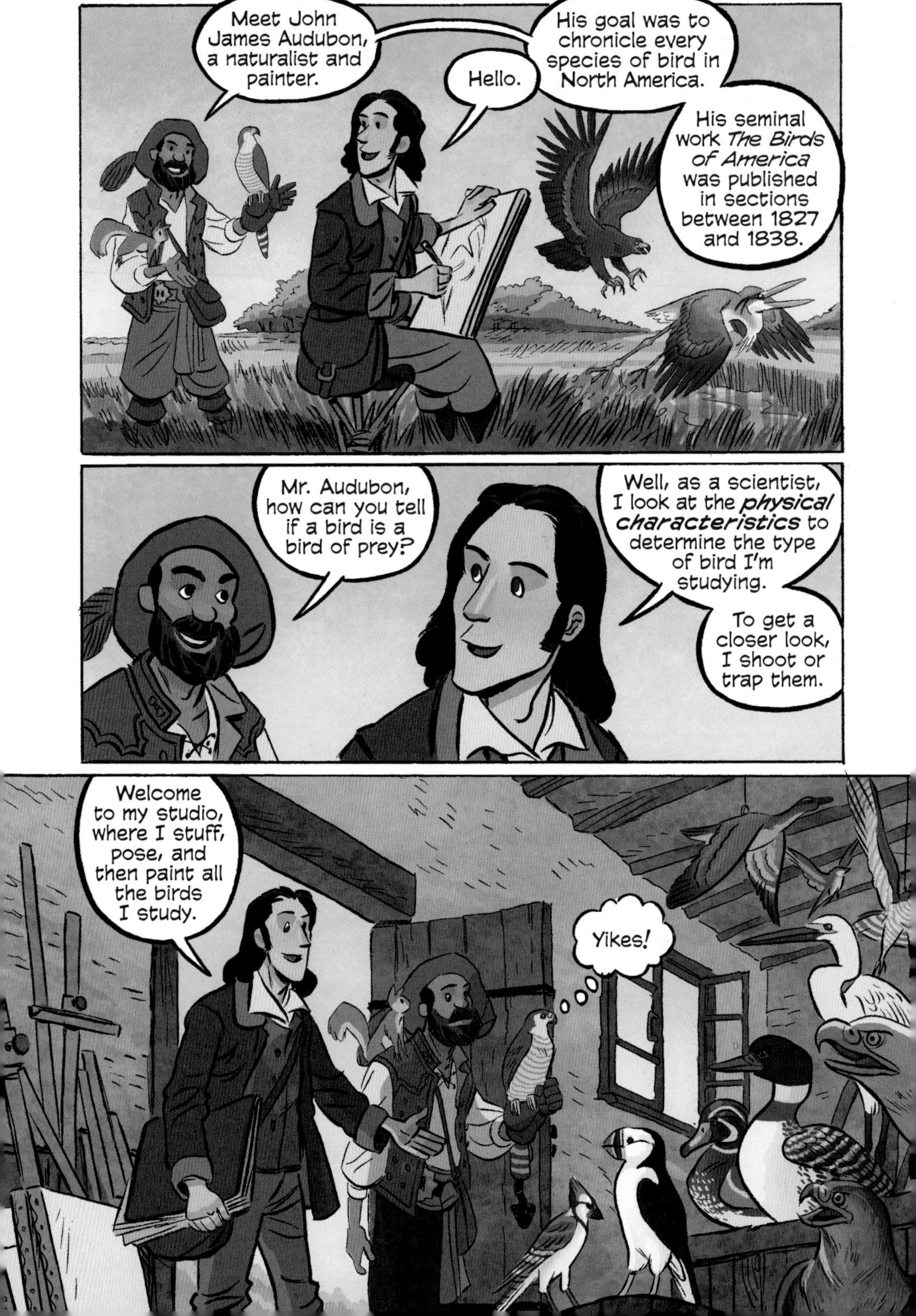

Meet John James Audubon, a naturalist and painter.
His goal was to chronicle every species of bird in North America.
Hello.
His seminal work *The Birds of America* was published in sections between 1827 and 1838.
Mr. Audubon, how can you tell if a bird is a bird of prey?
Well, as a scientist, I look at the ***physical characteristics*** to determine the type of bird I'm studying.
To get a closer look, I shoot or trap them.
Welcome to my studio, where I stuff, pose, and then paint all the birds I study.
Yikes!

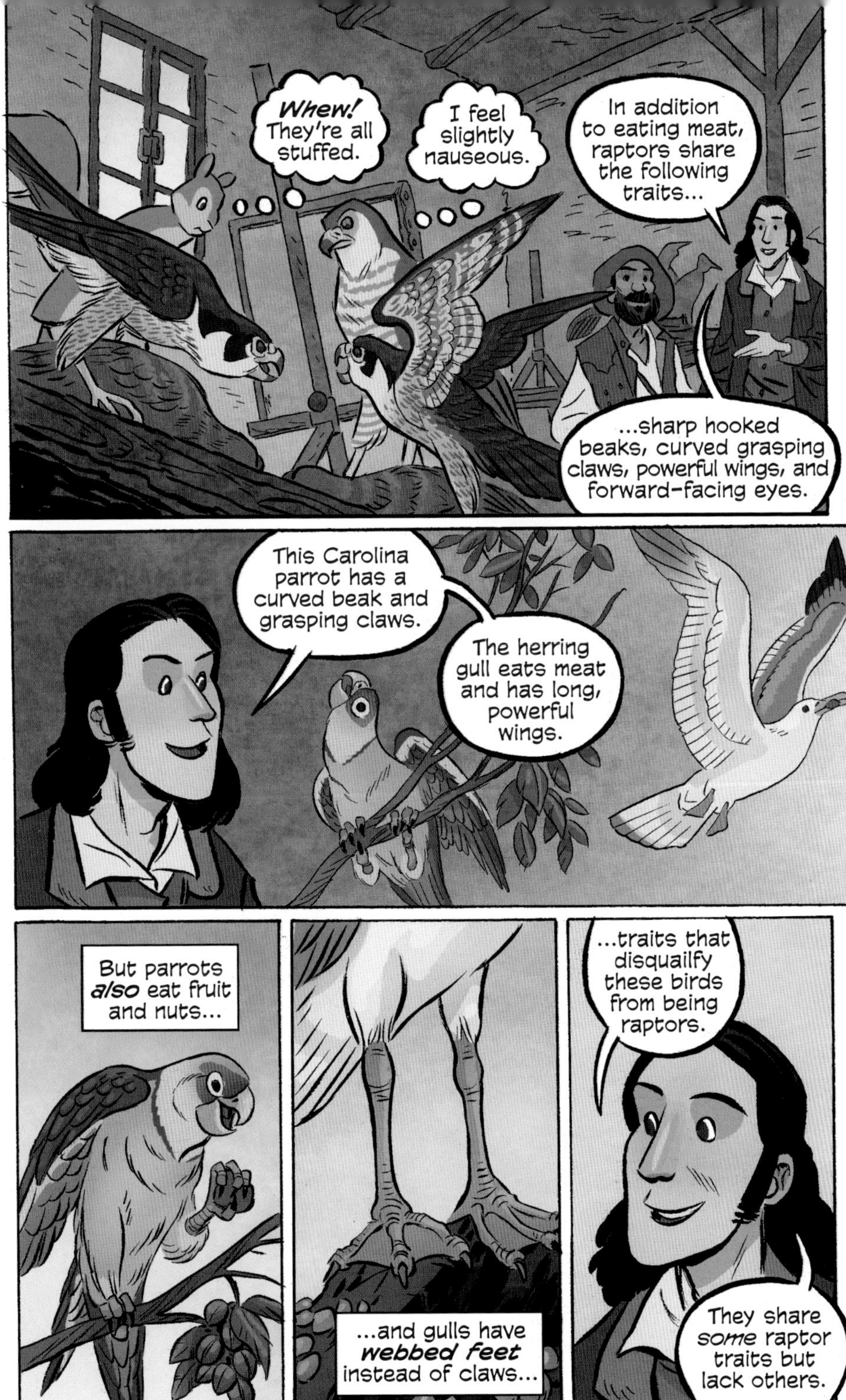
Whew! They're all stuffed.
I feel slightly nauseous.
In addition to eating meat, raptors share the following traits...
...sharp hooked beaks, curved grasping claws, powerful wings, and forward-facing eyes.
This Carolina parrot has a curved beak and grasping claws.
The herring gull eats meat and has long, powerful wings.
But parrots *also* eat fruit and nuts...
...and gulls have ***webbed feet*** instead of claws...
...traits that disquailfy these birds from being raptors.
They share *some* raptor traits but lack others.

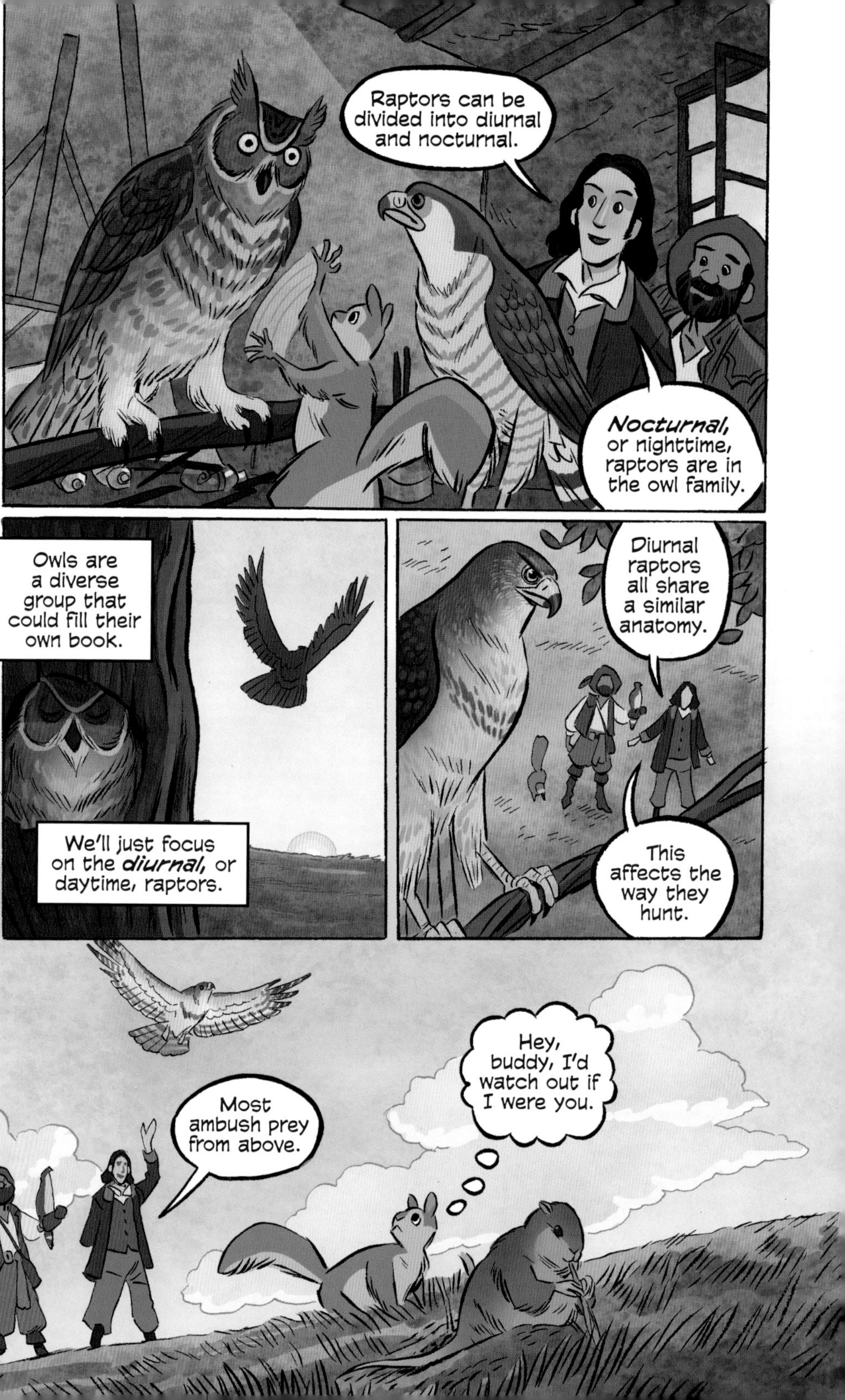

Raptors can be divided into diurnal and nocturnal.
Nocturnal, or nighttime, raptors are in the owl family.
Owls are a diverse group that could fill their own book.
We'll just focus on the *diurnal,* or daytime, raptors.
Diurnal raptors all share a similar anatomy.
This affects the way they hunt.
Most ambush prey from above.
Hey, buddy, I'd watch out if I were you.

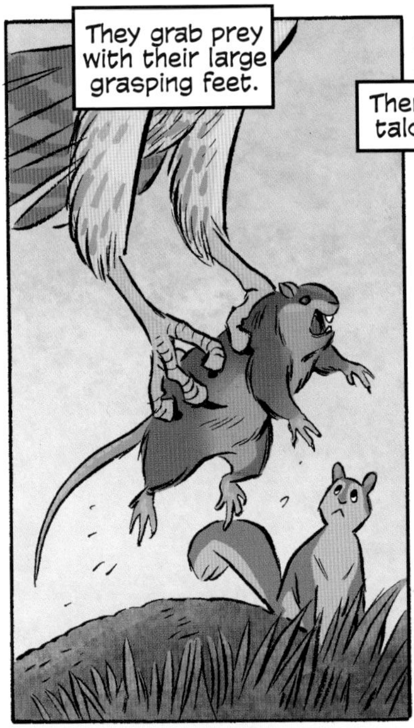
They grab prey with their large grasping feet.

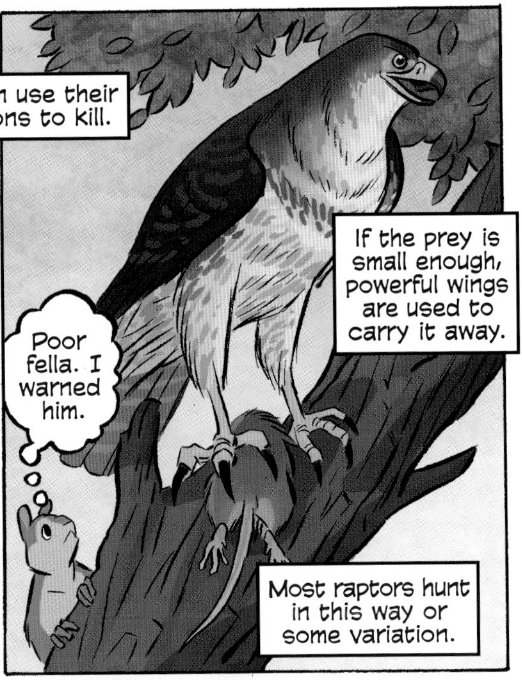
Then use their talons to kill.
If the prey is small enough, powerful wings are used to carry it away.
Poor fella. I warned him.
Most raptors hunt in this way or some variation.

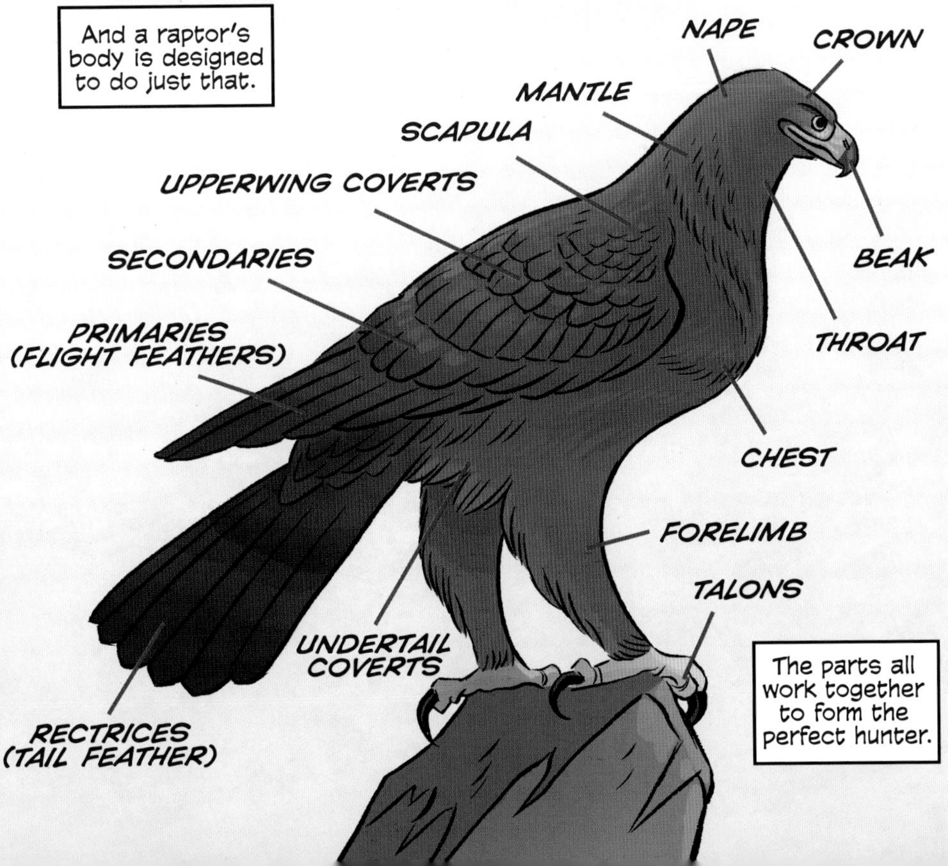
And a raptor's body is designed to do just that.
NAPE
CROWN
MANTLE
SCAPULA
UPPERWING COVERTS
BEAK
SECONDARIES
THROAT
PRIMARIES (FLIGHT FEATHERS)
CHEST
FORELIMB
TALONS
UNDERTAIL COVERTS
RECTRICES (TAIL FEATHER)
The parts all work together to form the perfect hunter.

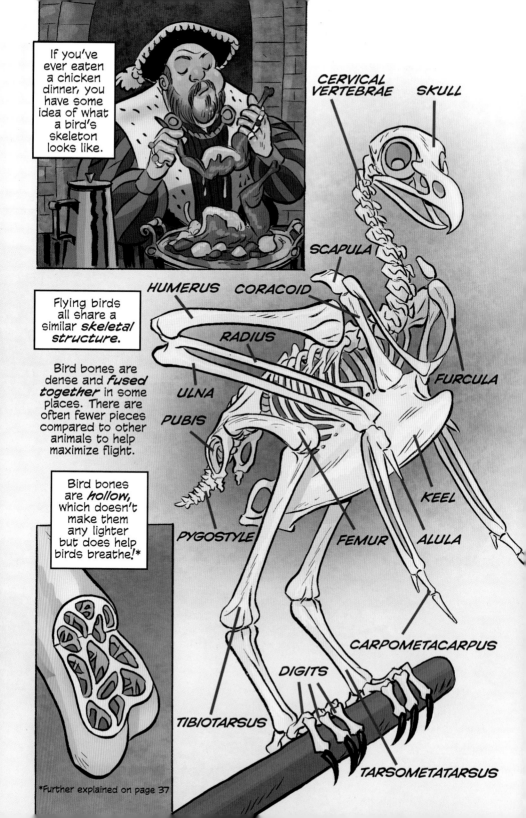

If you've ever eaten a chicken dinner, you have some idea of what a bird's skeleton looks like.

Flying birds all share a similar *skeletal structure.*

Bird bones are dense and *fused together* in some places. There are often fewer pieces compared to other animals to help maximize flight.

Bird bones are *hollow,* which doesn't make them any lighter but does help birds breathe!*

*Further explained on page 37

CERVICAL VERTEBRAE

SKULL

SCAPULA

HUMERUS

CORACOID

RADIUS

ULNA

PUBIS

FURCULA

PYGOSTYLE

FEMUR

KEEL

ALULA

CARPOMETACARPUS

DIGITS

TIBIOTARSUS

TARSOMETATARSUS

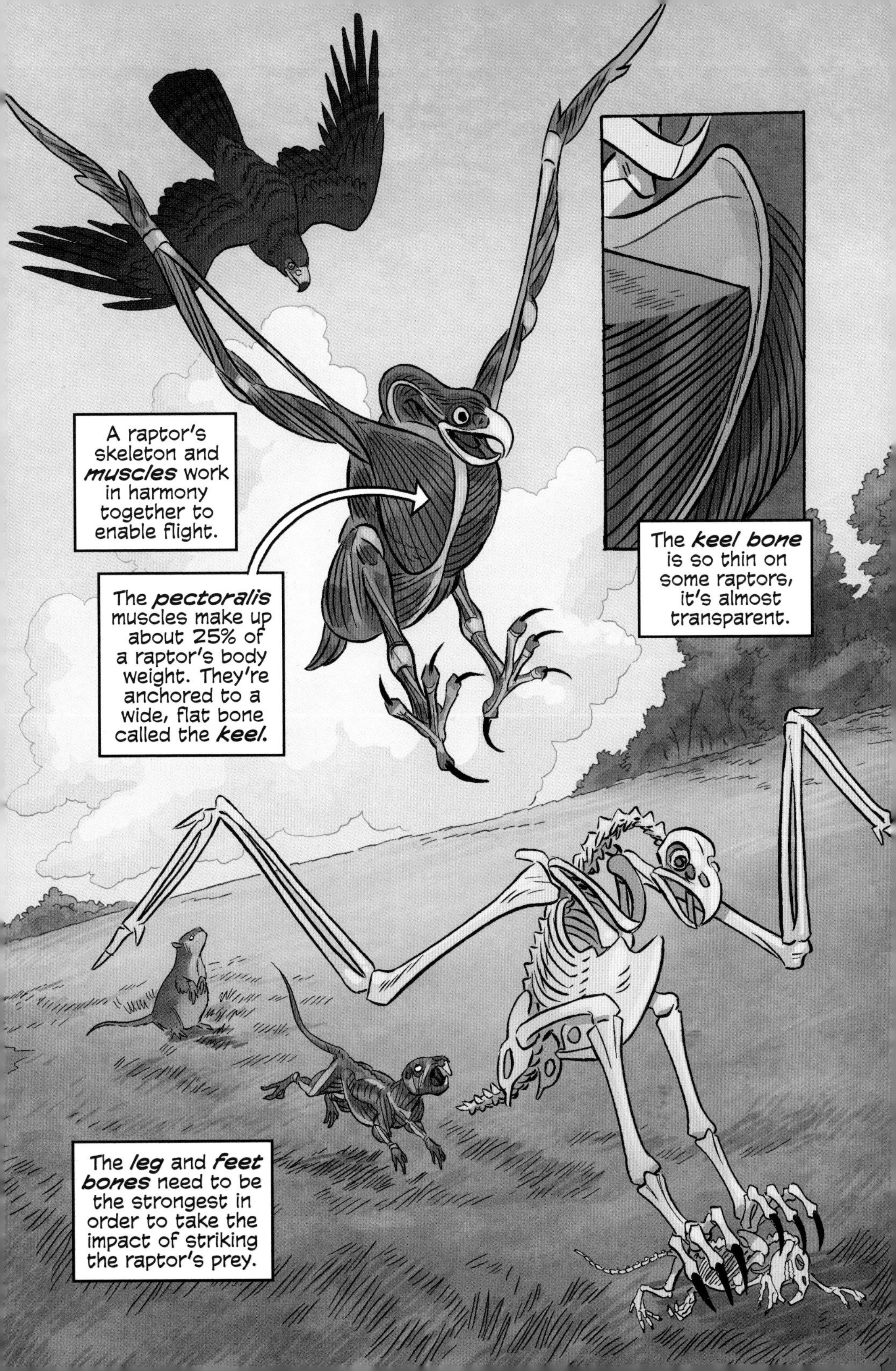
A raptor's skeleton and *muscles* work in harmony together to enable flight.
The *pectoralis* muscles make up about 25% of a raptor's body weight. They're anchored to a wide, flat bone called the *keel*.
The *keel bone* is so thin on some raptors, it's almost transparent.
The *leg* and *feet bones* need to be the strongest in order to take the impact of striking the raptor's prey.

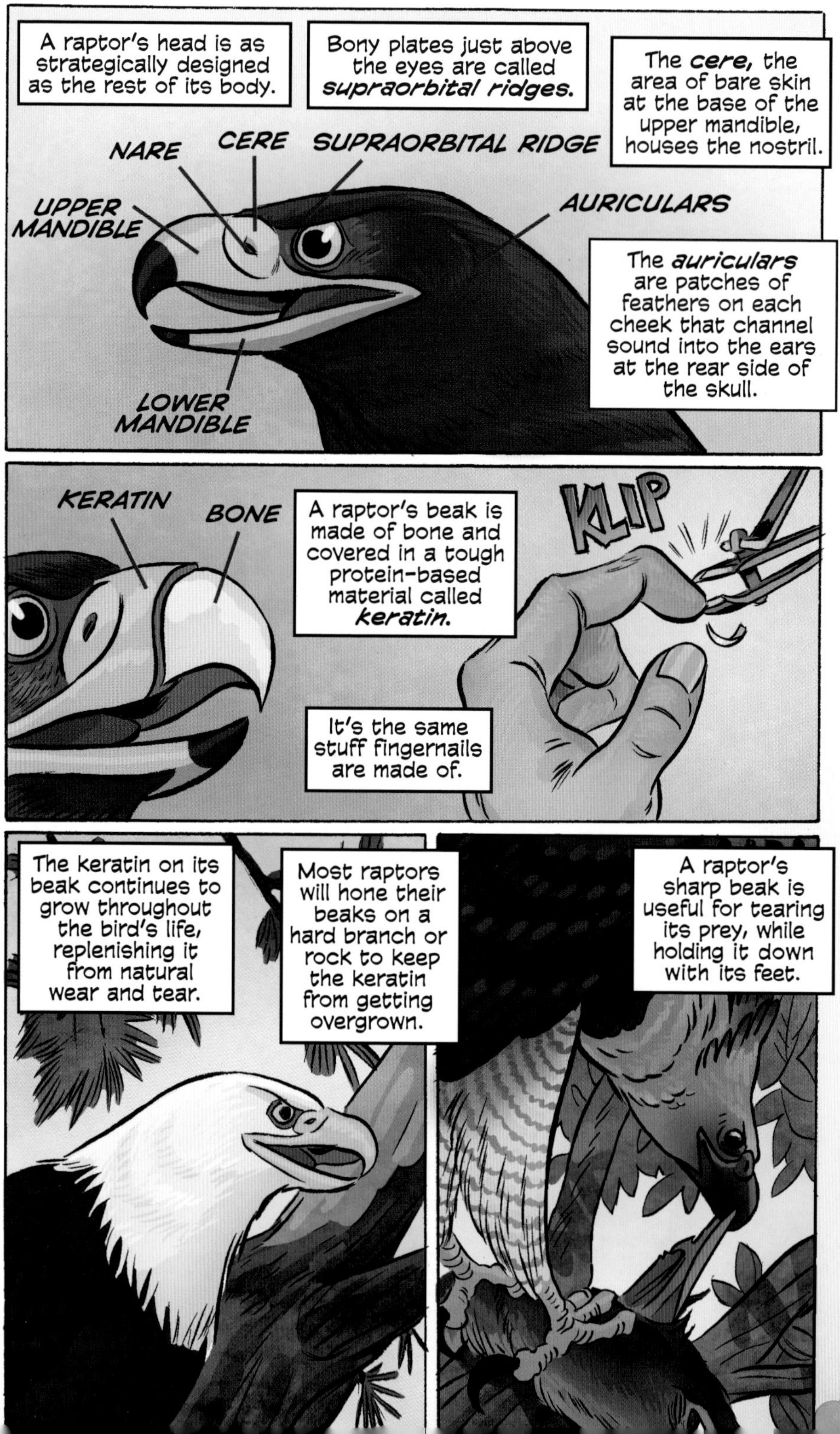
A raptor's head is as strategically designed as the rest of its body.
Bony plates just above the eyes are called *supraorbital ridges.*
The *cere,* the area of bare skin at the base of the upper mandible, houses the nostril.
NARE
CERE
SUPRAORBITAL RIDGE
UPPER MANDIBLE
AURICULARS
The *auriculars* are patches of feathers on each cheek that channel sound into the ears at the rear side of the skull.
LOWER MANDIBLE
KERATIN
BONE
A raptor's beak is made of bone and covered in a tough protein-based material called *keratin.*
KLIP
It's the same stuff fingernails are made of.
The keratin on its beak continues to grow throughout the bird's life, replenishing it from natural wear and tear.
Most raptors will hone their beaks on a hard branch or rock to keep the keratin from getting overgrown.
A raptor's sharp beak is useful for tearing its prey, while holding it down with its feet.

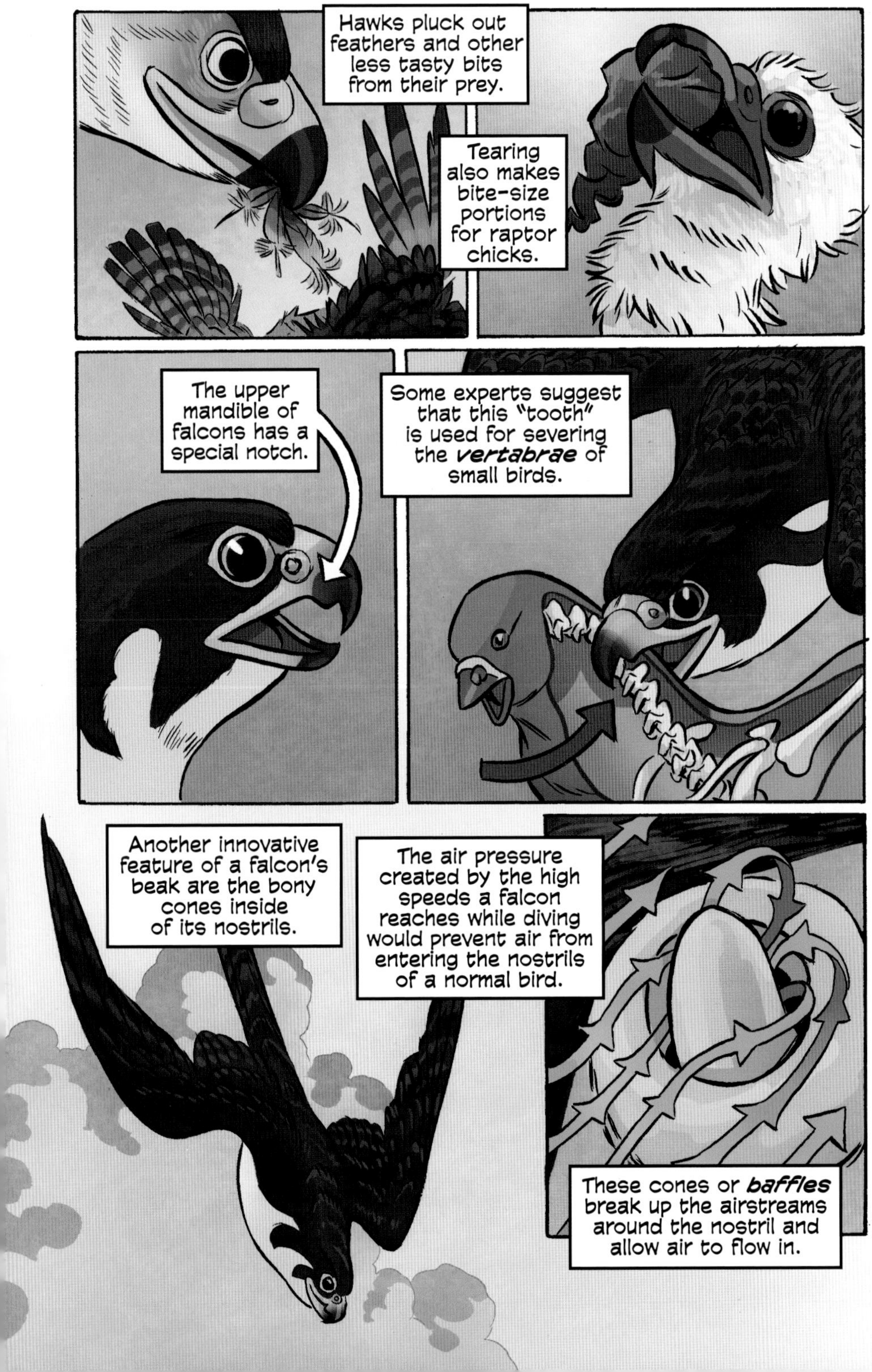
Hawks pluck out feathers and other less tasty bits from their prey.
Tearing also makes bite-size portions for raptor chicks.
The upper mandible of falcons has a special notch.
Some experts suggest that this "tooth" is used for severing the *vertabrae* of small birds.
Another innovative feature of a falcon's beak are the bony cones inside of its nostrils.
The air pressure created by the high speeds a falcon reaches while diving would prevent air from entering the nostrils of a normal bird.
These cones or *baffles* break up the airstreams around the nostril and allow air to flow in.

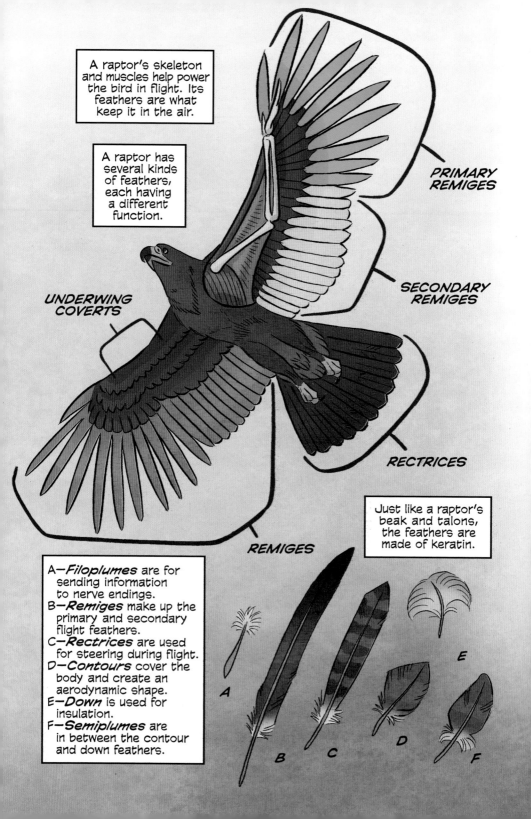

A raptor's skeleton and muscles help power the bird in flight. Its feathers are what keep it in the air.

A raptor has several kinds of feathers, each having a different function.

PRIMARY REMIGES

SECONDARY REMIGES

UNDERWING COVERTS

RECTRICES

REMIGES

Just like a raptor's beak and talons, the feathers are made of keratin.

A—*Filoplumes* are for sending information to nerve endings.
B—*Remiges* make up the primary and secondary flight feathers.
C—*Rectrices* are used for steering during flight.
D—*Contours* cover the body and create an aerodynamic shape.
E—*Down* is used for insulation.
F—*Semiplumes* are in between the contour and down feathers.

A
B
C
D
E
F

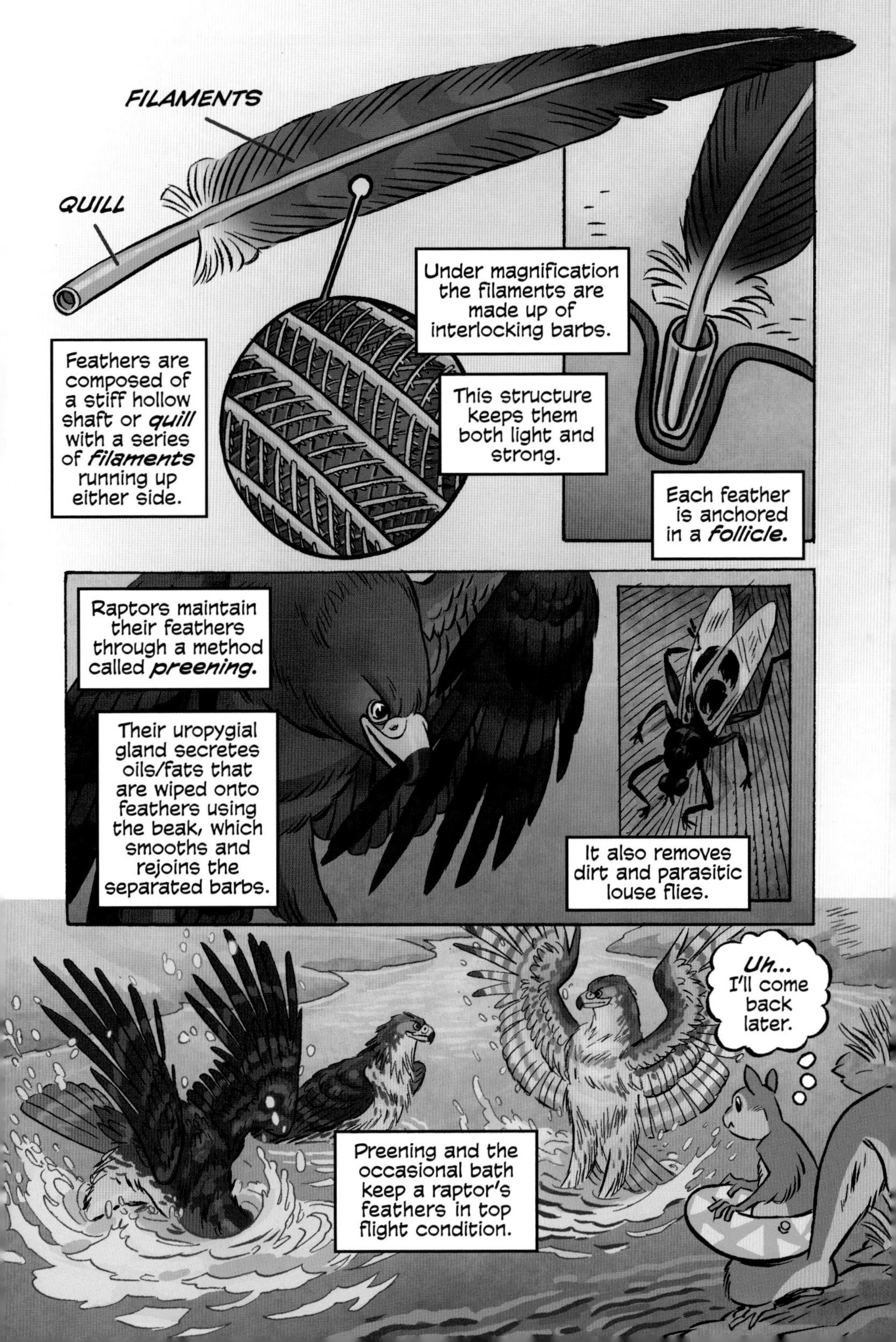
FILAMENTS
QUILL
Feathers are composed of a stiff hollow shaft or *quill* with a series of *filaments* running up either side.
Under magnification the filaments are made up of interlocking barbs.
This structure keeps them both light and strong.
Each feather is anchored in a *follicle.*
Raptors maintain their feathers through a method called *preening.*
Their uropygial gland secretes oils/fats that are wiped onto feathers using the beak, which smooths and rejoins the separated barbs.
It also removes dirt and parasitic louse flies.
Uh... I'll come back later.
Preening and the occasional bath keep a raptor's feathers in top flight condition.

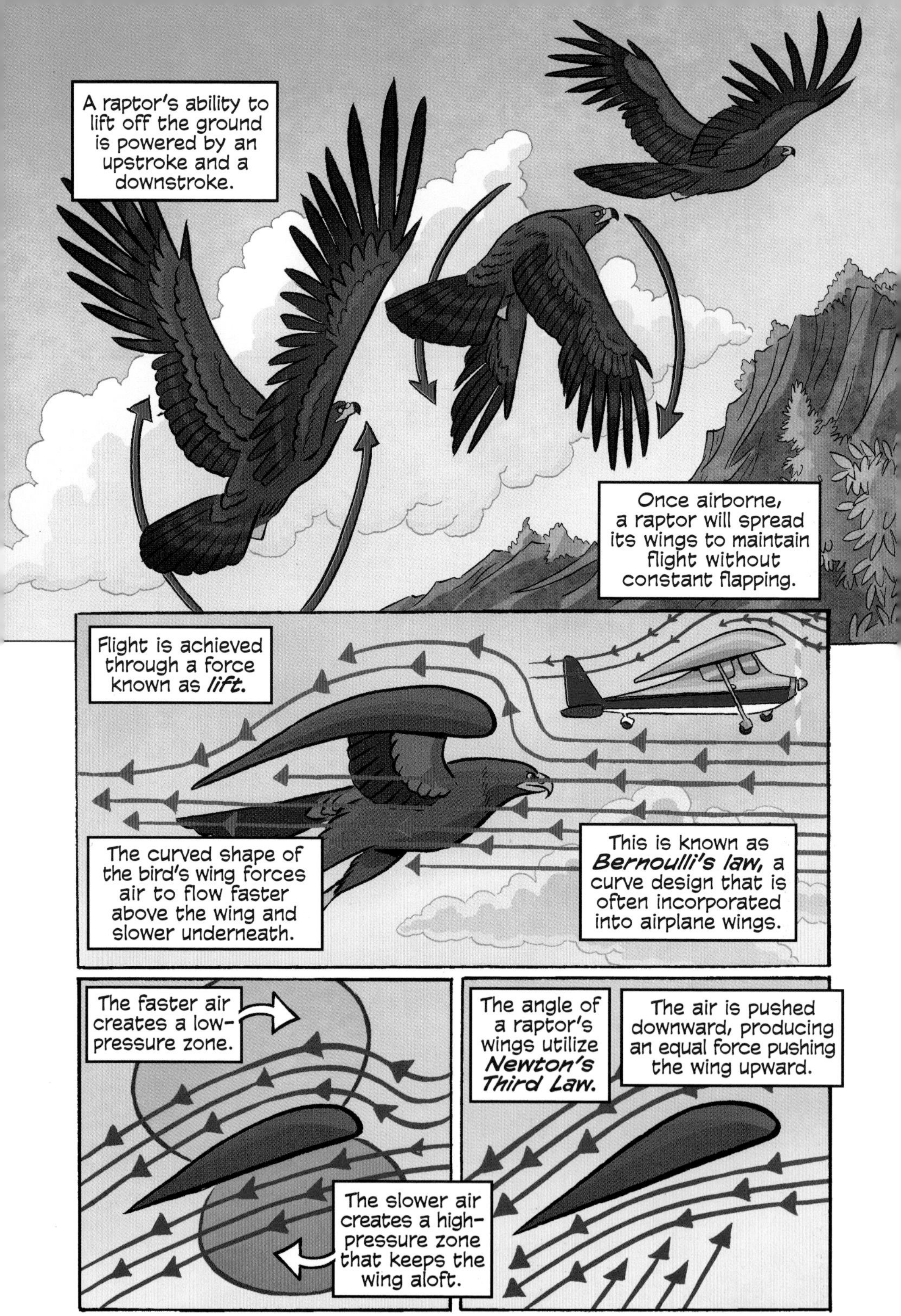
A raptor's ability to lift off the ground is powered by an upstroke and a downstroke.
Once airborne, a raptor will spread its wings to maintain flight without constant flapping.
Flight is achieved through a force known as *lift*.
The curved shape of the bird's wing forces air to flow faster above the wing and slower underneath.
This is known as ***Bernoulli's law,*** a curve design that is often incorporated into airplane wings.
The faster air creates a low-pressure zone.
The slower air creates a high-pressure zone that keeps the wing aloft.
The angle of a raptor's wings utilize ***Newton's Third Law.***
The air is pushed downward, producing an equal force pushing the wing upward.

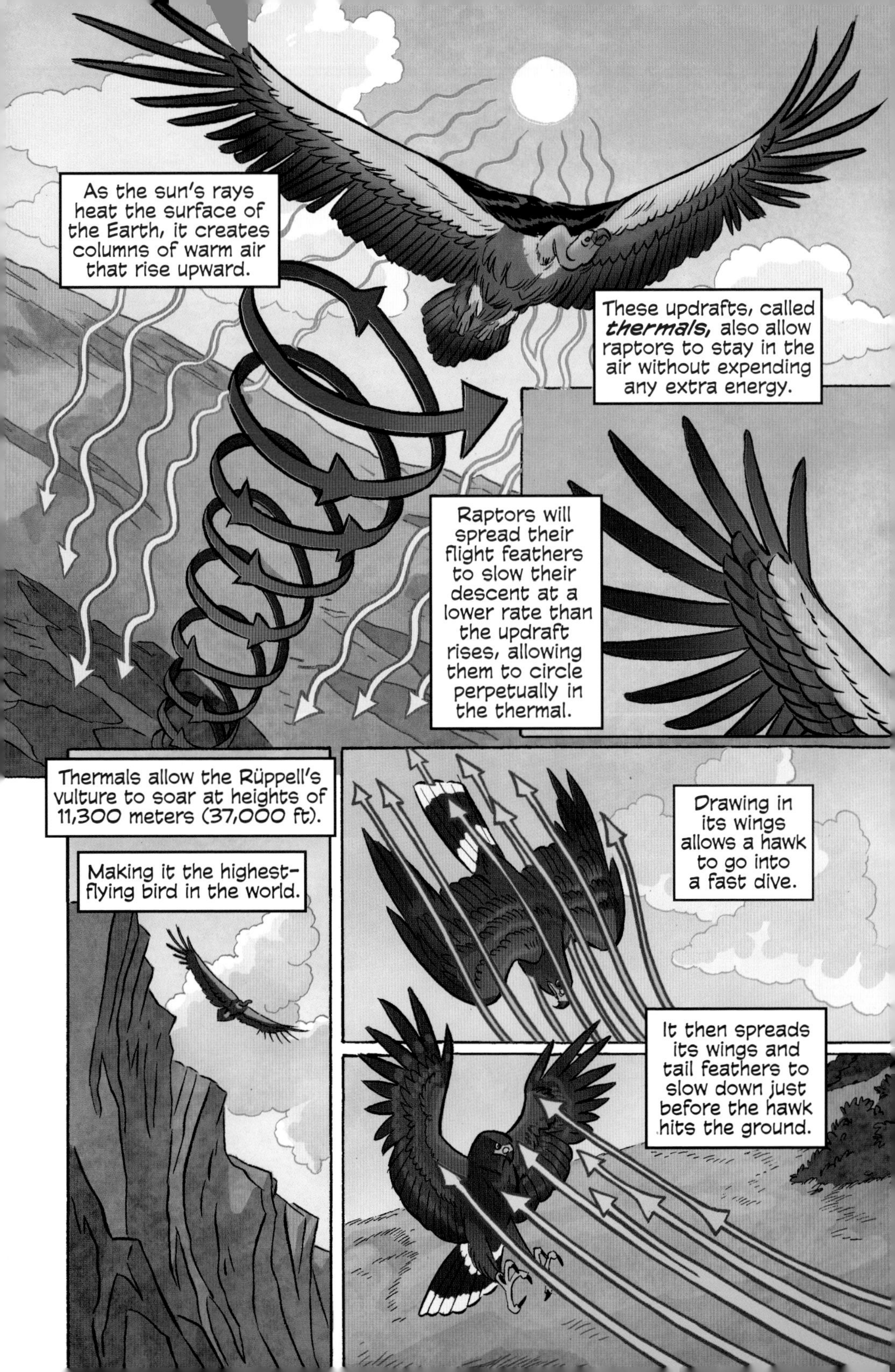
As the sun's rays heat the surface of the Earth, it creates columns of warm air that rise upward.
These updrafts, called *thermals,* also allow raptors to stay in the air without expending any extra energy.
Raptors will spread their flight feathers to slow their descent at a lower rate than the updraft rises, allowing them to circle perpetually in the thermal.
Thermals allow the Rüppell's vulture to soar at heights of 11,300 meters (37,000 ft).
Making it the highest-flying bird in the world.
Drawing in its wings allows a hawk to go into a fast dive.
It then spreads its wings and tail feathers to slow down just before the hawk hits the ground.

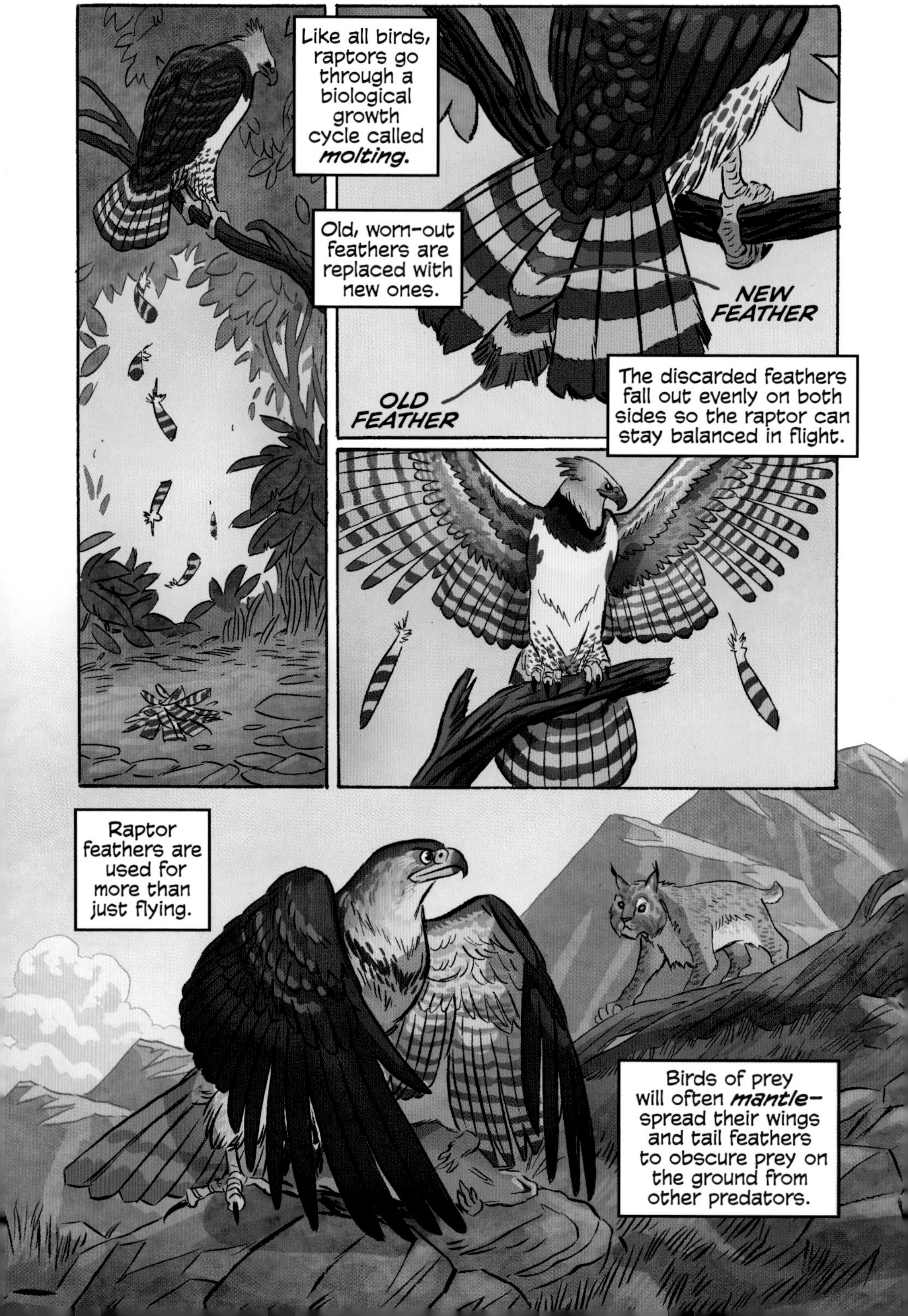
Like all birds, raptors go through a biological growth cycle called *molting*.
Old, worn-out feathers are replaced with new ones.
NEW FEATHER
OLD FEATHER
The discarded feathers fall out evenly on both sides so the raptor can stay balanced in flight.
Raptor feathers are used for more than just flying.
Birds of prey will often *mantle*—spread their wings and tail feathers to obscure prey on the ground from other predators.

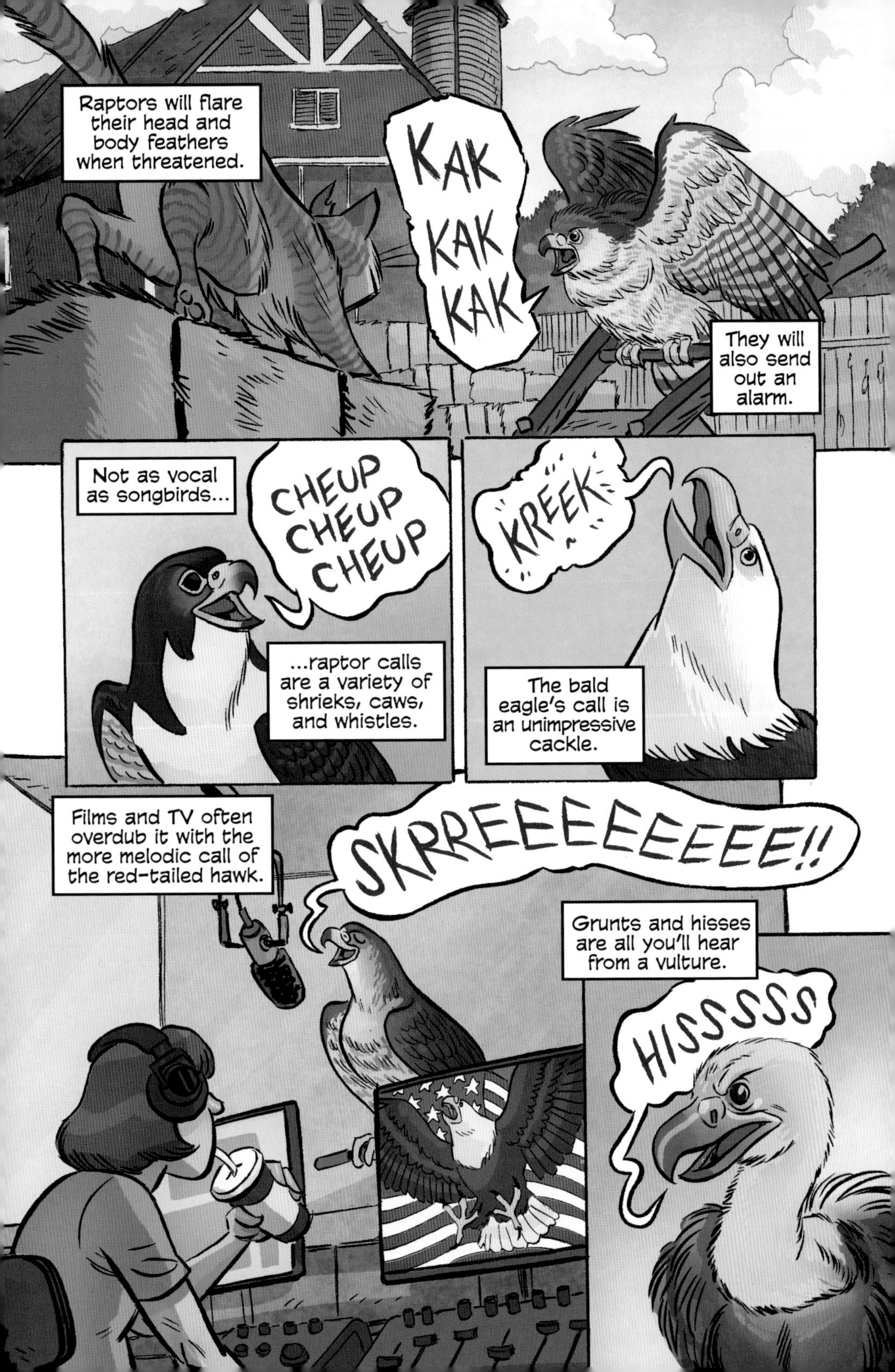

Raptors will flare their head and body feathers when threatened.
KAK KAK KAK
They will also send out an alarm.
Not as vocal as songbirds...
CHEUP CHEUP CHEUP
...raptor calls are a variety of shrieks, caws, and whistles.
KREEK
The bald eagle's call is an unimpressive cackle.
Films and TV often overdub it with the more melodic call of the red-tailed hawk.
SKRREEEEEEEEEE!!
Grunts and hisses are all you'll hear from a vulture.
HISSSSS

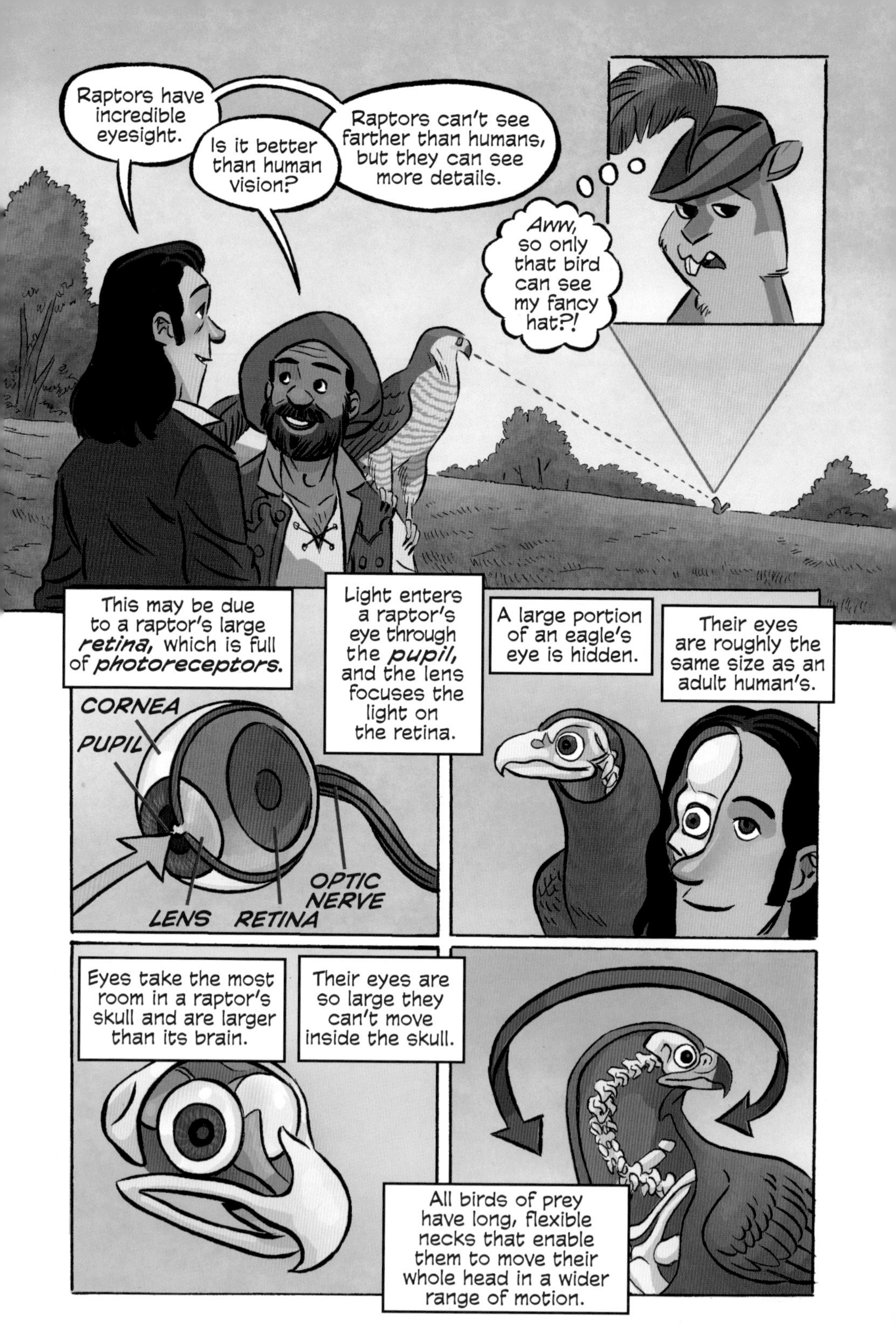
Raptors have incredible eyesight.
Is it better than human vision?
Raptors can't see farther than humans, but they can see more details.
Aww, so only that bird can see my fancy hat?!
This may be due to a raptor's large *retina,* which is full of *photoreceptors.*
CORNEA
PUPIL
LENS
RETINA
OPTIC NERVE
Light enters a raptor's eye through the *pupil,* and the lens focuses the light on the retina.
A large portion of an eagle's eye is hidden.
Their eyes are roughly the same size as an adult human's.
Eyes take the most room in a raptor's skull and are larger than its brain.
Their eyes are so large they can't move inside the skull.
All birds of prey have long, flexible necks that enable them to move their whole head in a wider range of motion.

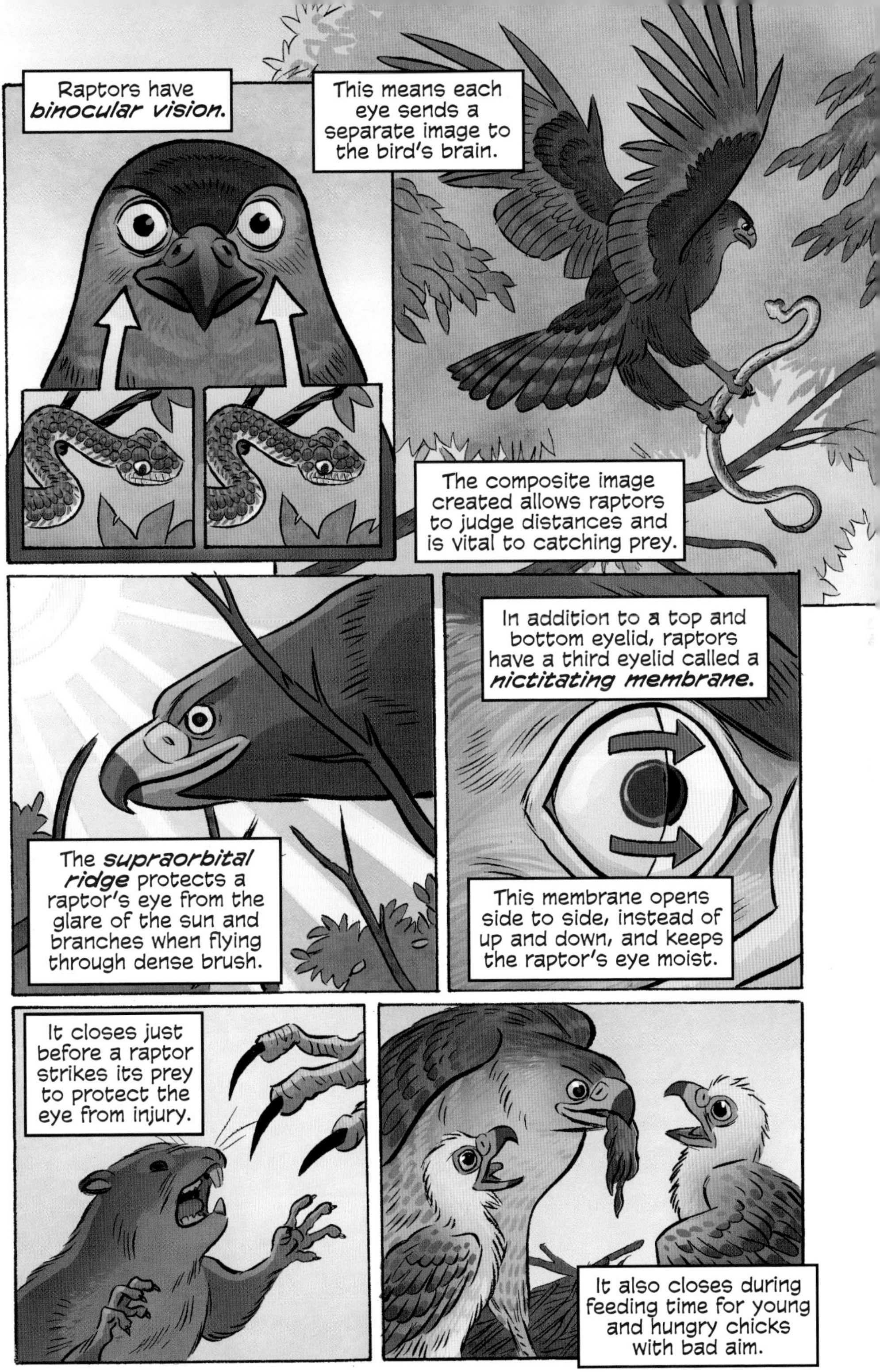
Raptors have *binocular vision.*
This means each eye sends a separate image to the bird's brain.
The composite image created allows raptors to judge distances and is vital to catching prey.
The *supraorbital ridge* protects a raptor's eye from the glare of the sun and branches when flying through dense brush.
In addition to a top and bottom eyelid, raptors have a third eyelid called a *nictitating membrane.*
This membrane opens side to side, instead of up and down, and keeps the raptor's eye moist.
It closes just before a raptor strikes its prey to protect the eye from injury.
It also closes during feeding time for young and hungry chicks with bad aim.

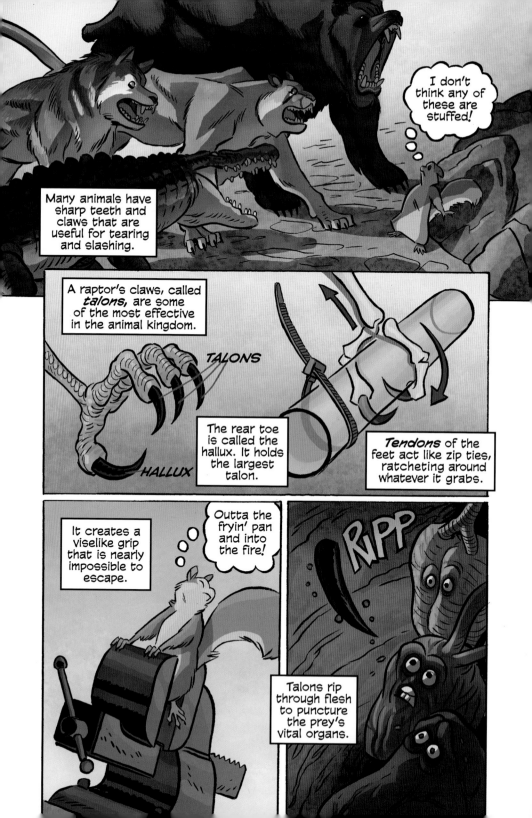

I don't think any of these are stuffed!

Many animals have sharp teeth and claws that are useful for tearing and slashing.

A raptor's claws, called *talons,* are some of the most effective in the animal kingdom.

TALONS

HALLUX

The rear toe is called the hallux. It holds the largest talon.

Tendons of the feet act like zip ties, ratcheting around whatever it grabs.

It creates a viselike grip that is nearly impossible to escape.

Outta the fryin' pan and into the fire!

RIPP

Talons rip through flesh to puncture the prey's vital organs.

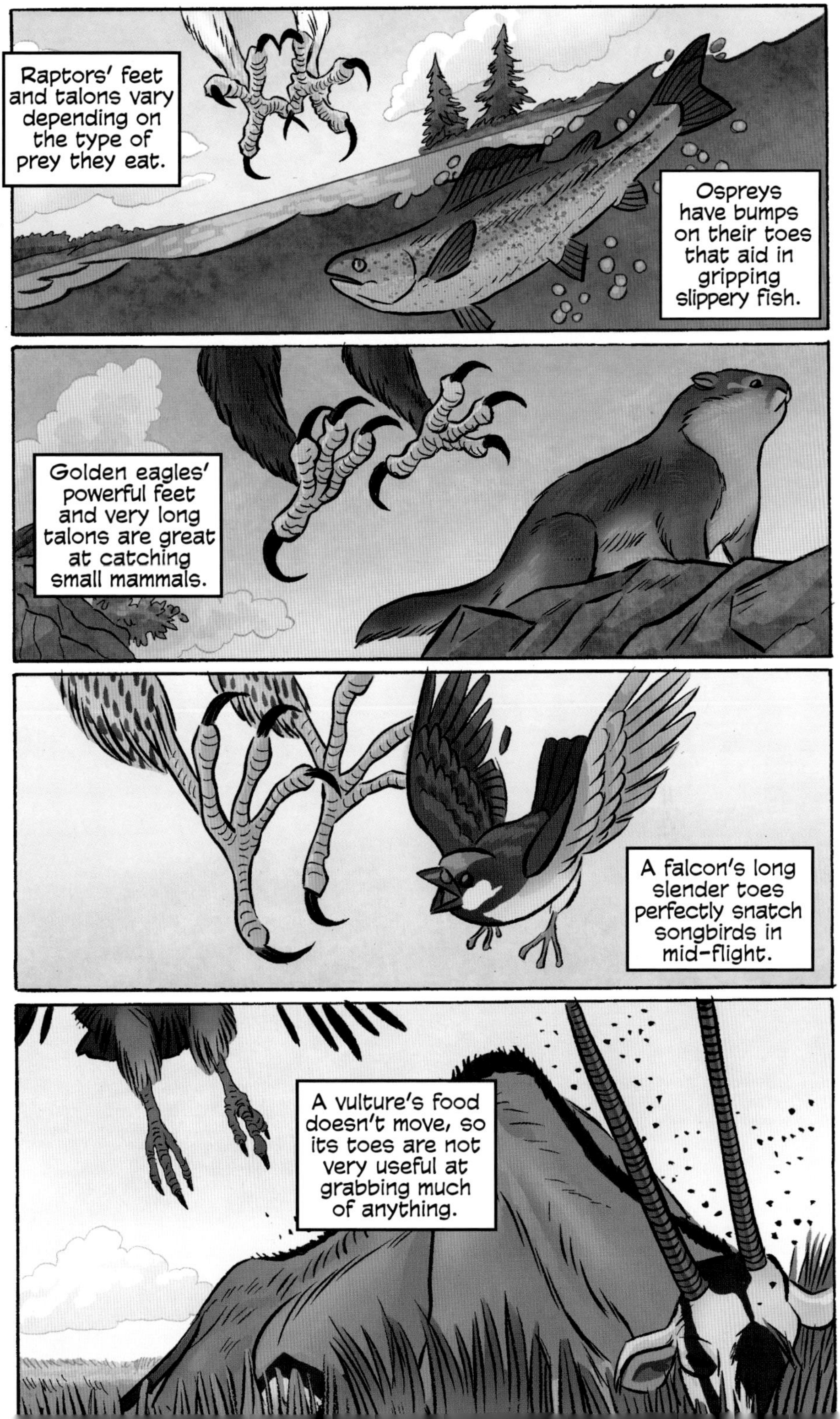
Raptors' feet and talons vary depending on the type of prey they eat.
Ospreys have bumps on their toes that aid in gripping slippery fish.
Golden eagles' powerful feet and very long talons are great at catching small mammals.
A falcon's long slender toes perfectly snatch songbirds in mid-flight.
A vulture's food doesn't move, so its toes are not very useful at grabbing much of anything.

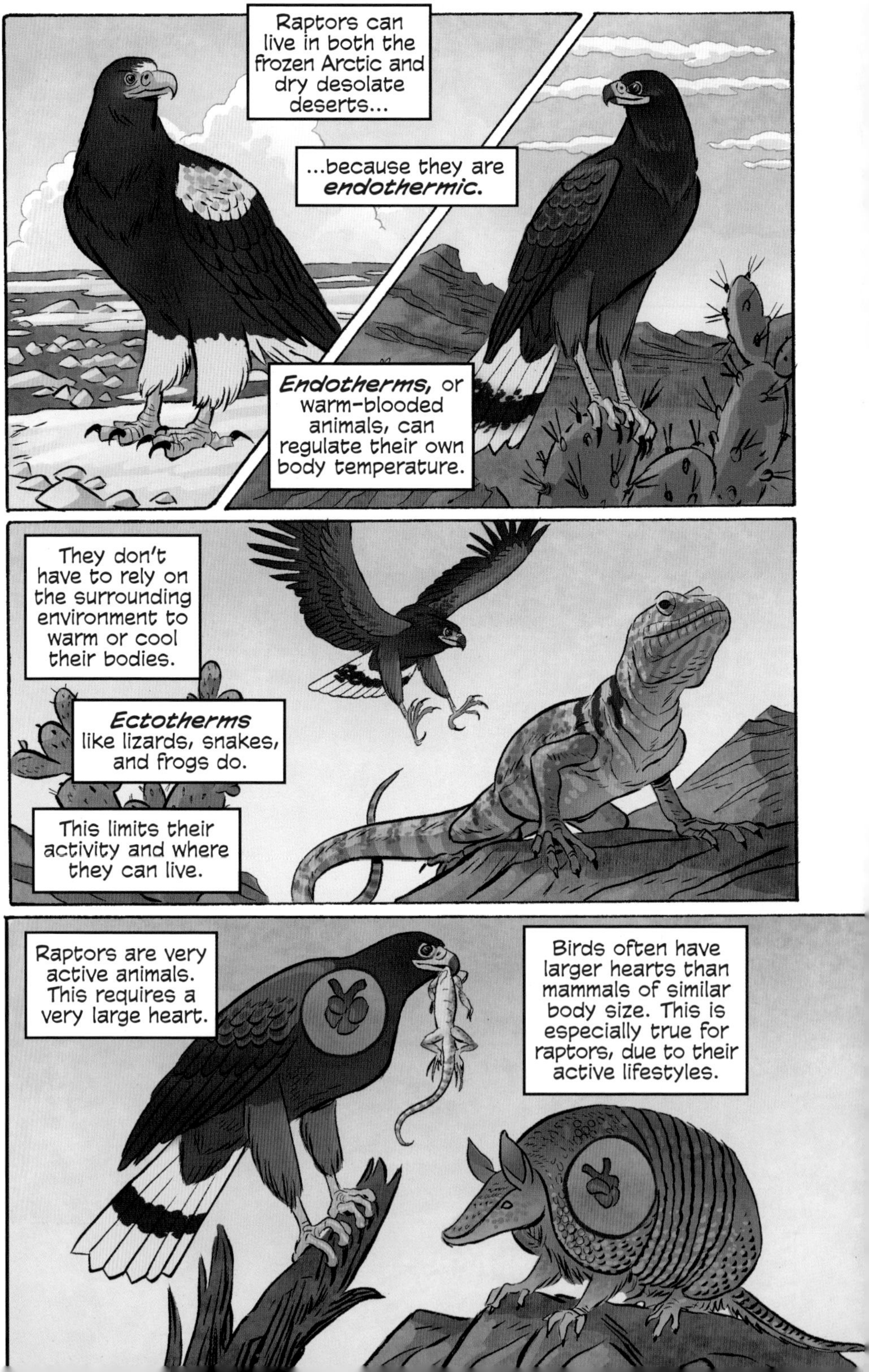
Raptors can live in both the frozen Arctic and dry desolate deserts...
...because they are *endothermic.*
Endotherms, or warm-blooded animals, can regulate their own body temperature.
They don't have to rely on the surrounding environment to warm or cool their bodies.
Ectotherms like lizards, snakes, and frogs do.
This limits their activity and where they can live.
Raptors are very active animals. This requires a very large heart.
Birds often have larger hearts than mammals of similar body size. This is especially true for raptors, due to their active lifestyles.

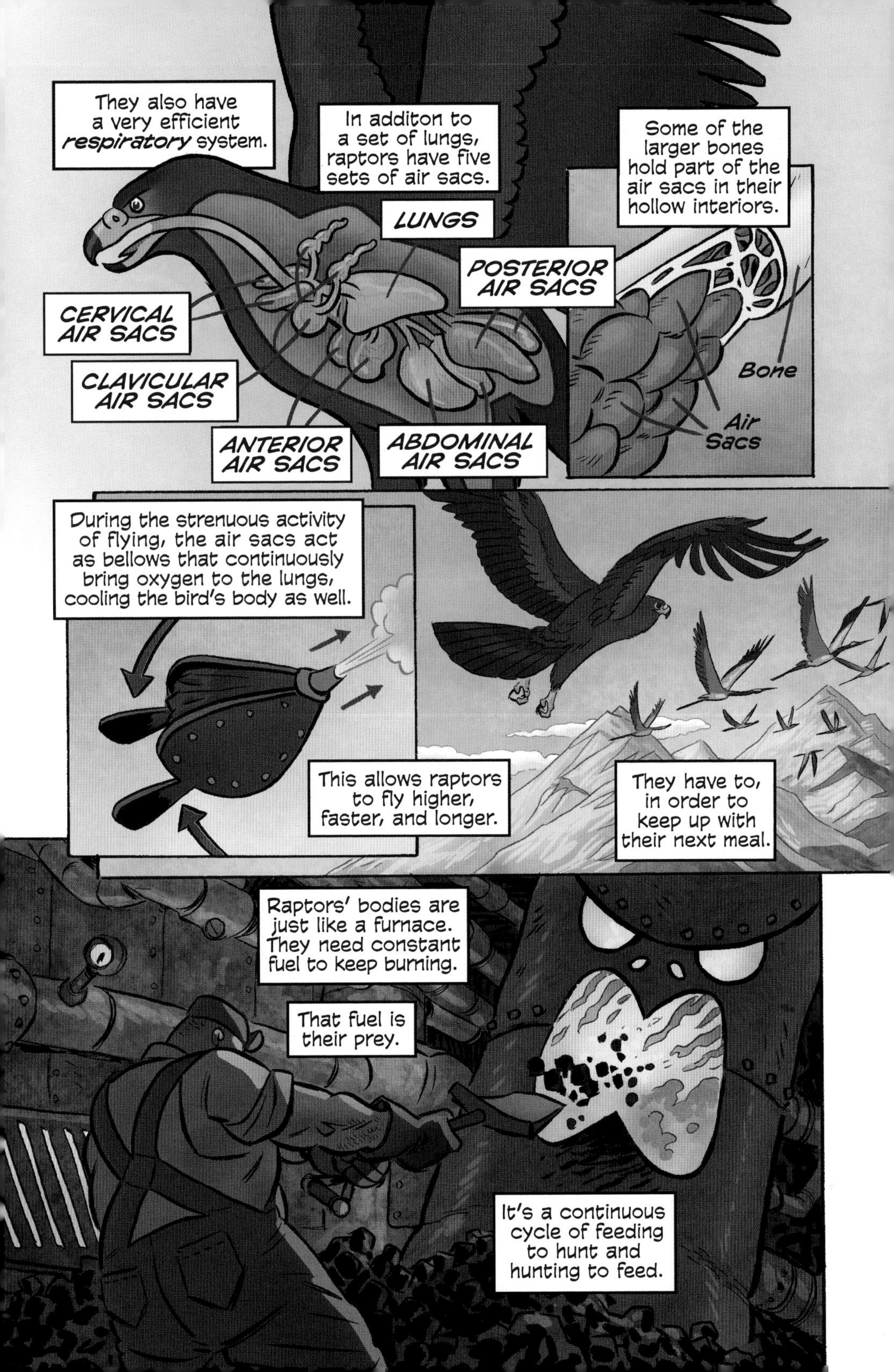
They also have a very efficient *respiratory* system.
In additon to a set of lungs, raptors have five sets of air sacs.
Some of the larger bones hold part of the air sacs in their hollow interiors.
LUNGS
POSTERIOR AIR SACS
CERVICAL AIR SACS
CLAVICULAR AIR SACS
ANTERIOR AIR SACS
ABDOMINAL AIR SACS
Bone
Air Sacs
During the strenuous activity of flying, the air sacs act as bellows that continuously bring oxygen to the lungs, cooling the bird's body as well.
This allows raptors to fly higher, faster, and longer.
They have to, in order to keep up with their next meal.
Raptors' bodies are just like a furnace. They need constant fuel to keep burning.
That fuel is their prey.
It's a continuous cycle of feeding to hunt and hunting to feed.

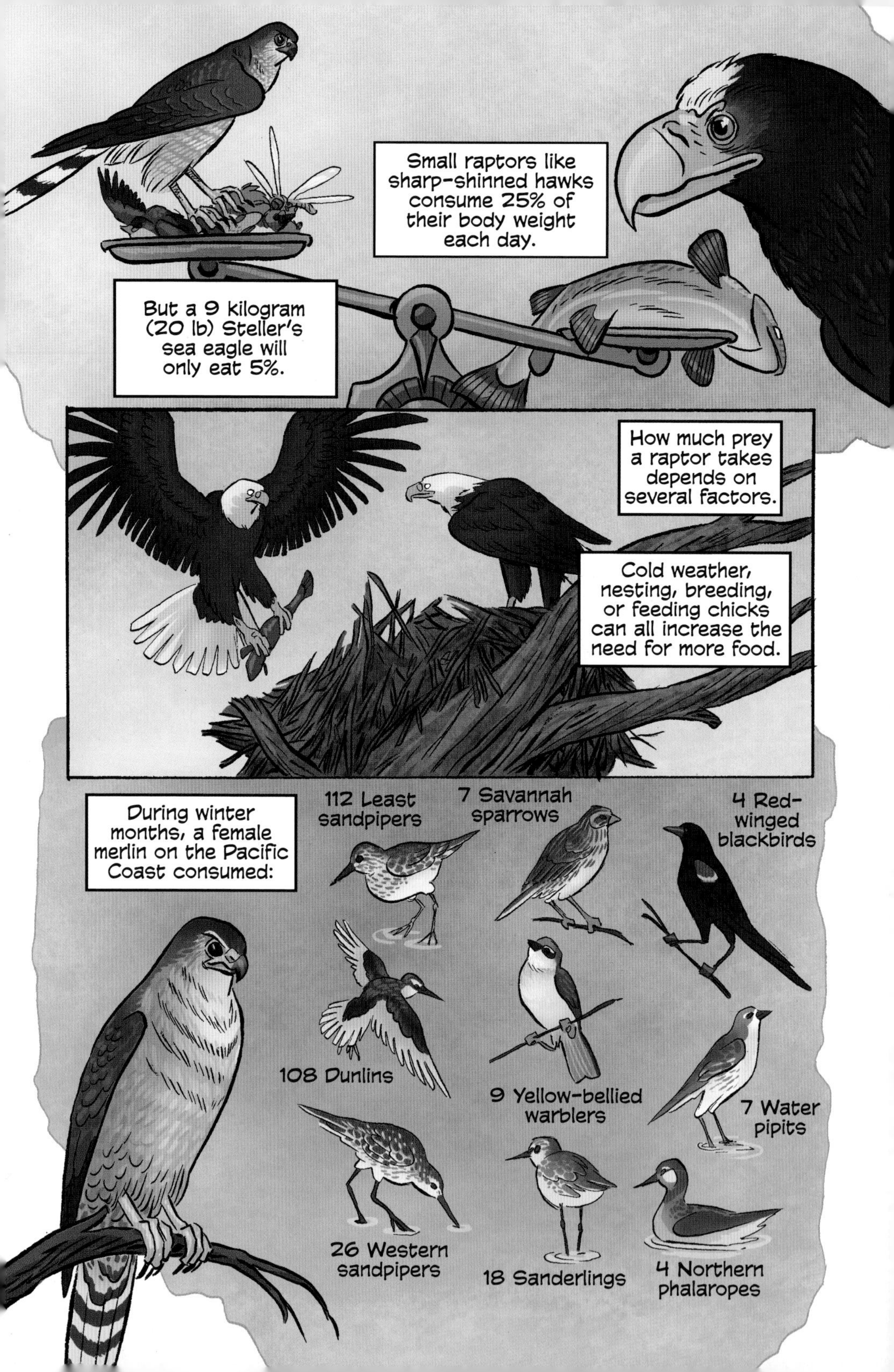

Small raptors like sharp-shinned hawks consume 25% of their body weight each day.
But a 9 kilogram (20 lb) Steller's sea eagle will only eat 5%.
How much prey a raptor takes depends on several factors.
Cold weather, nesting, breeding, or feeding chicks can all increase the need for more food.
During winter months, a female merlin on the Pacific Coast consumed:
112 Least sandpipers
7 Savannah sparrows
4 Red-winged blackbirds
108 Dunlins
9 Yellow-bellied warblers
7 Water pipits
26 Western sandpipers
18 Sanderlings
4 Northern phalaropes

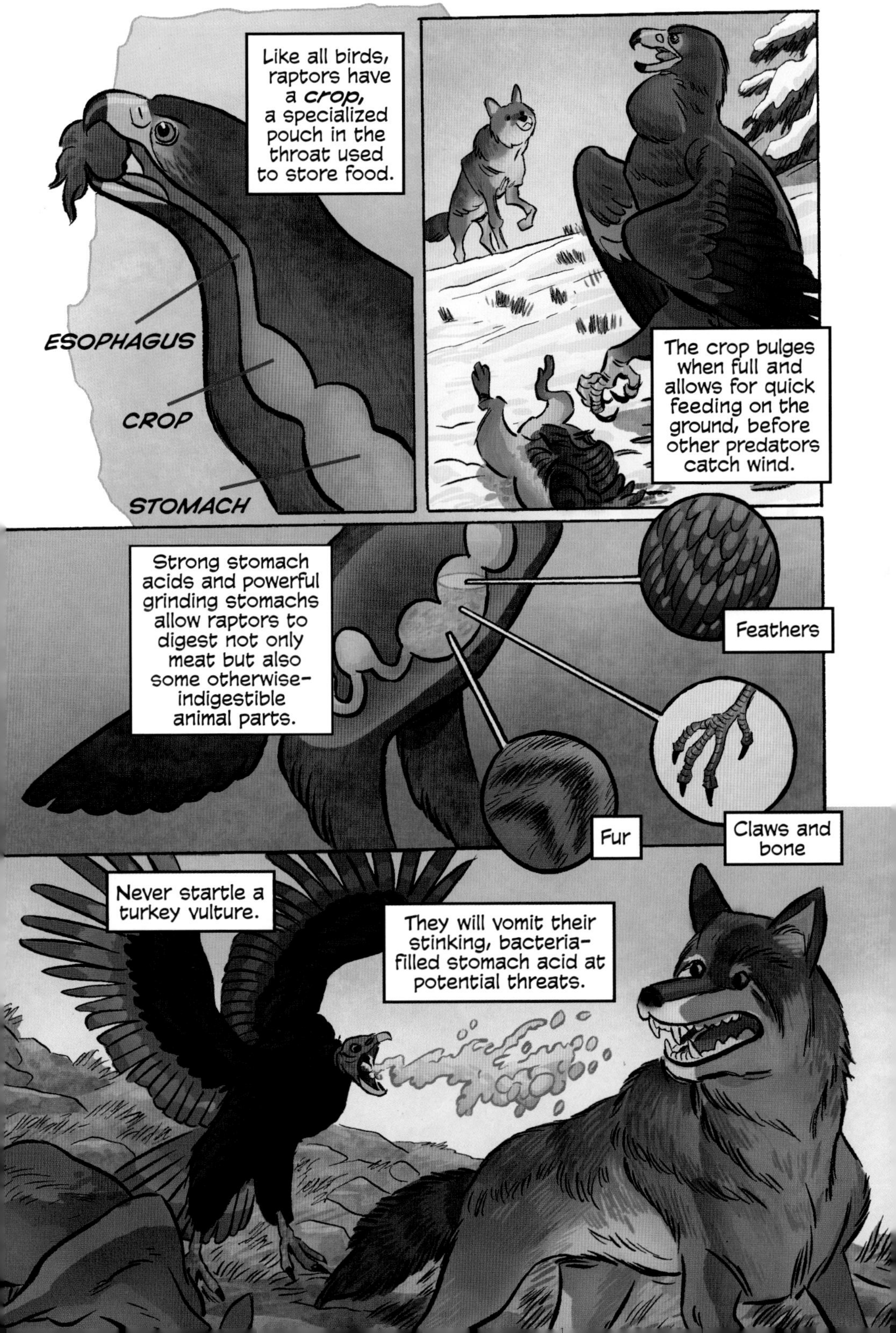
Like all birds, raptors have a *crop,* a specialized pouch in the throat used to store food.
ESOPHAGUS
CROP
STOMACH
The crop bulges when full and allows for quick feeding on the ground, before other predators catch wind.
Strong stomach acids and powerful grinding stomachs allow raptors to digest not only meat but also some otherwise-indigestible animal parts.
Feathers
Fur
Claws and bone
Never startle a turkey vulture.
They will vomit their stinking, bacteria-filled stomach acid at potential threats.

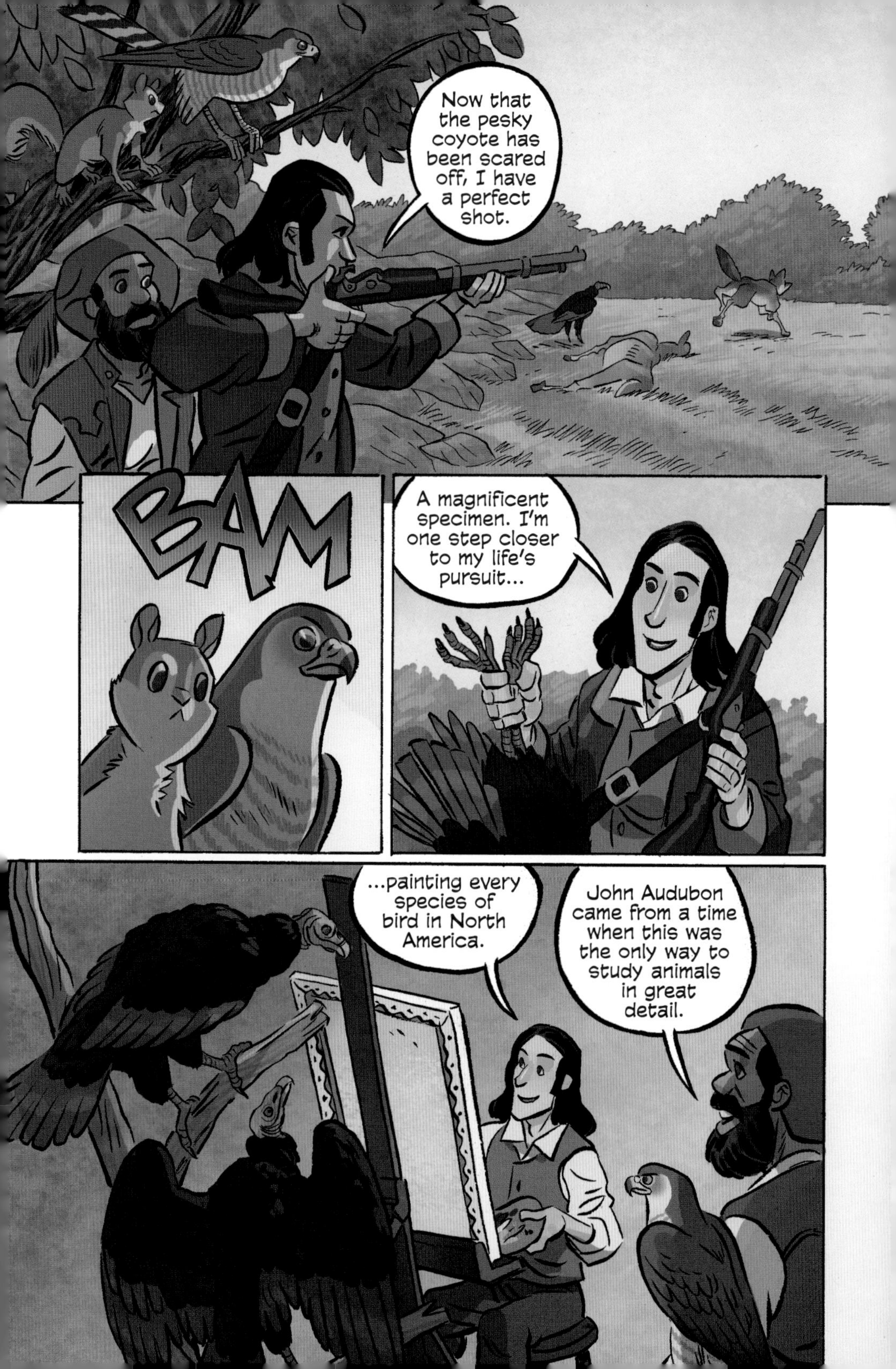

Now that the pesky coyote has been scared off, I have a perfect shot.
BAM
A magnificent specimen. I'm one step closer to my life's pursuit...
...painting every species of bird in North America.
John Audubon came from a time when this was the only way to study animals in great detail.

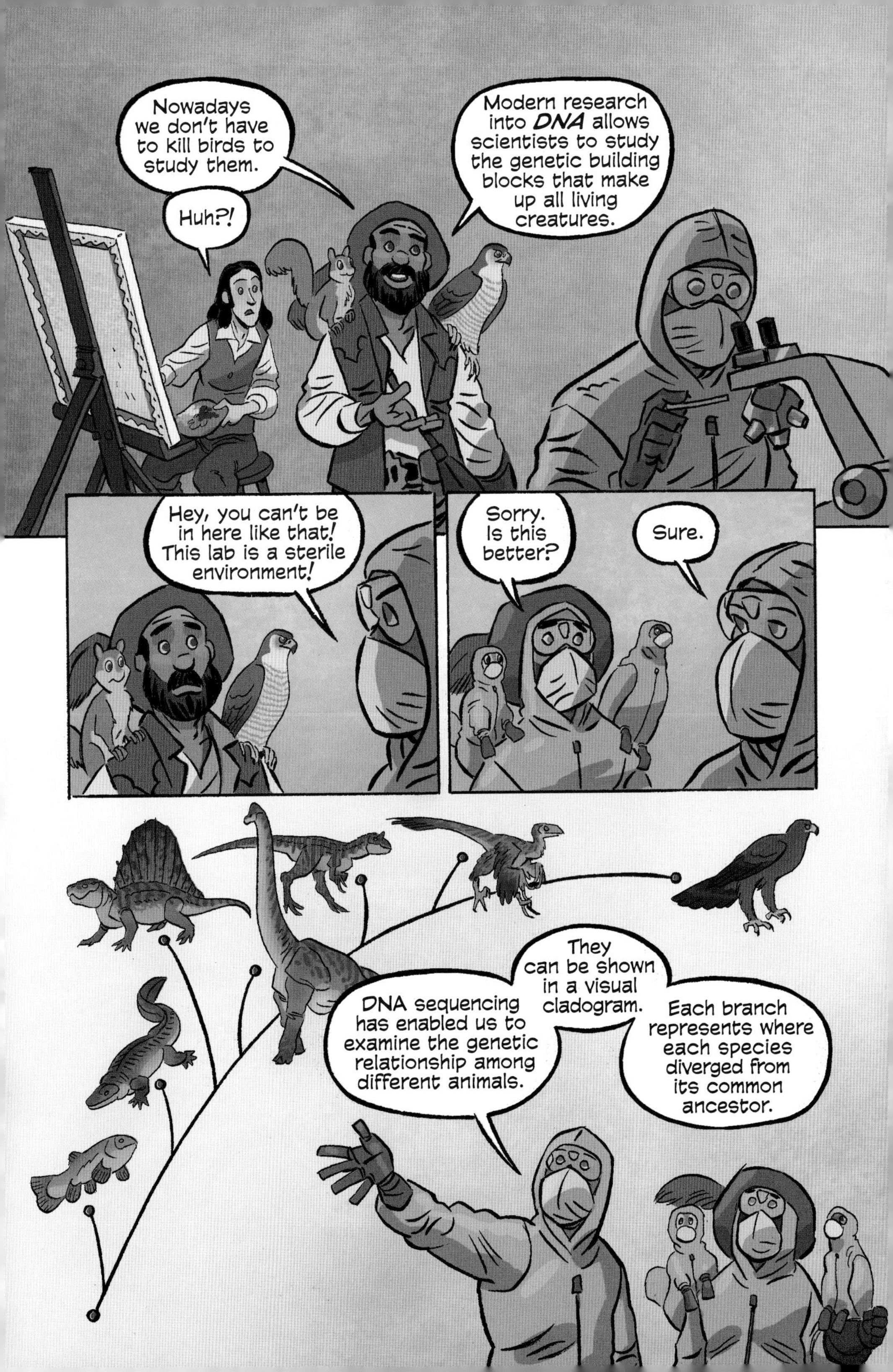

Nowadays we don't have to kill birds to study them.
Huh?!
Modern research into DNA allows scientists to study the genetic building blocks that make up all living creatures.
Hey, you can't be in here like that! This lab is a sterile environment!
Sorry. Is this better?
Sure.
DNA sequencing has enabled us to examine the genetic relationship among different animals.
They can be shown in a visual cladogram.
Each branch represents where each species diverged from its common ancestor.

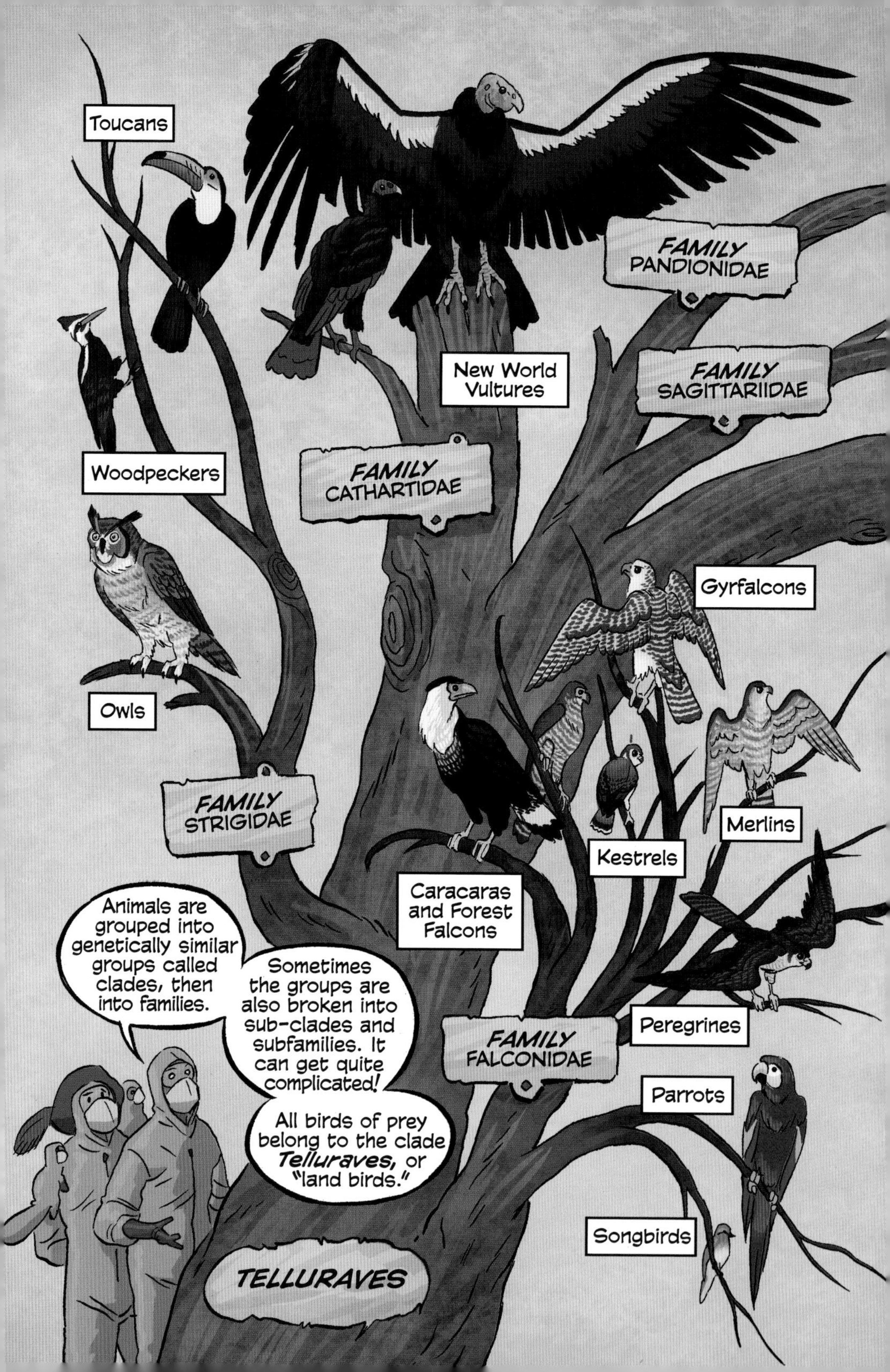

Toucans
FAMILY PANDIONIDAE
New World Vultures
FAMILY SAGITTARIIDAE
Woodpeckers
FAMILY CATHARTIDAE
Gyrfalcons
Owls
FAMILY STRIGIDAE
Merlins
Kestrels
Caracaras and Forest Falcons
Animals are grouped into genetically similar groups called clades, then into families.
Sometimes the groups are also broken into sub-clades and subfamilies. It can get quite complicated!
All birds of prey belong to the clade *Telluraves,* or "land birds."
Peregrines
FAMILY FALCONIDAE
Parrots
Songbirds
TELLURAVES

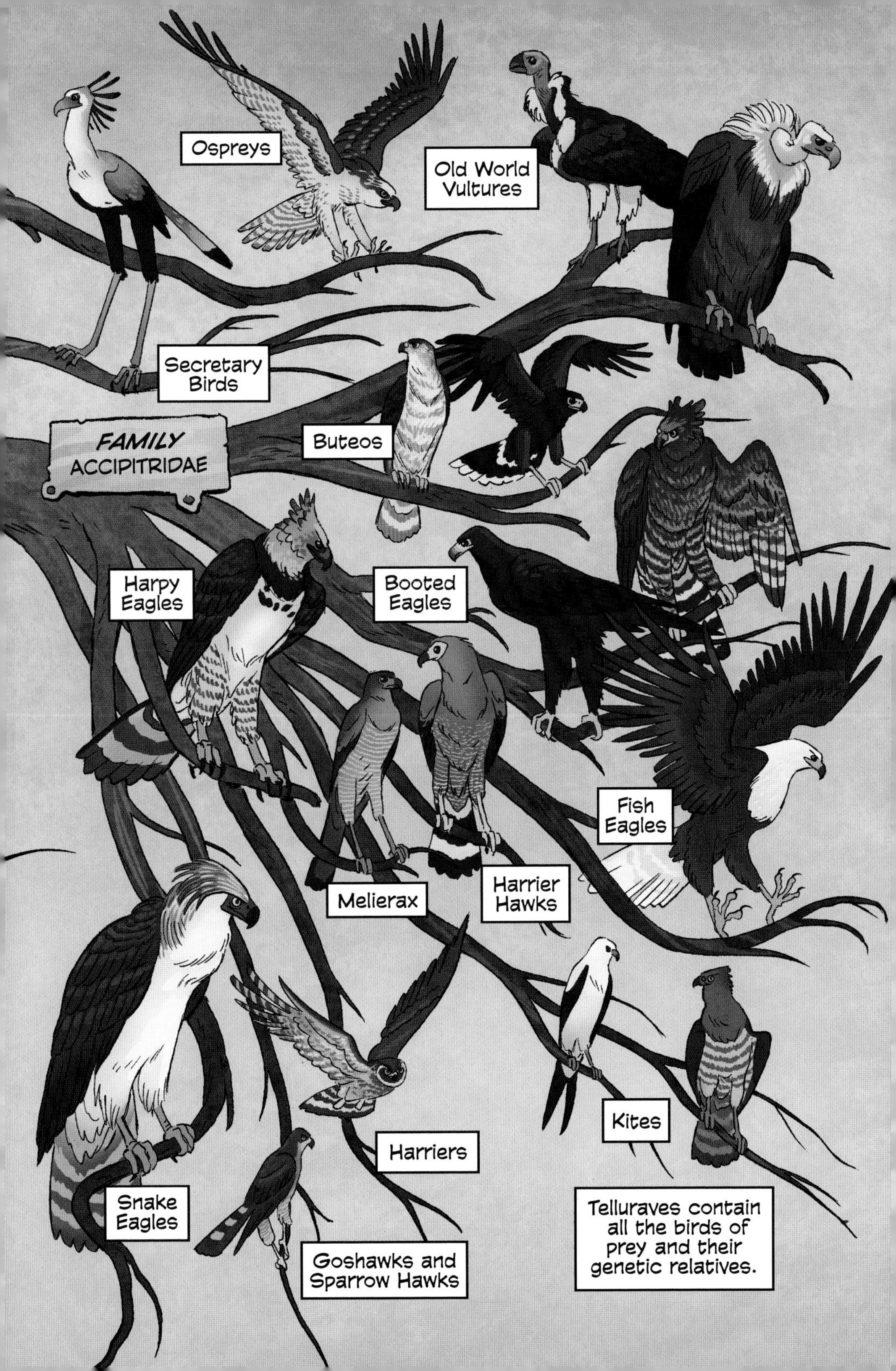

Ospreys
Old World Vultures
Secretary Birds
FAMILY ACCIPITRIDAE
Buteos
Harpy Eagles
Booted Eagles
Fish Eagles
Melierax
Harrier Hawks
Kites
Harriers
Snake Eagles
Goshawks and Sparrow Hawks
Telluraves contain all the birds of prey and their genetic relatives.

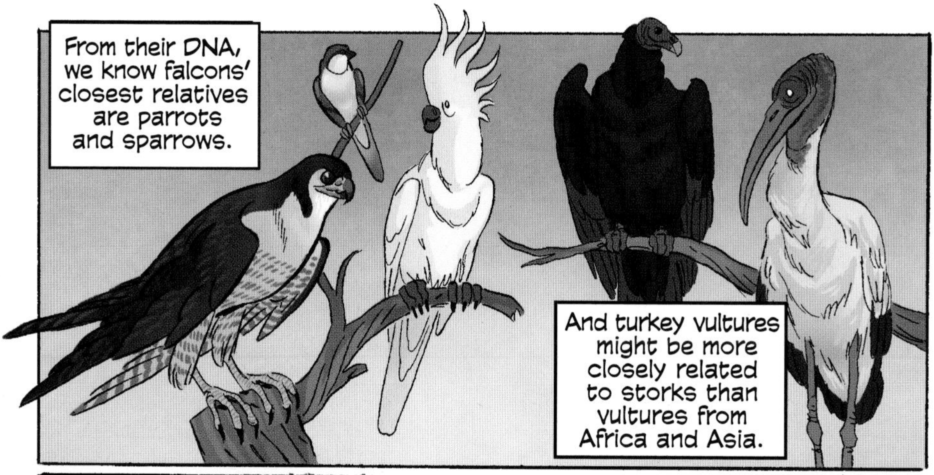
From their DNA, we know falcons' closest relatives are parrots and sparrows.
And turkey vultures might be more closely related to storks than vultures from Africa and Asia.

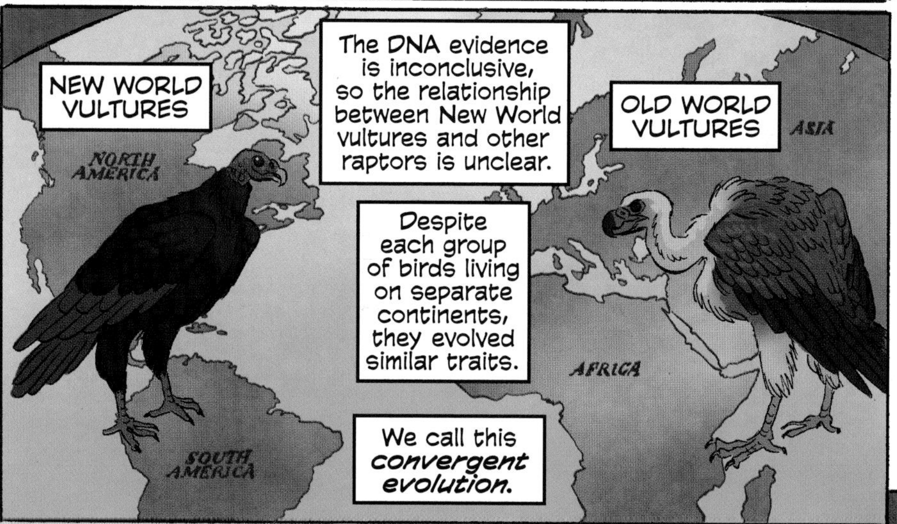
NEW WORLD VULTURES
NORTH AMERICA
SOUTH AMERICA
The DNA evidence is inconclusive, so the relationship between New World vultures and other raptors is unclear.
OLD WORLD VULTURES
ASIA
AFRICA
Despite each group of birds living on separate continents, they evolved similar traits.
We call this ***convergent evolution.***

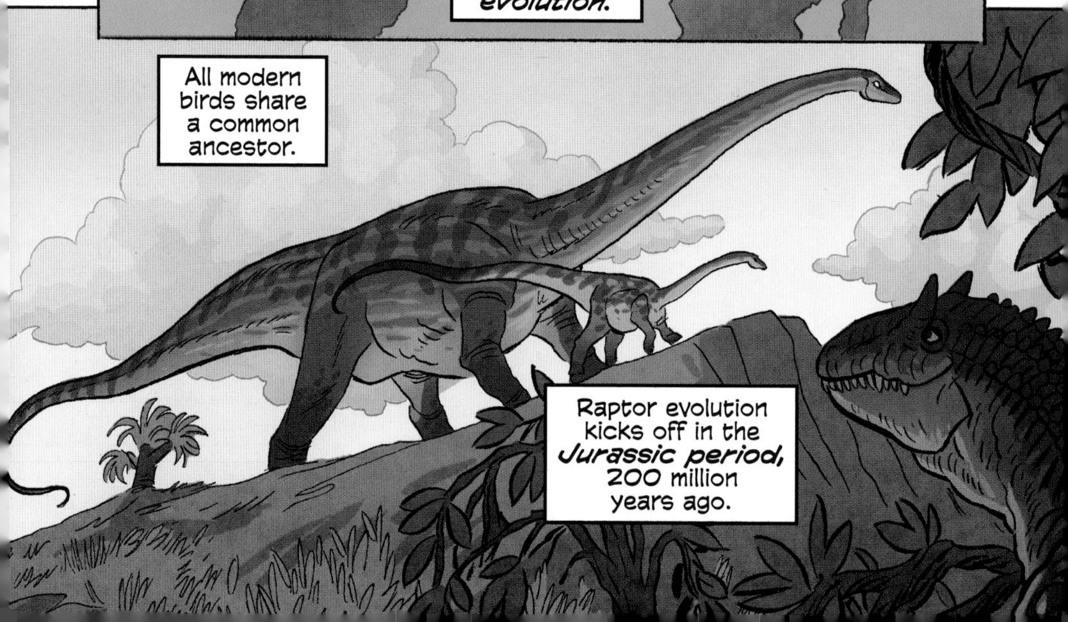
All modern birds share a common ancestor.
Raptor evolution kicks off in the ***Jurassic period,*** 200 million years ago.

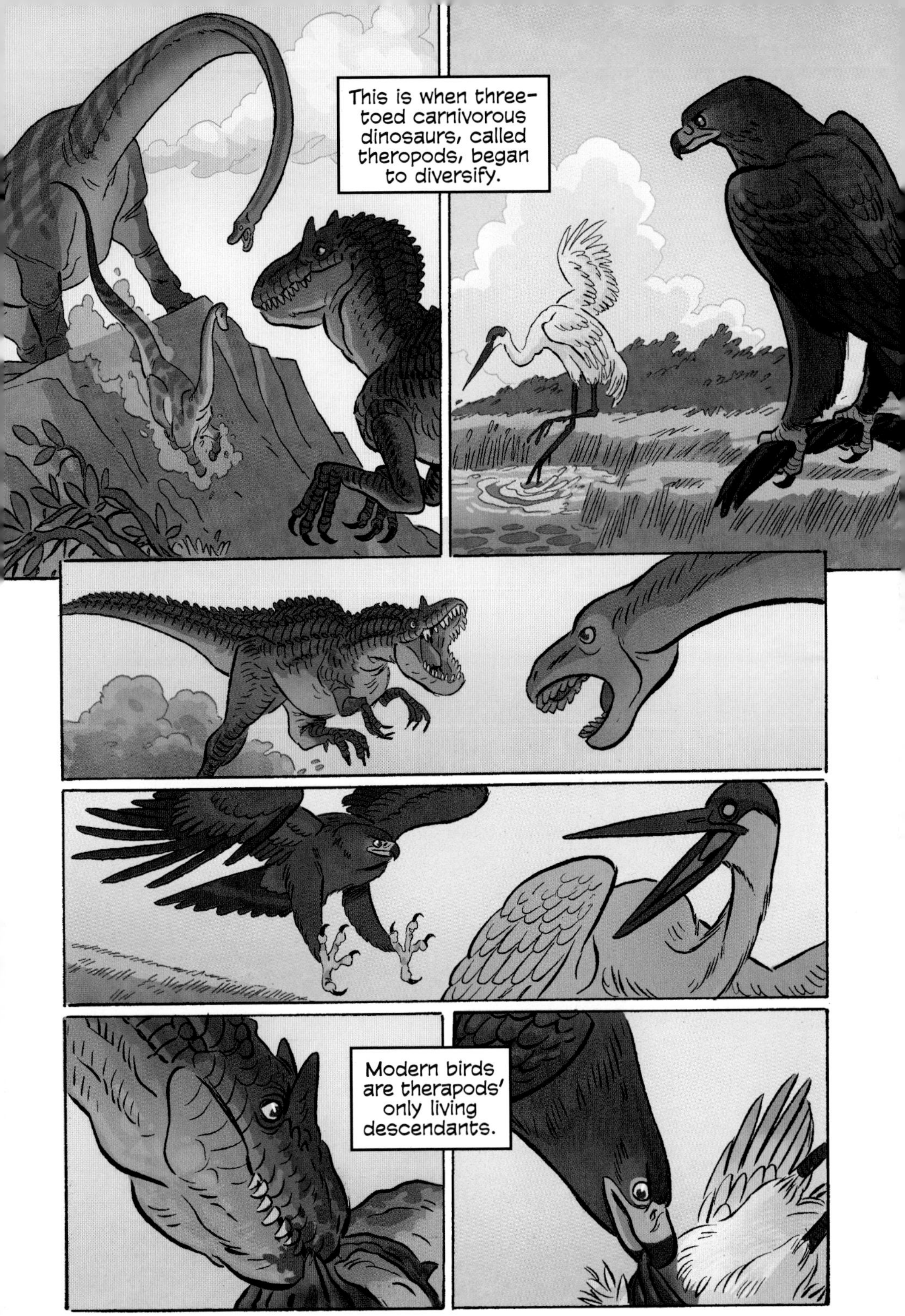
This is when three-toed carnivorous dinosaurs, called theropods, began to diversify.
Modern birds are therapods' only living descendants.

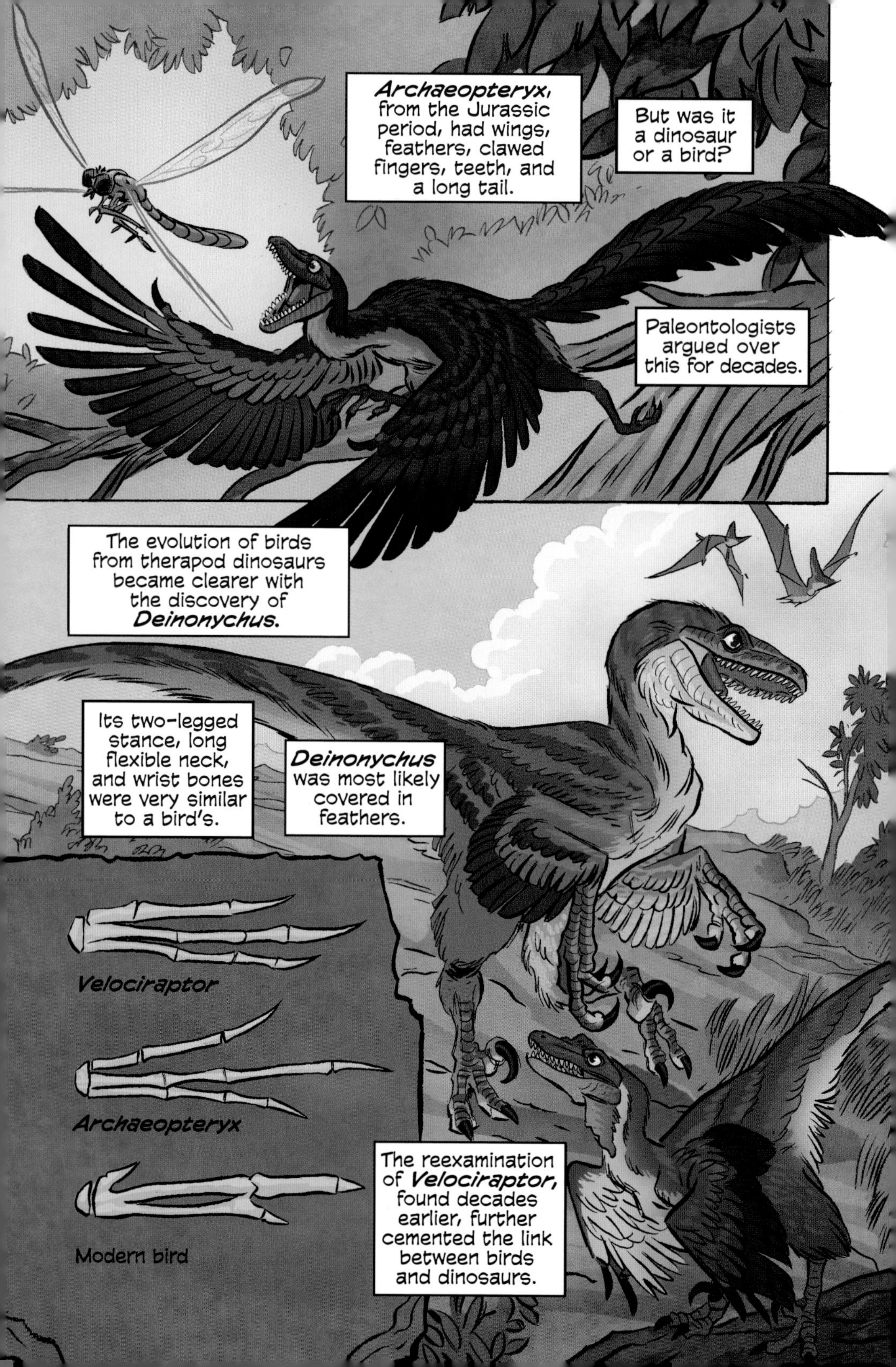
Archaeopteryx, from the Jurassic period, had wings, feathers, clawed fingers, teeth, and a long tail.
But was it a dinosaur or a bird?
Paleontologists argued over this for decades.
The evolution of birds from therapod dinosaurs became clearer with the discovery of ***Deinonychus***.
Its two-legged stance, long flexible neck, and wrist bones were very similar to a bird's.
Deinonychus was most likely covered in feathers.
Velociraptor
Archaeopteryx
Modern bird
The reexamination of ***Velociraptor***, found decades earlier, further cemented the link between birds and dinosaurs.

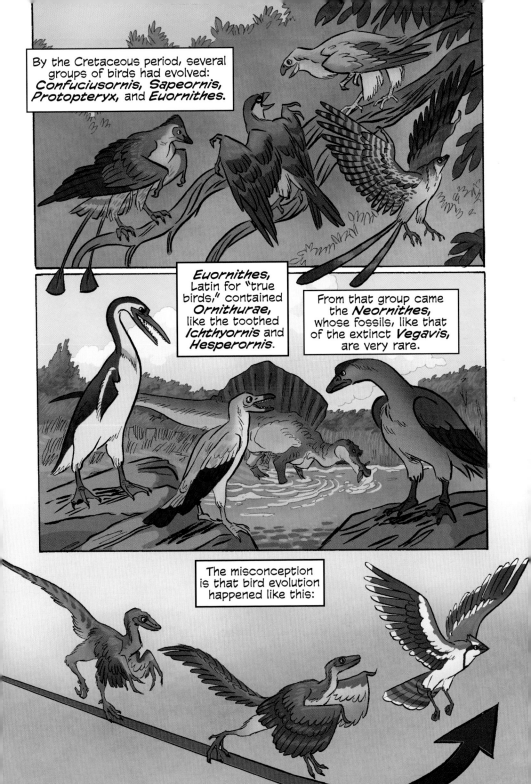

By the Cretaceous period, several groups of birds had evolved: *Confuciusornis*, *Sapeornis*, *Protopteryx*, and *Euornithes*.

Euornithes, Latin for "true birds," contained *Ornithurae*, like the toothed *Ichthyornis* and *Hesperornis*.

From that group came the *Neornithes*, whose fossils, like that of the extinct *Vegavis*, are very rare.

The misconception is that bird evolution happened like this:

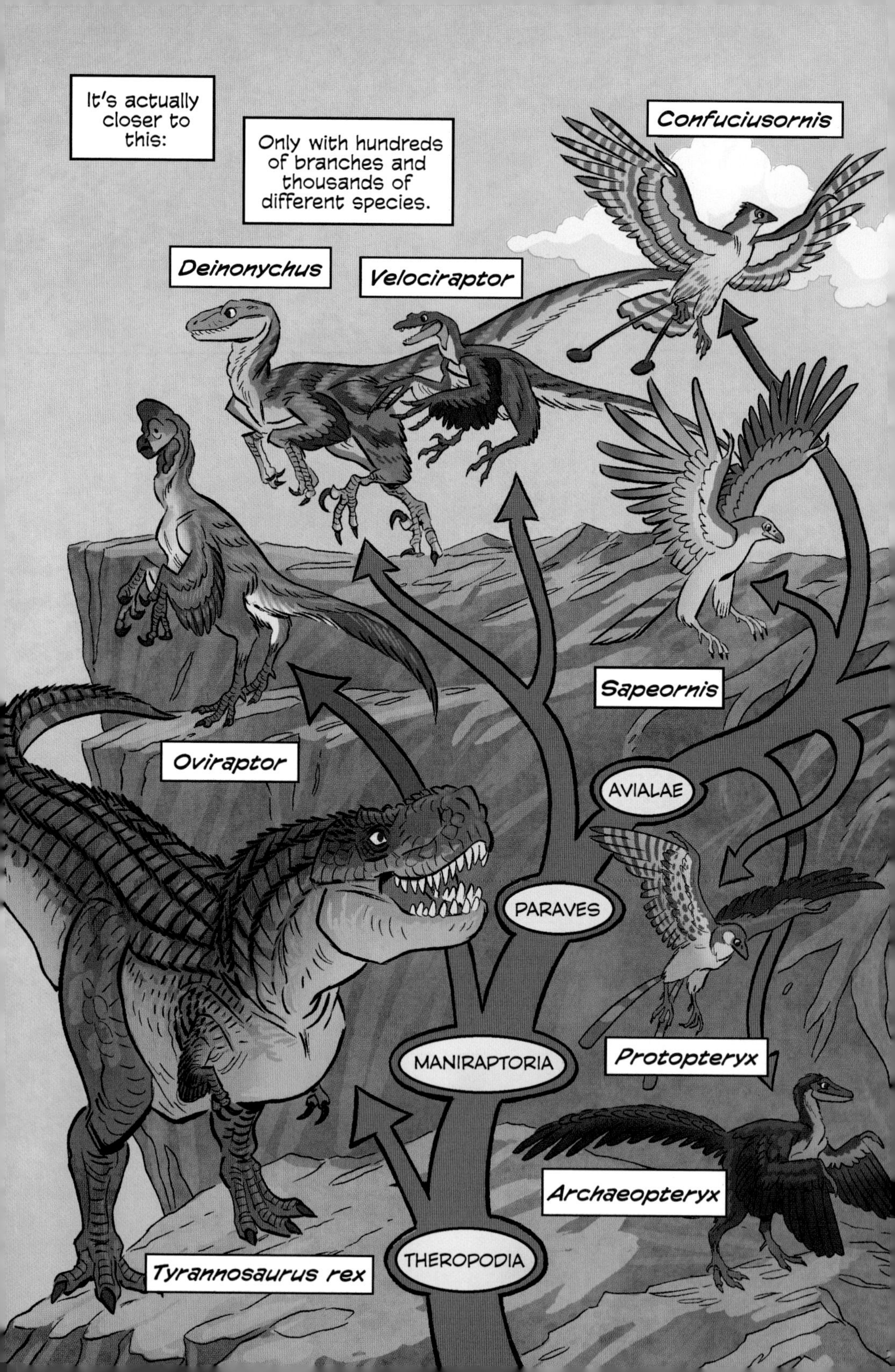
It's actually closer to this:
Only with hundreds of branches and thousands of different species.
Confuciusornis
Deinonychus
Velociraptor
Sapeornis
Oviraptor
AVIALAE
PARAVES
MANIRAPTORIA
Protopteryx
Archaeopteryx
THEROPODIA
Tyrannosaurus rex

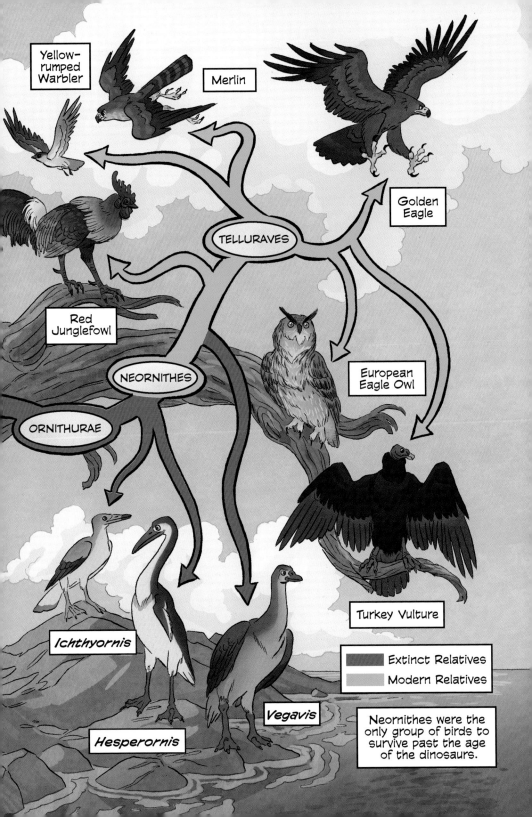

Yellow-rumped Warbler

Merlin

Golden Eagle

TELLURAVES

Red Junglefowl

NEORNITHES

European Eagle Owl

ORNITHURAE

Turkey Vulture

Ichthyornis

Vegavis

Hesperornis

Extinct Relatives
Modern Relatives

Neornithes were the only group of birds to survive past the age of the dinosaurs.

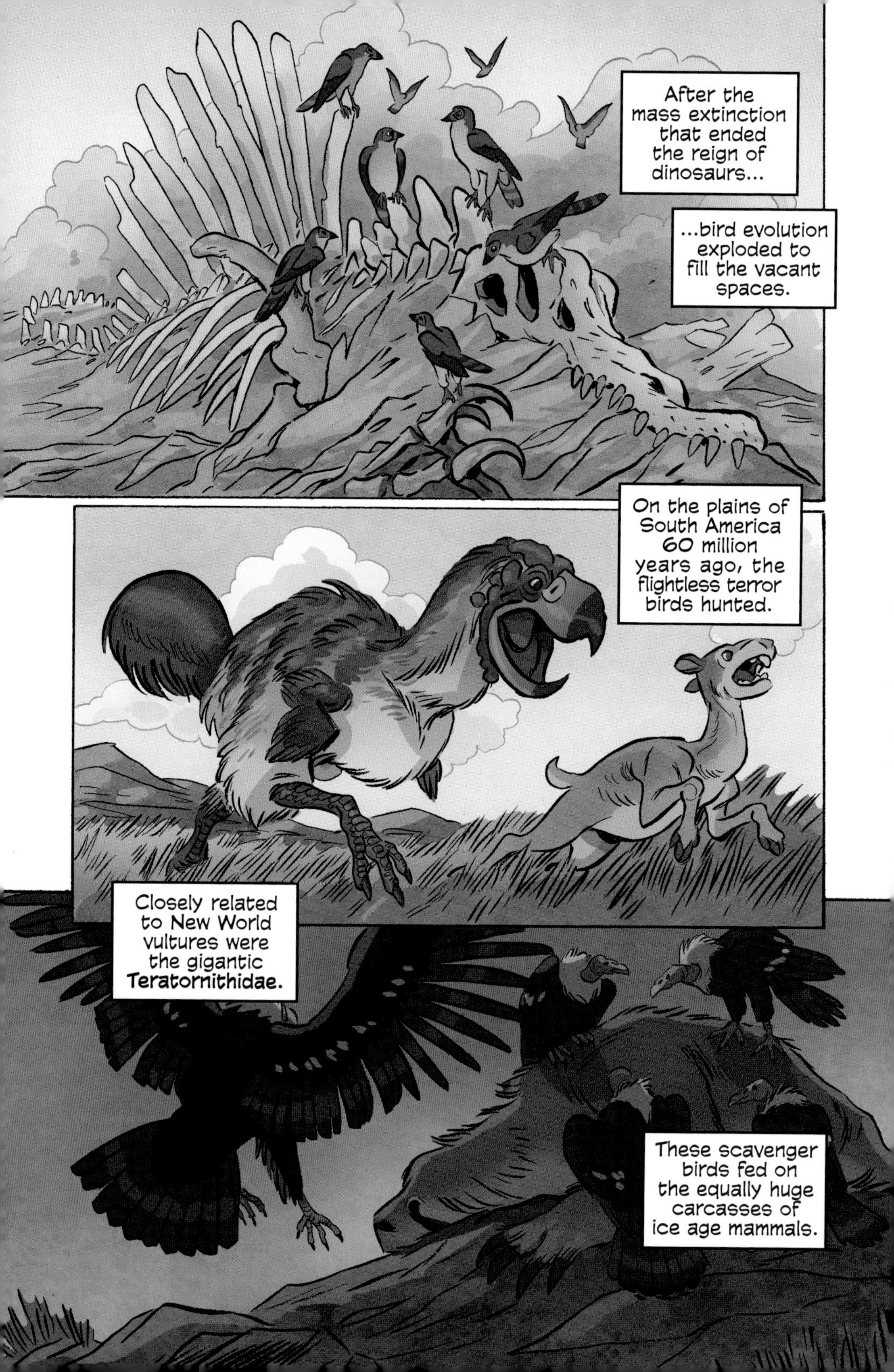

After the mass extinction that ended the reign of dinosaurs...
...bird evolution exploded to fill the vacant spaces.
On the plains of South America 60 million years ago, the flightless terror birds hunted.
Closely related to New World vultures were the gigantic **Teratornithidae**.
These scavenger birds fed on the equally huge carcasses of ice age mammals.

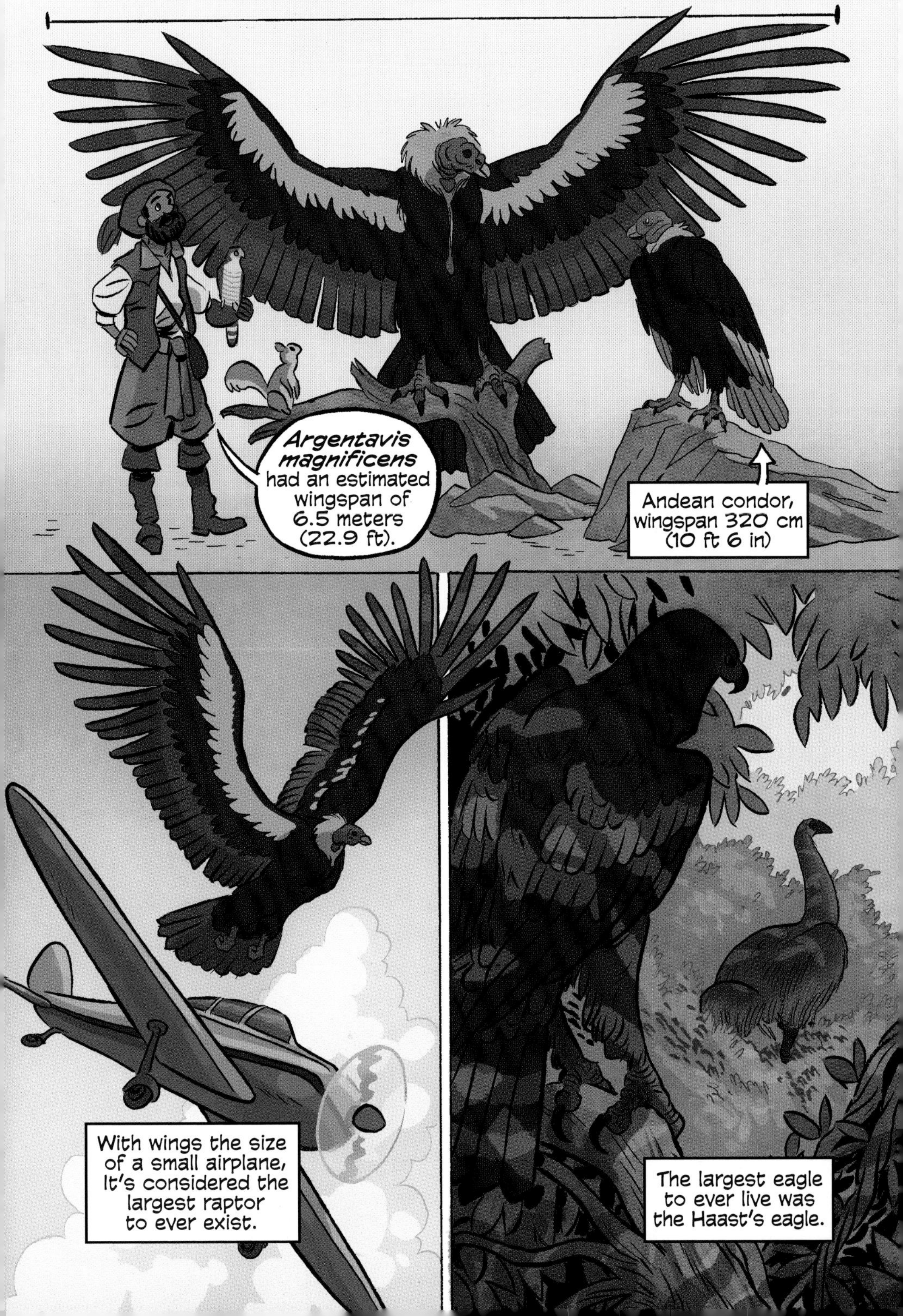
Argentavis magnificens had an estimated wingspan of 6.5 meters (22.9 ft).
Andean condor, wingspan 320 cm (10 ft 6 in)
With wings the size of a small airplane, it's considered the largest raptor to ever exist.
The largest eagle to ever live was the Haast's eagle.

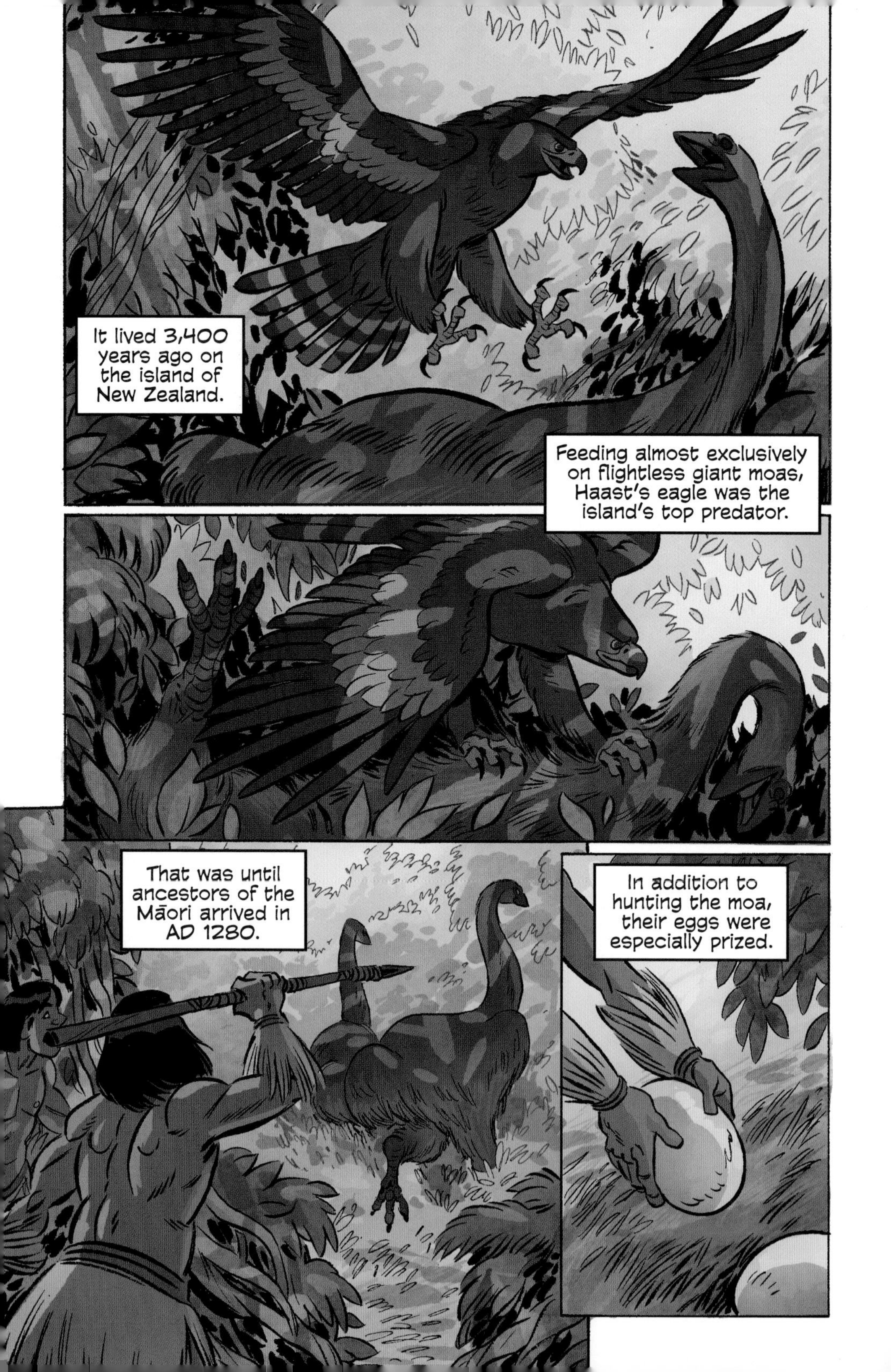
It lived 3,400 years ago on the island of New Zealand.
Feeding almost exclusively on flightless giant moas, Haast's eagle was the island's top predator.
That was until ancestors of the Māori arrived in AD 1280.
In addition to hunting the moa, their eggs were especially prized.

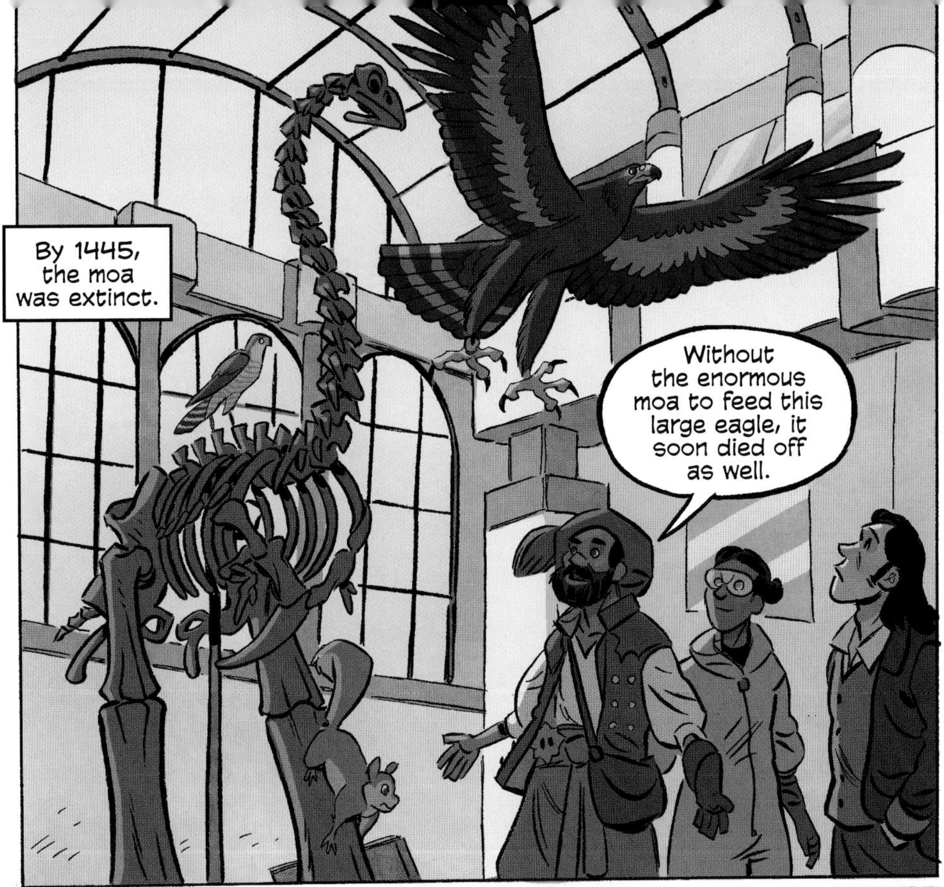
By 1445, the moa was extinct.
Without the enormous moa to feed this large eagle, it soon died off as well.

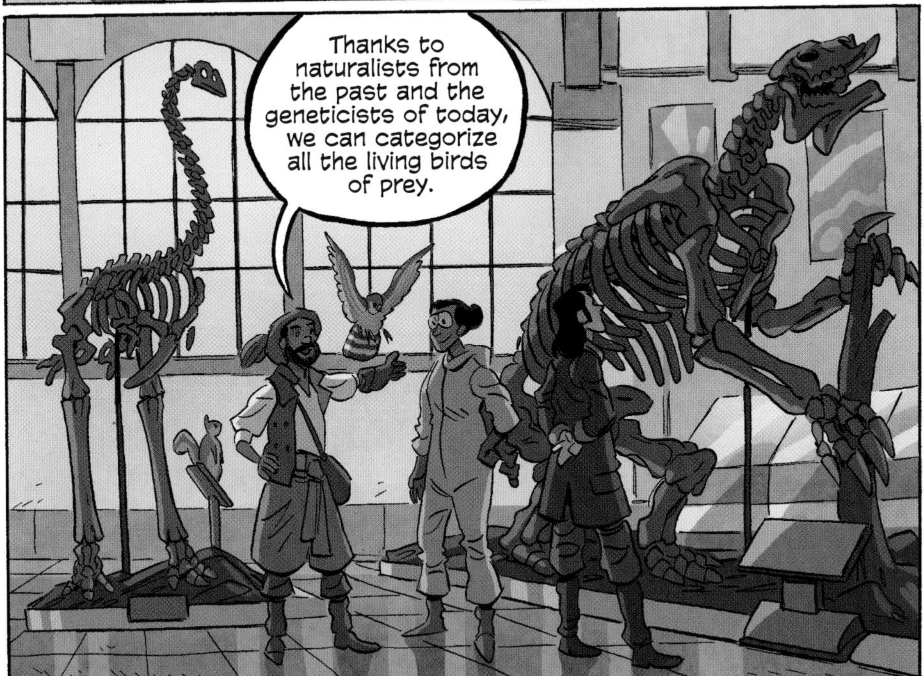
Thanks to naturalists from the past and the geneticists of today, we can categorize all the living birds of prey.

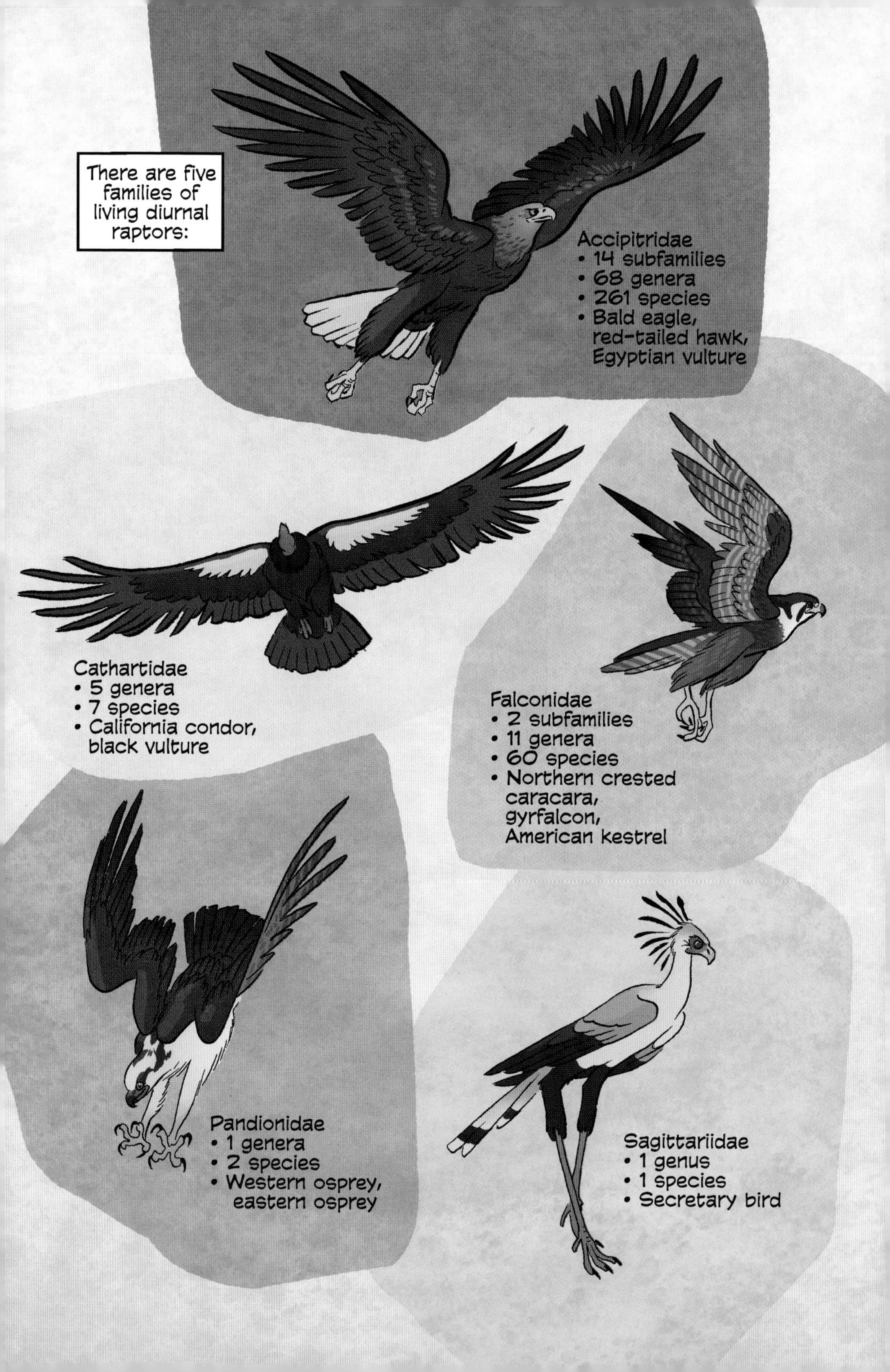
There are five families of living diurnal raptors:
Accipitridae
• 14 subfamilies
• 68 genera
• 261 species
• Bald eagle, red-tailed hawk, Egyptian vulture
Cathartidae
• 5 genera
• 7 species
• California condor, black vulture
Falconidae
• 2 subfamilies
• 11 genera
• 60 species
• Northern crested caracara, gyrfalcon, American kestrel
Pandionidae
• 1 genera
• 2 species
• Western osprey, eastern osprey
Sagittariidae
• 1 genus
• 1 species
• Secretary bird

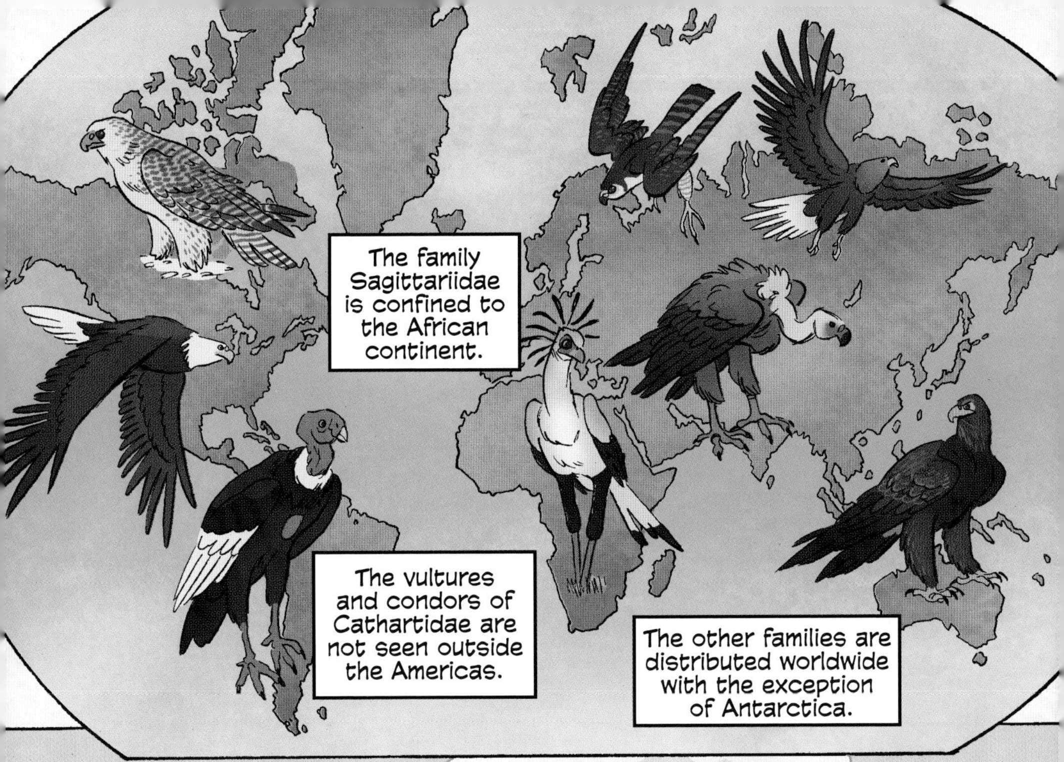
The family Sagittariidae is confined to the African continent.
The vultures and condors of Cathartidae are not seen outside the Americas.
The other families are distributed worldwide with the exception of Antarctica.

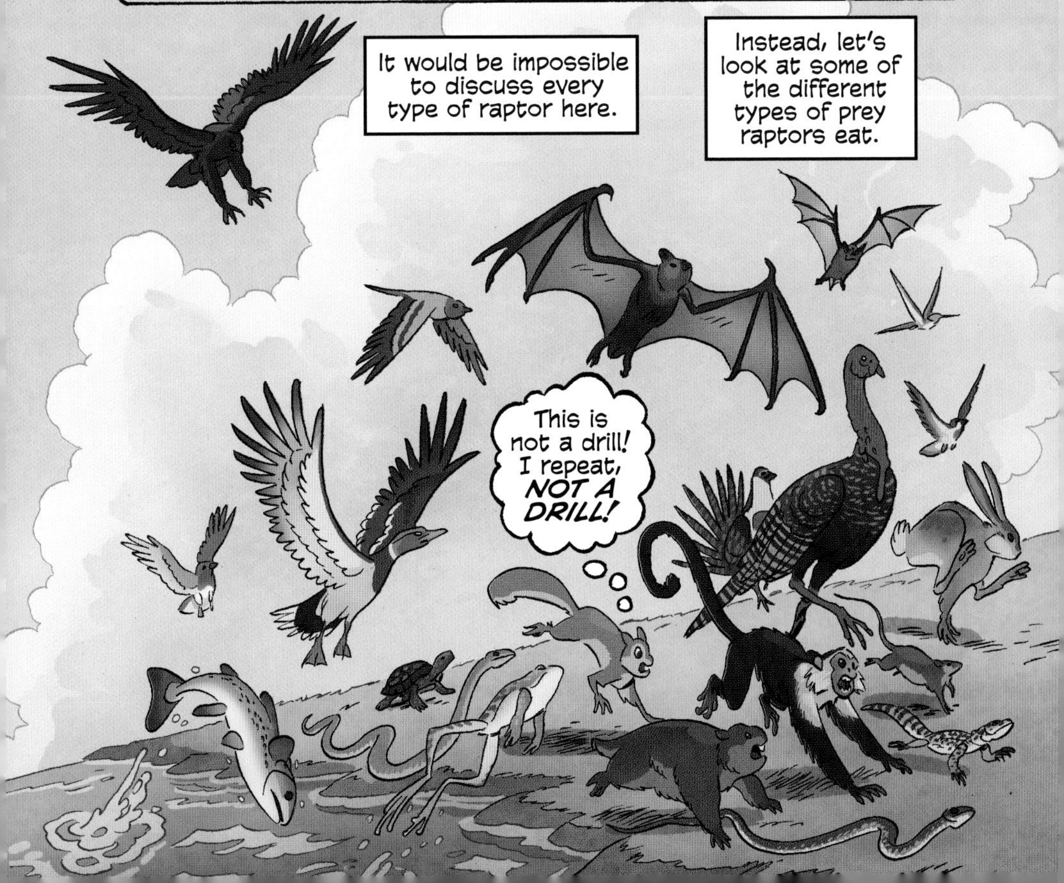
It would be impossible to discuss every type of raptor here.
Instead, let's look at some of the different types of prey raptors eat.
This is not a drill! I repeat, NOT A DRILL!

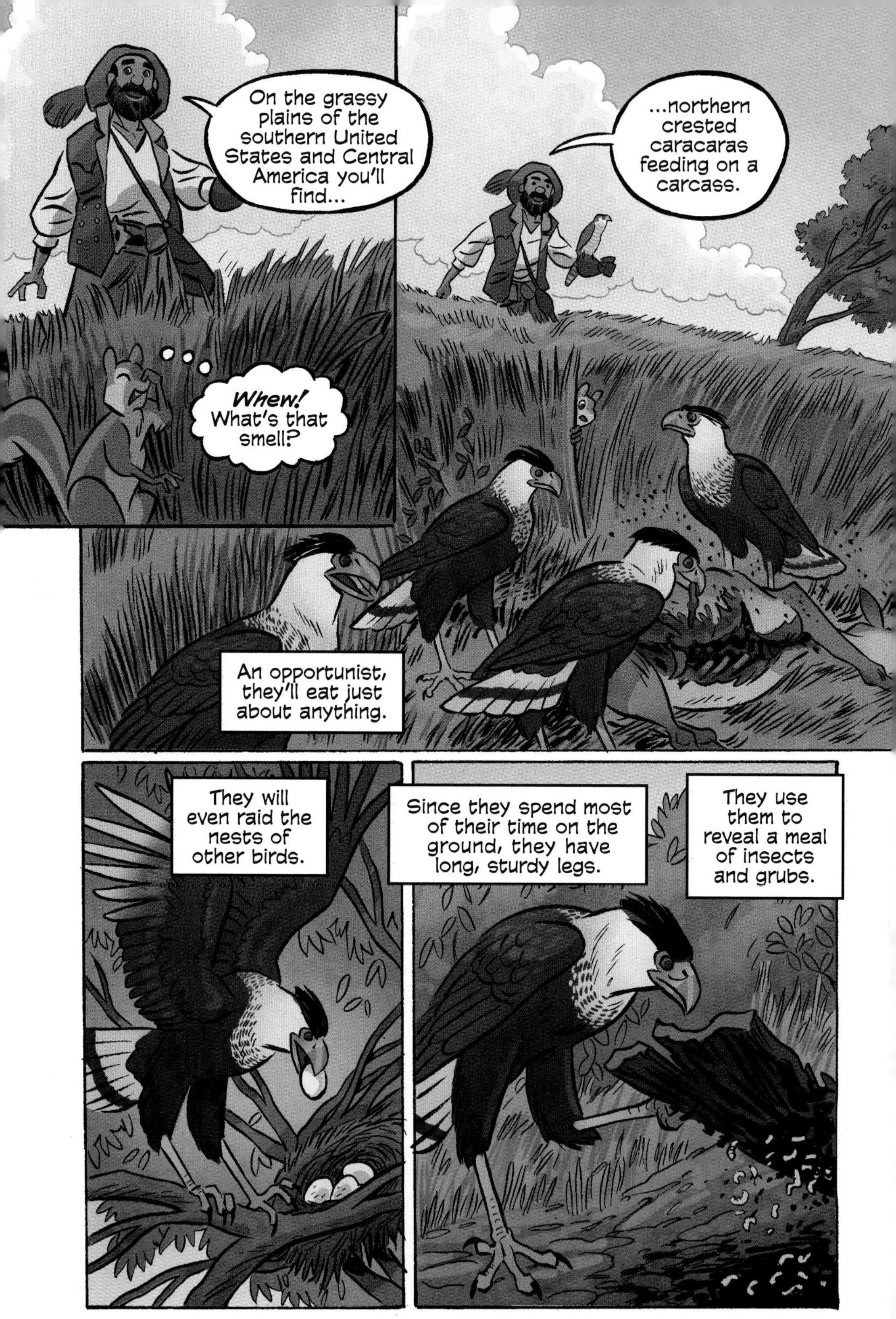
On the grassy plains of the southern United States and Central America you'll find...
Whew! What's that smell?
...northern crested caracaras feeding on a carcass.
An opportunist, they'll eat just about anything.
They will even raid the nests of other birds.
Since they spend most of their time on the ground, they have long, sturdy legs.
They use them to reveal a meal of insects and grubs.

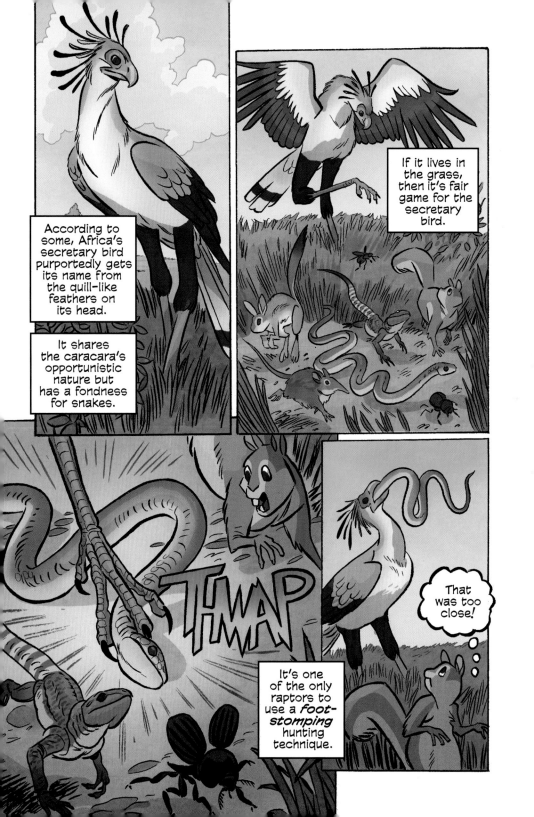

According to some, Africa's secretary bird purportedly gets its name from the quill-like feathers on its head.

It shares the caracara's opportunistic nature but has a fondness for snakes.

If it lives in the grass, then it's fair game for the secretary bird.

THWAP

That was too close!

It's one of the only raptors to use a *foot-stomping* hunting technique.

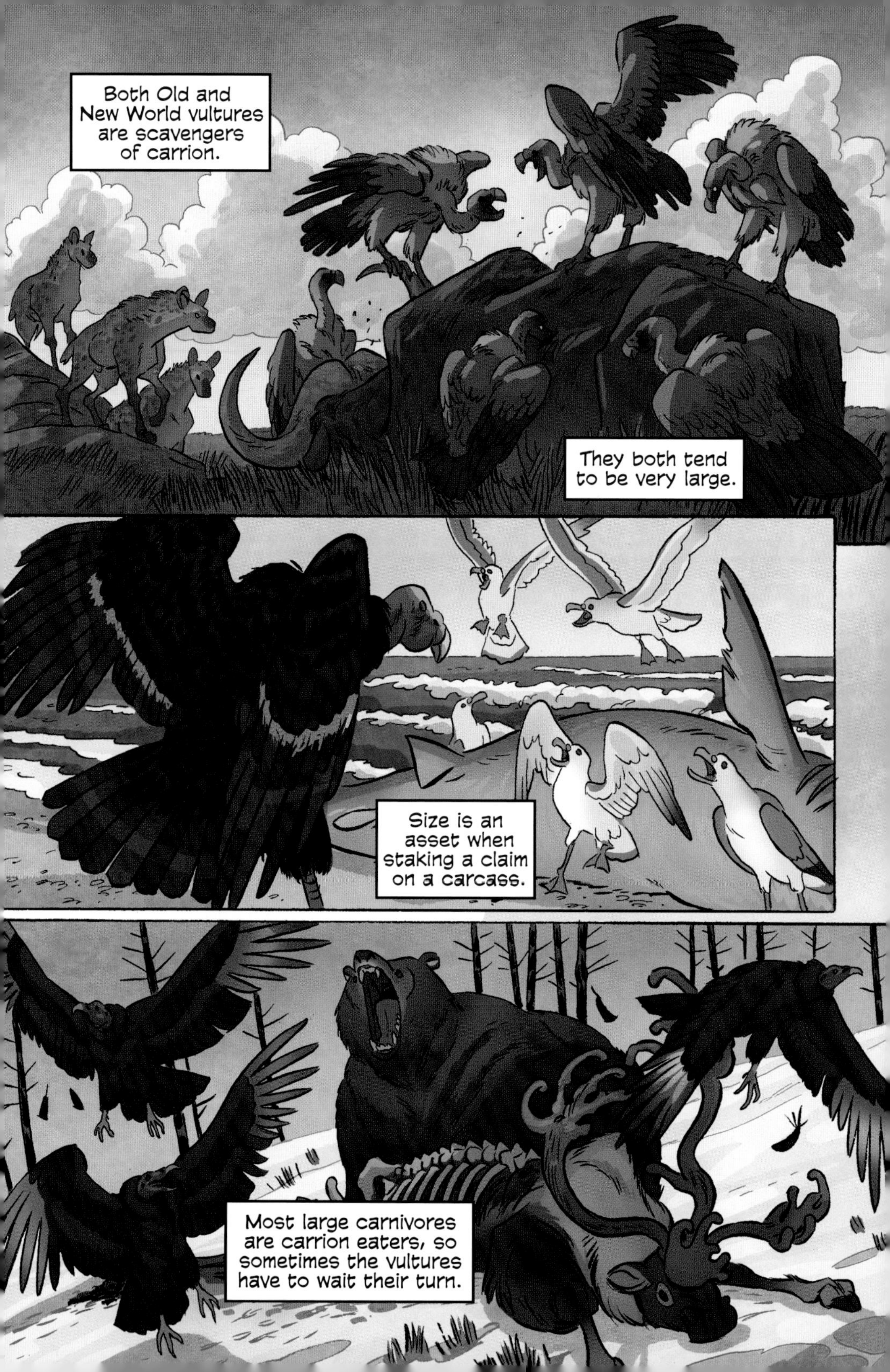
Both Old and New World vultures are scavengers of carrion.
They both tend to be very large.
Size is an asset when staking a claim on a carcass.
Most large carnivores are carrion eaters, so sometimes the vultures have to wait their turn.

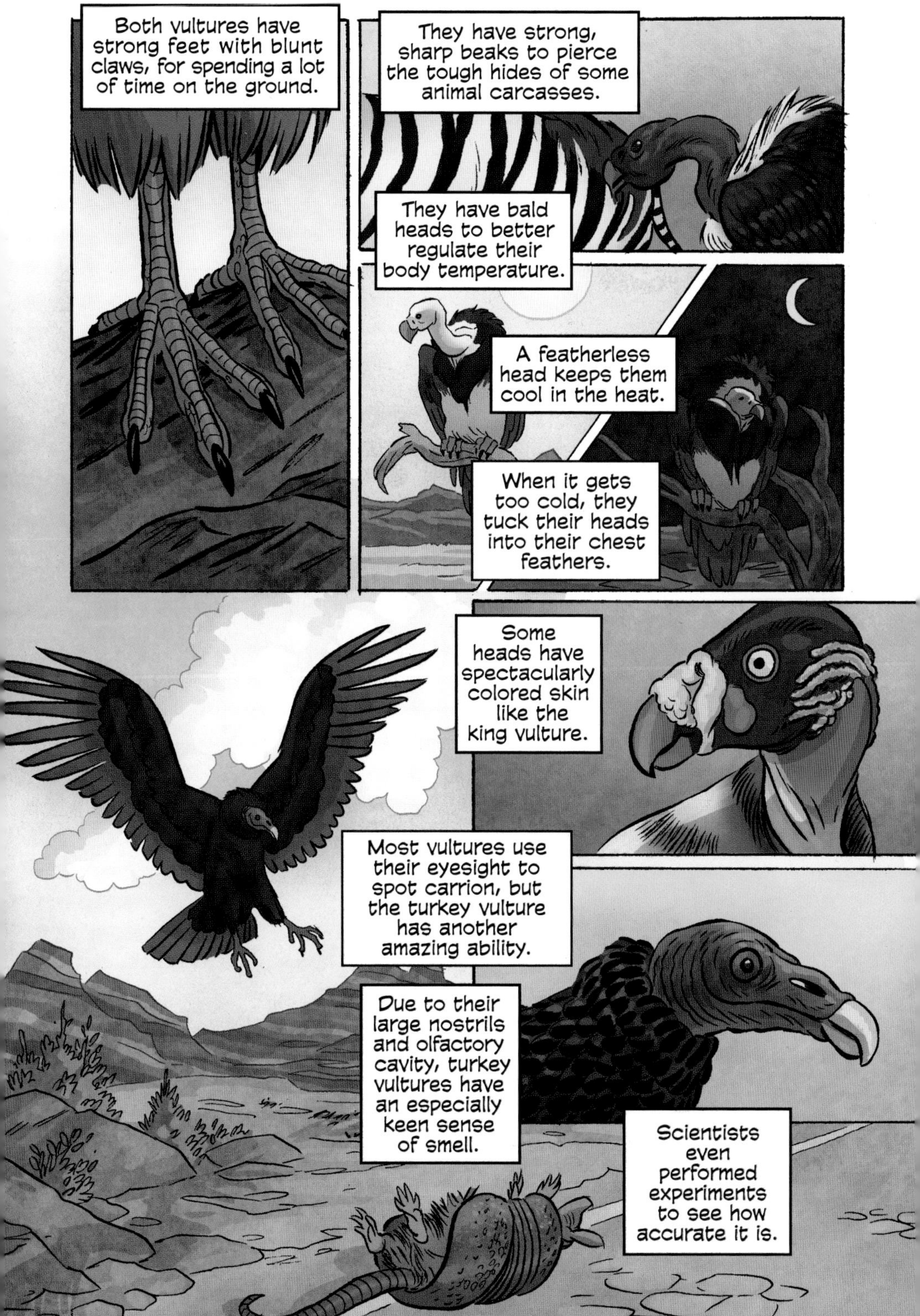
Both vultures have strong feet with blunt claws, for spending a lot of time on the ground.
They have strong, sharp beaks to pierce the tough hides of some animal carcasses.
They have bald heads to better regulate their body temperature.
A featherless head keeps them cool in the heat.
When it gets too cold, they tuck their heads into their chest feathers.
Some heads have spectacularly colored skin like the king vulture.
Most vultures use their eyesight to spot carrion, but the turkey vulture has another amazing ability.
Due to their large nostrils and olfactory cavity, turkey vultures have an especially keen sense of smell.
Scientists even performed experiments to see how accurate it is.

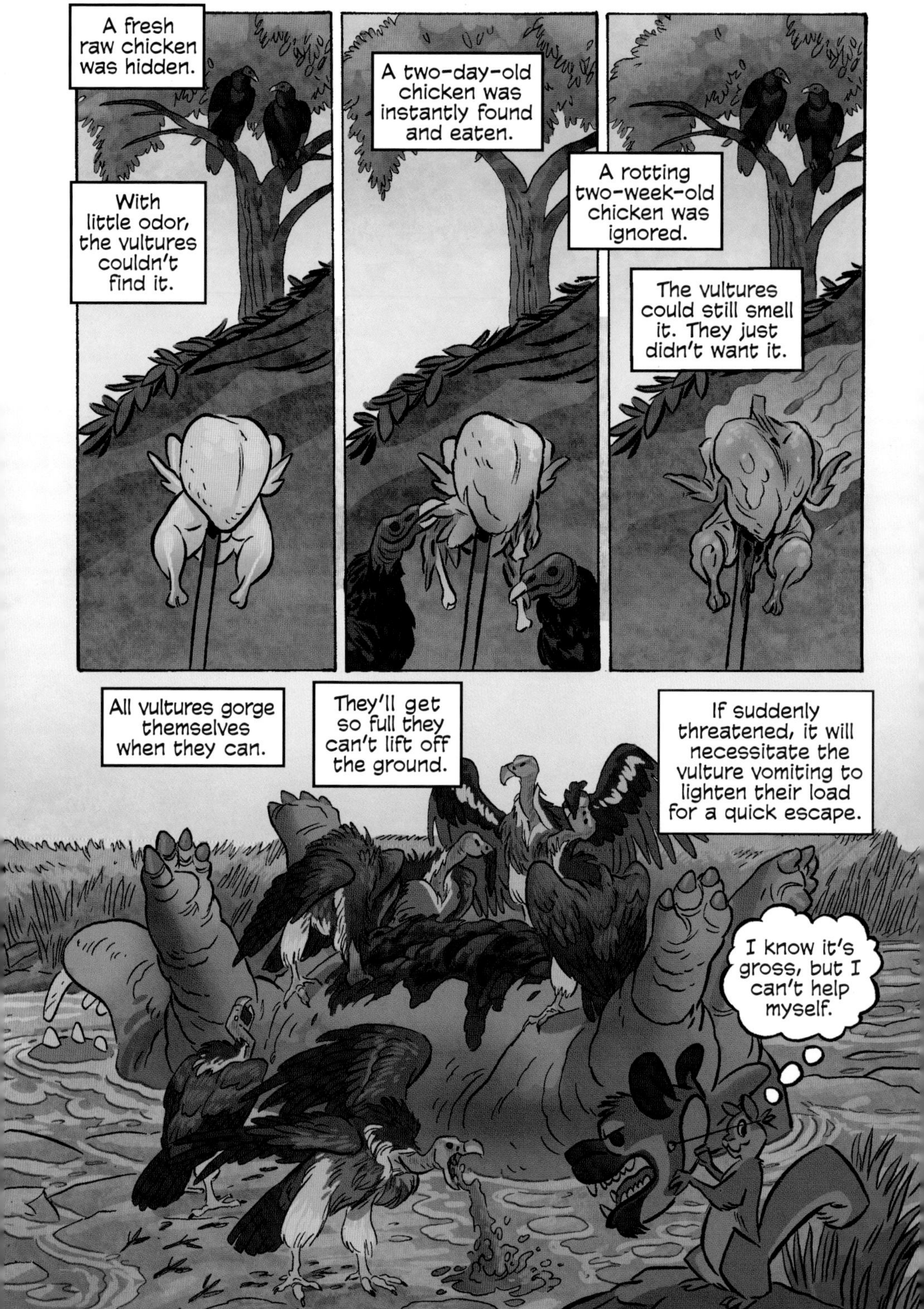
A fresh raw chicken was hidden.
With little odor, the vultures couldn't find it.
A two-day-old chicken was instantly found and eaten.
A rotting two-week-old chicken was ignored.
The vultures could still smell it. They just didn't want it.
All vultures gorge themselves when they can.
They'll get so full they can't lift off the ground.
If suddenly threatened, it will necessitate the vulture vomiting to lighten their load for a quick escape.
I know it's gross, but I can't help myself.

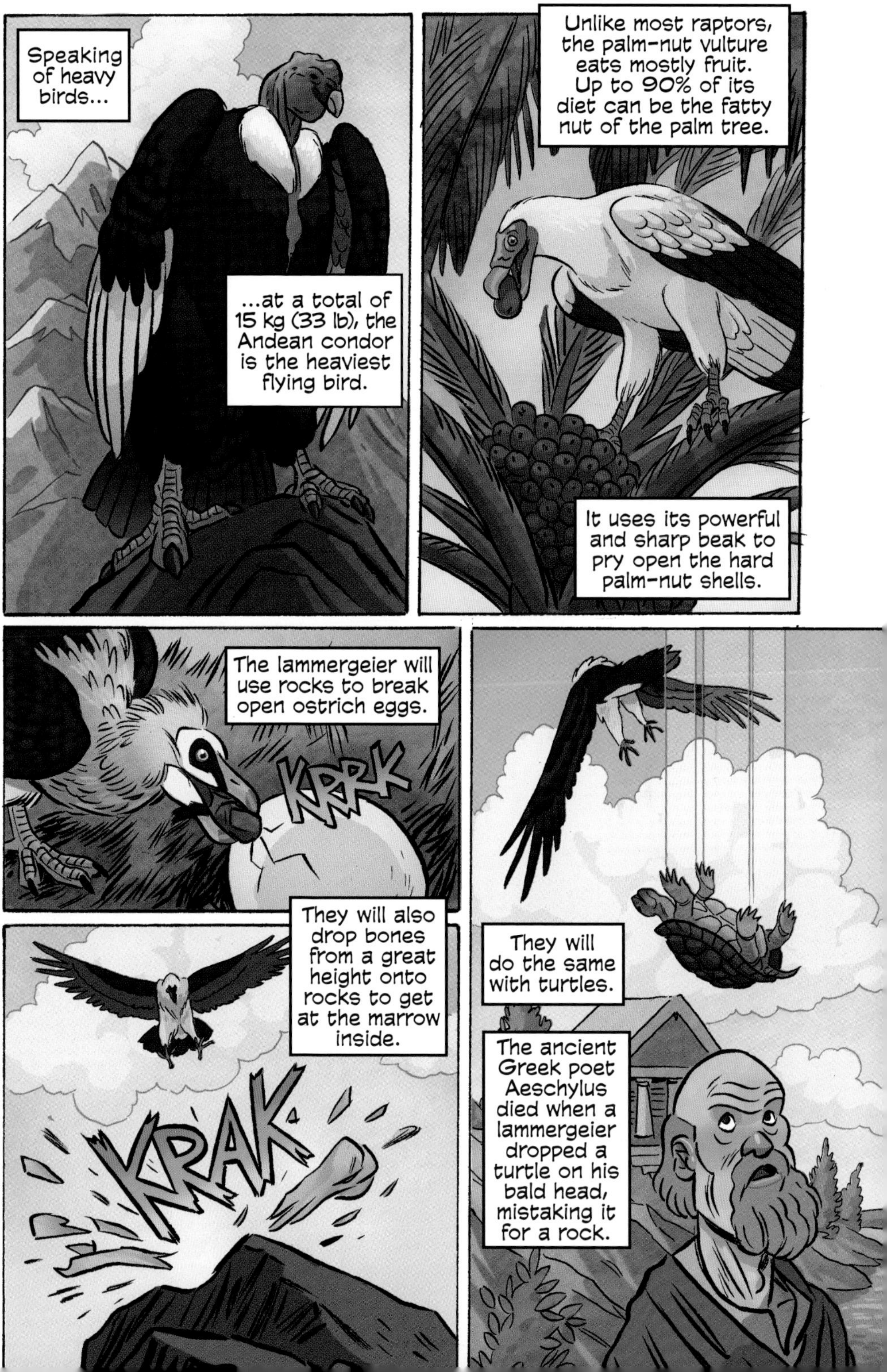
Speaking of heavy birds...
...at a total of 15 kg (33 lb), the Andean condor is the heaviest flying bird.
Unlike most raptors, the palm-nut vulture eats mostly fruit. Up to 90% of its diet can be the fatty nut of the palm tree.
It uses its powerful and sharp beak to pry open the hard palm-nut shells.
The lammergeier will use rocks to break open ostrich eggs.
KRRK
They will also drop bones from a great height onto rocks to get at the marrow inside.
KRAK
They will do the same with turtles.
The ancient Greek poet Aeschylus died when a lammergeier dropped a turtle on his bald head, mistaking it for a rock.

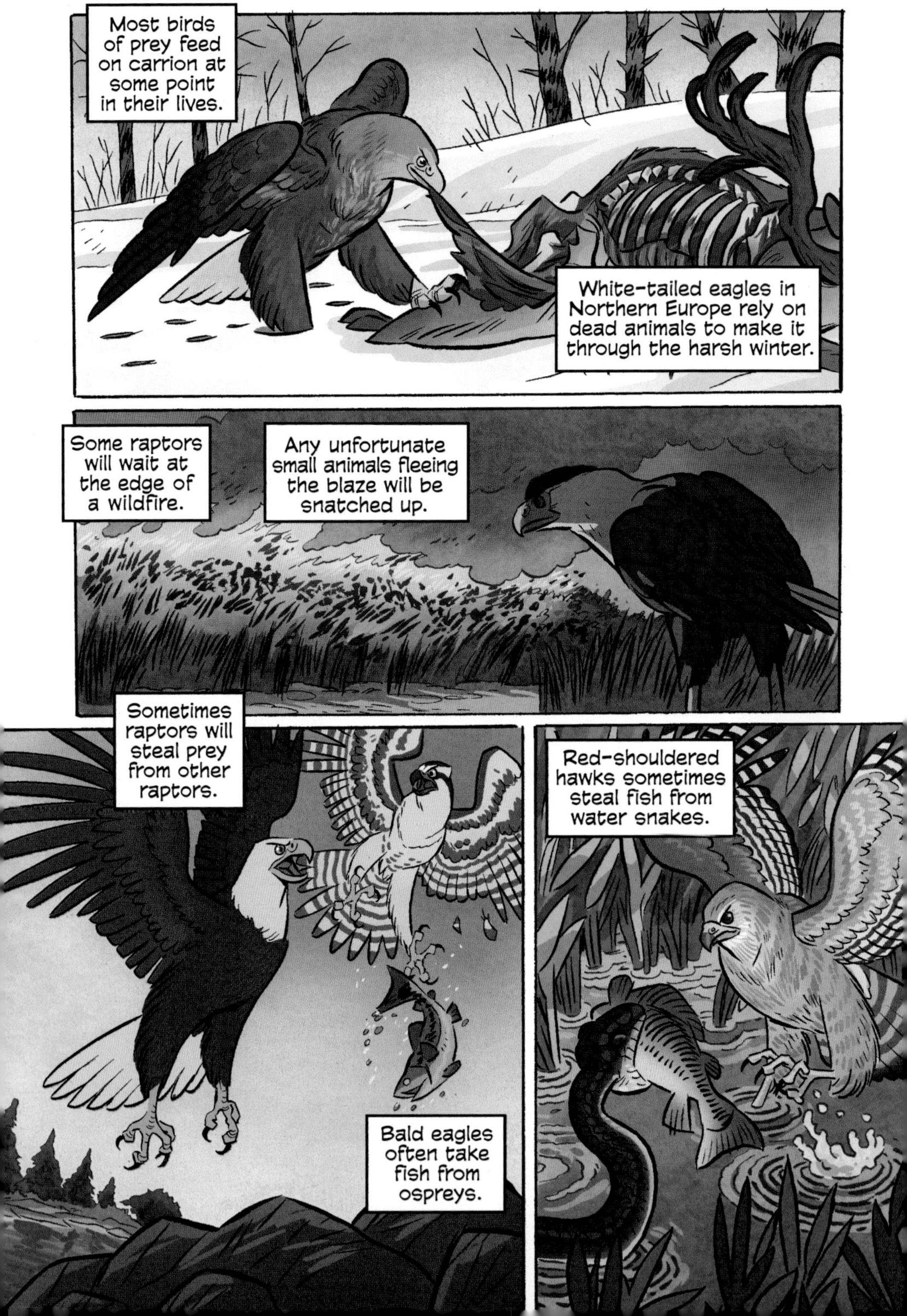
Most birds of prey feed on carrion at some point in their lives.
White-tailed eagles in Northern Europe rely on dead animals to make it through the harsh winter.
Some raptors will wait at the edge of a wildfire.
Any unfortunate small animals fleeing the blaze will be snatched up.
Sometimes raptors will steal prey from other raptors.
Bald eagles often take fish from ospreys.
Red-shouldered hawks sometimes steal fish from water snakes.

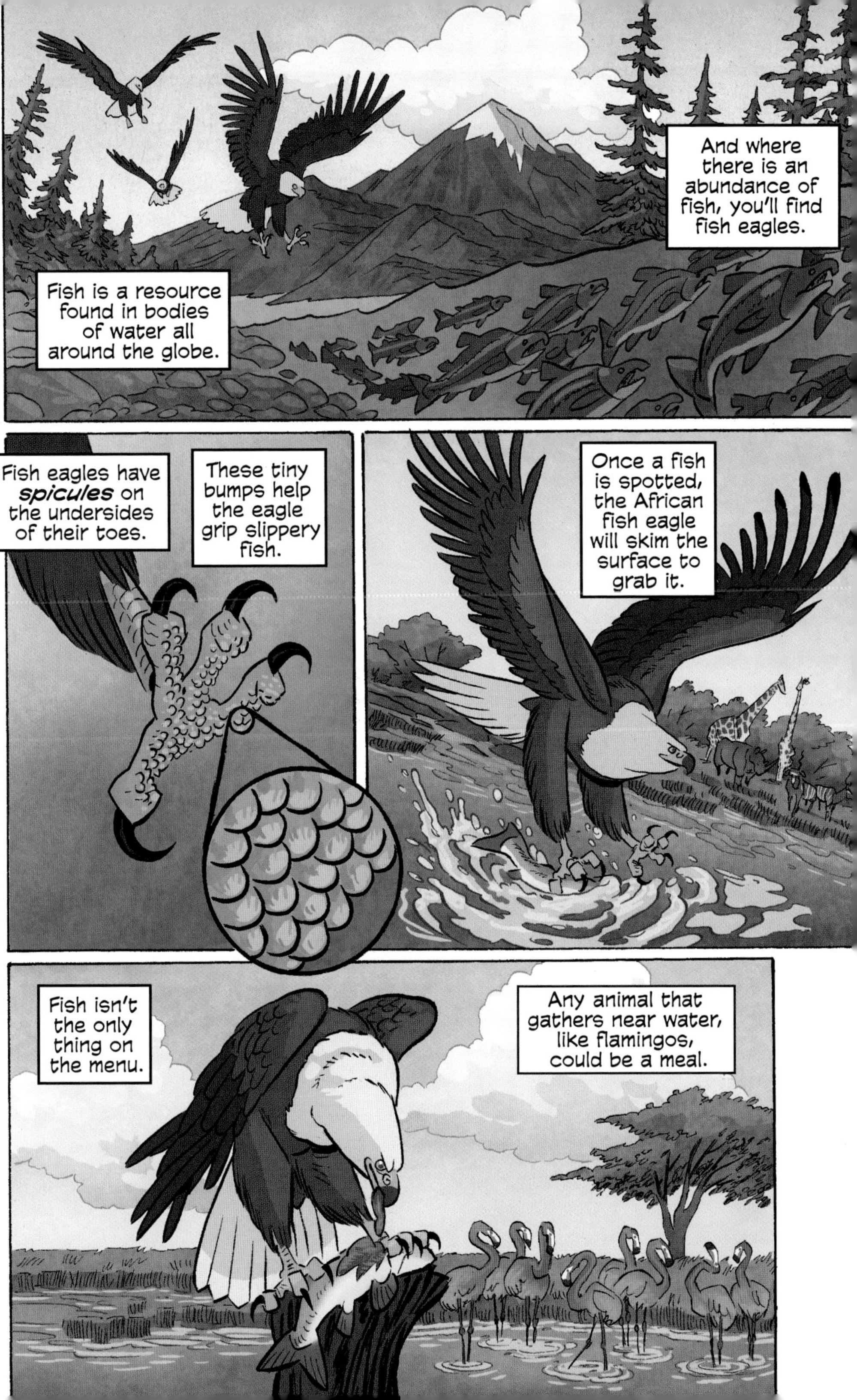

Fish is a resource found in bodies of water all around the globe.
And where there is an abundance of fish, you'll find fish eagles.
Fish eagles have *spicules* on the undersides of their toes.
These tiny bumps help the eagle grip slippery fish.
Once a fish is spotted, the African fish eagle will skim the surface to grab it.
Fish isn't the only thing on the menu.
Any animal that gathers near water, like flamingos, could be a meal.

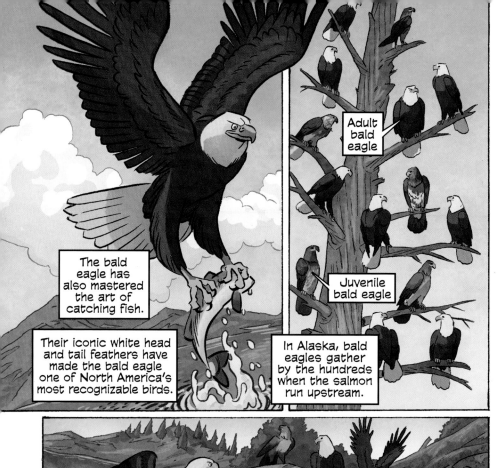

The bald eagle has also mastered the art of catching fish.

Their iconic white head and tail feathers have made the bald eagle one of North America's most recognizable birds.

Adult bald eagle

Juvenile bald eagle

In Alaska, bald eagles gather by the hundreds when the salmon run upstream.

When a salmon is too heavy to fly away with, the eagle will paddle to shore.

Even when there's plenty to eat, bald eagles still fight over prime fishing spots.

The osprey also hunts fish, but it belongs to its own separate family, Pandionidae.

Once a fish is spotted near the surface, an osprey plunges feetfirst...

...nearly submerging itself.

Lifting off with a fish, it shakes off the heavy water.

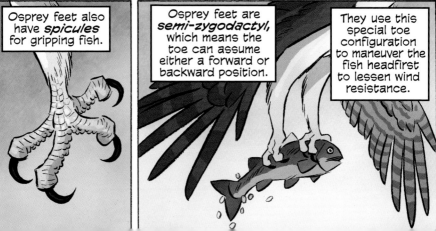

Osprey feet also have *spicules* for gripping fish.

Osprey feet are *semi-zygodactyl*, which means the toe can assume either a forward or backward position.

They use this special toe configuration to maneuver the fish headfirst to lessen wind resistance.

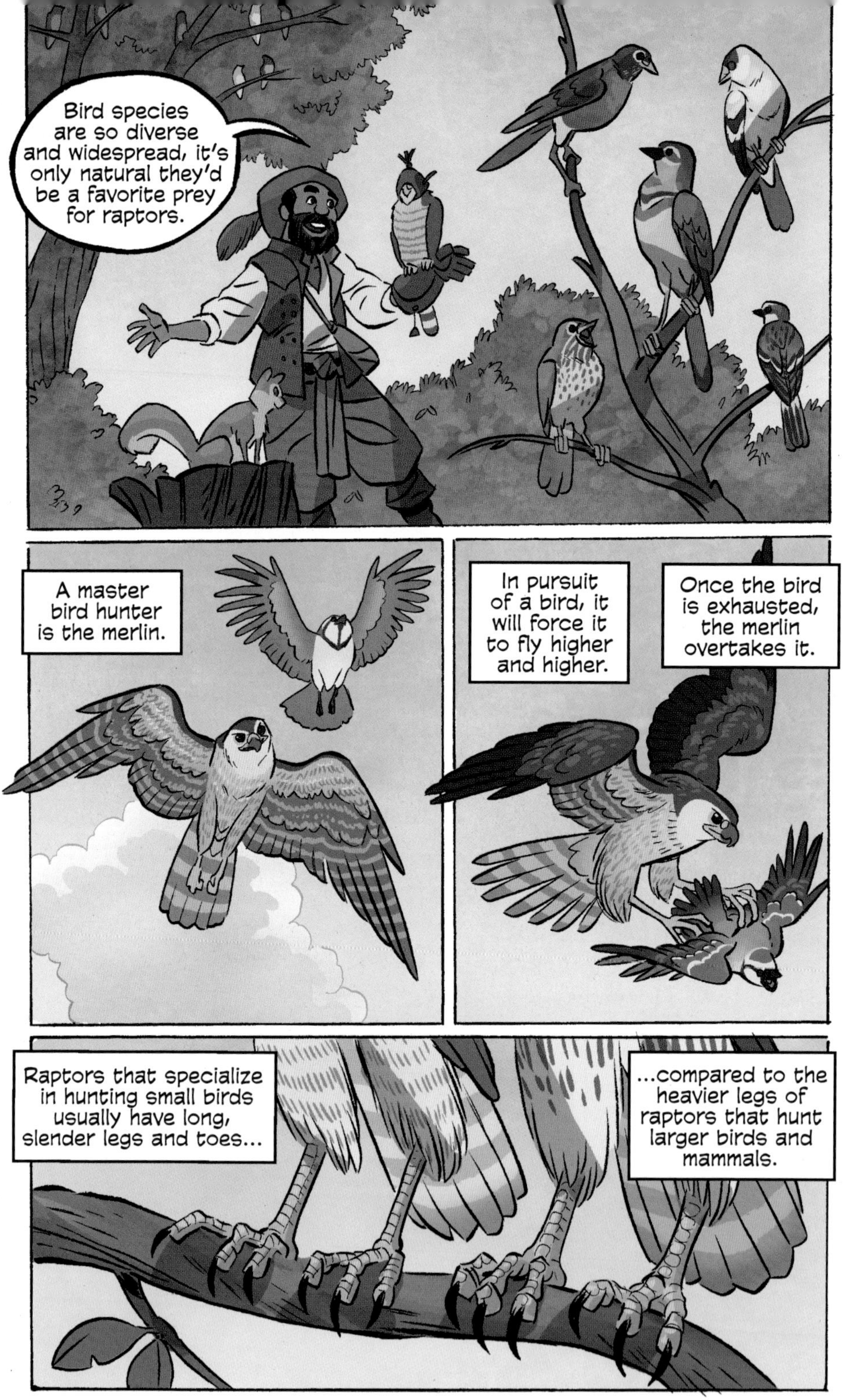
Bird species are so diverse and widespread, it's only natural they'd be a favorite prey for raptors.
A master bird hunter is the merlin.
In pursuit of a bird, it will force it to fly higher and higher.
Once the bird is exhausted, the merlin overtakes it.
Raptors that specialize in hunting small birds usually have long, slender legs and toes...
...compared to the heavier legs of raptors that hunt larger birds and mammals.

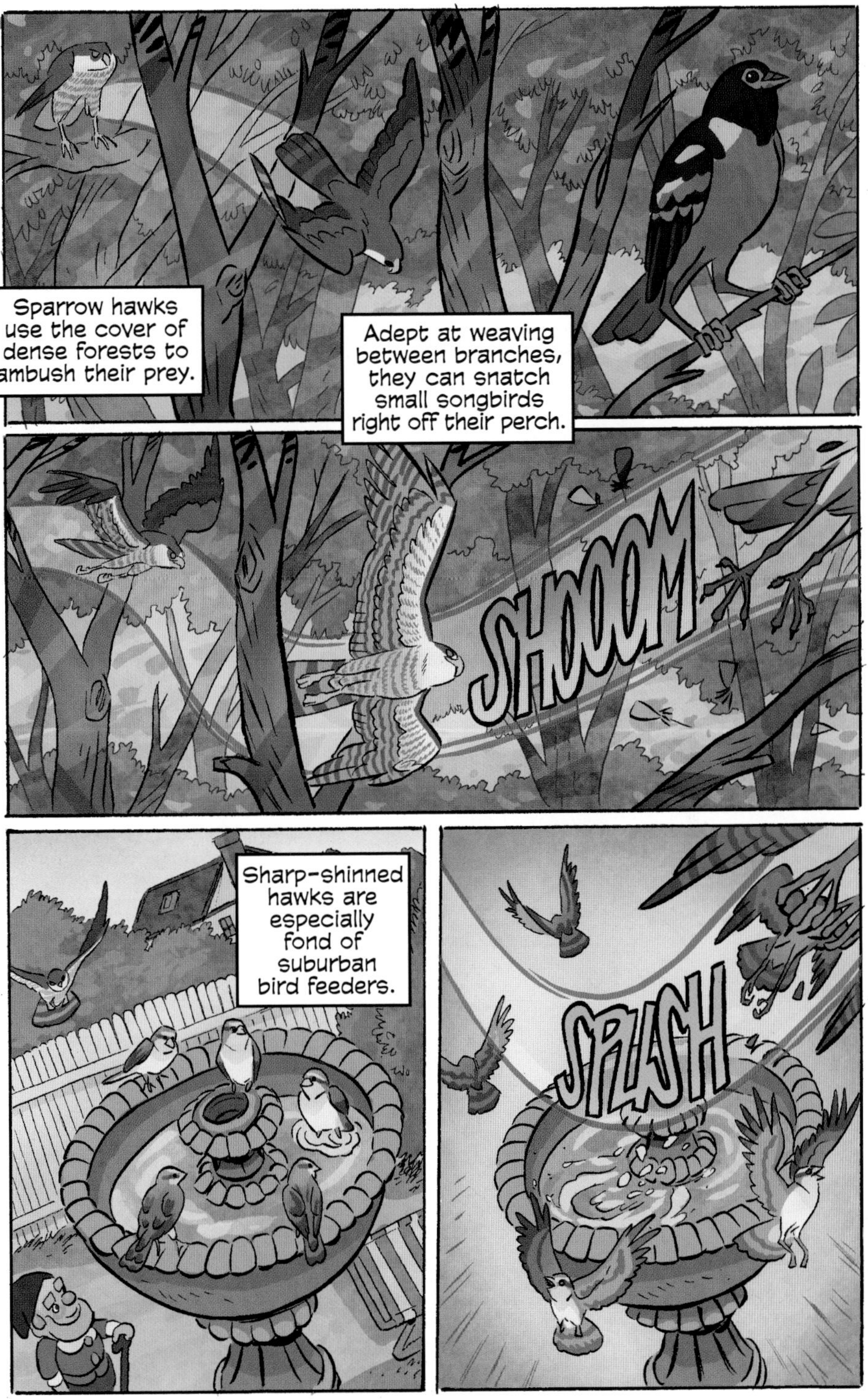
Sparrow hawks use the cover of dense forests to ambush their prey.
Adept at weaving between branches, they can snatch small songbirds right off their perch.
SHOOOM
Sharp-shinned hawks are especially fond of suburban bird feeders.
SPLASH

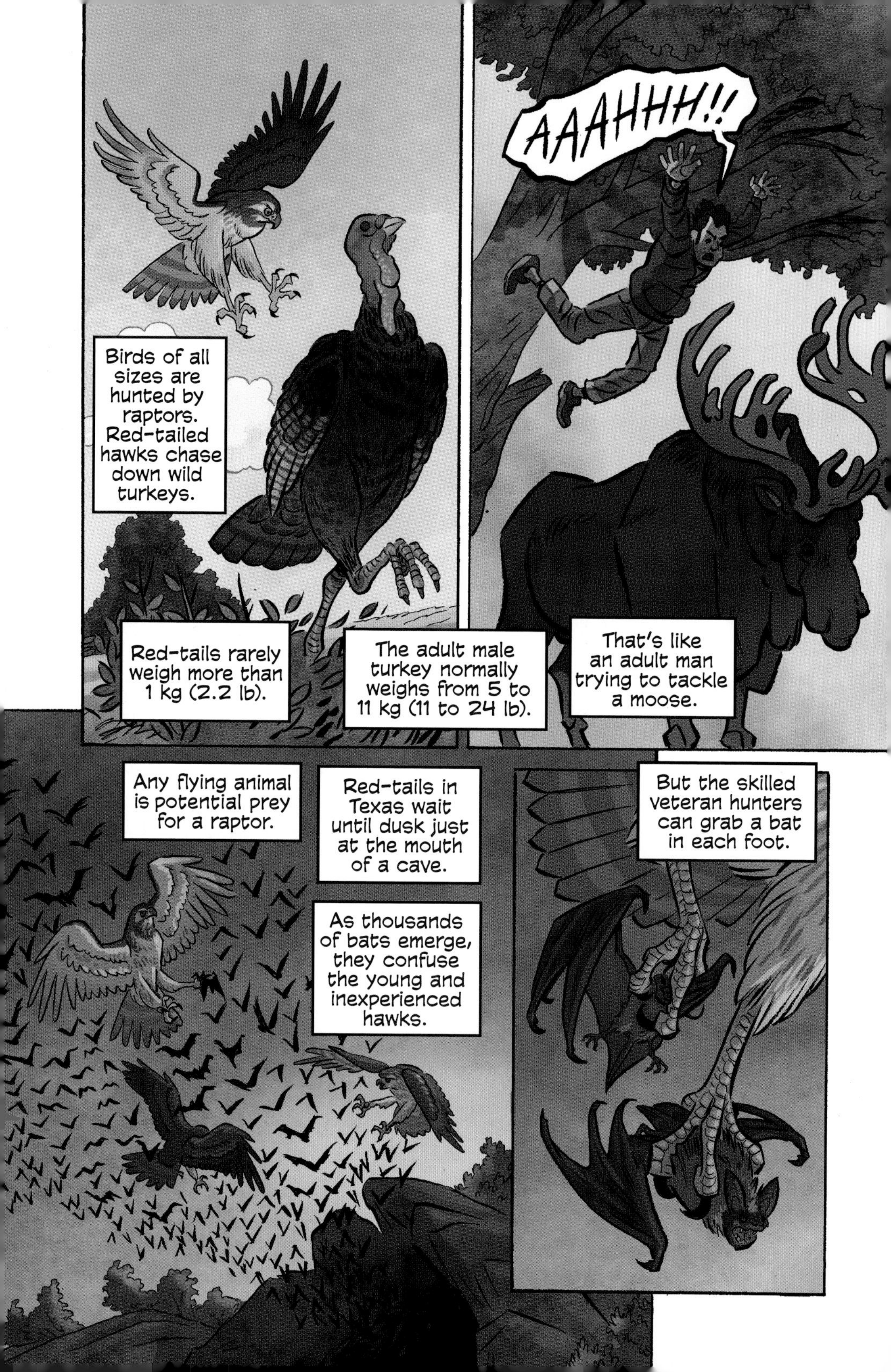
Birds of all sizes are hunted by raptors. Red-tailed hawks chase down wild turkeys.
Red-tails rarely weigh more than 1 kg (2.2 lb).
The adult male turkey normally weighs from 5 to 11 kg (11 to 24 lb).
AAAHHH!!
That's like an adult man trying to tackle a moose.
Any flying animal is potential prey for a raptor.
Red-tails in Texas wait until dusk just at the mouth of a cave.
As thousands of bats emerge, they confuse the young and inexperienced hawks.
But the skilled veteran hunters can grab a bat in each foot.

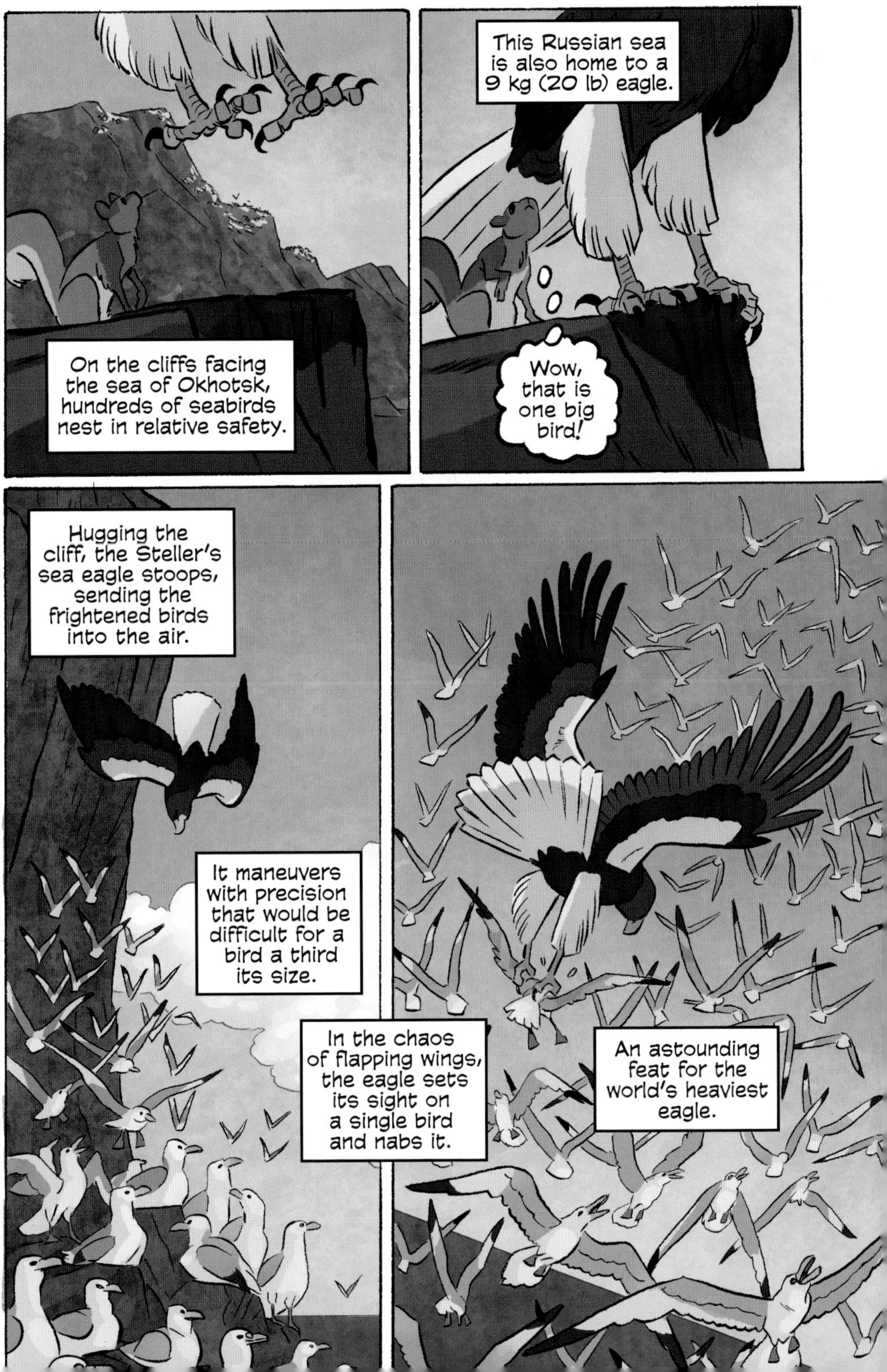

On the cliffs facing the sea of Okhotsk, hundreds of seabirds nest in relative safety.
This Russian sea is also home to a 9 kg (20 lb) eagle.
Wow, that is one big bird!
Hugging the cliff, the Steller's sea eagle stoops, sending the frightened birds into the air.
It maneuvers with precision that would be difficult for a bird a third its size.
In the chaos of flapping wings, the eagle sets its sight on a single bird and nabs it.
An astounding feat for the world's heaviest eagle.

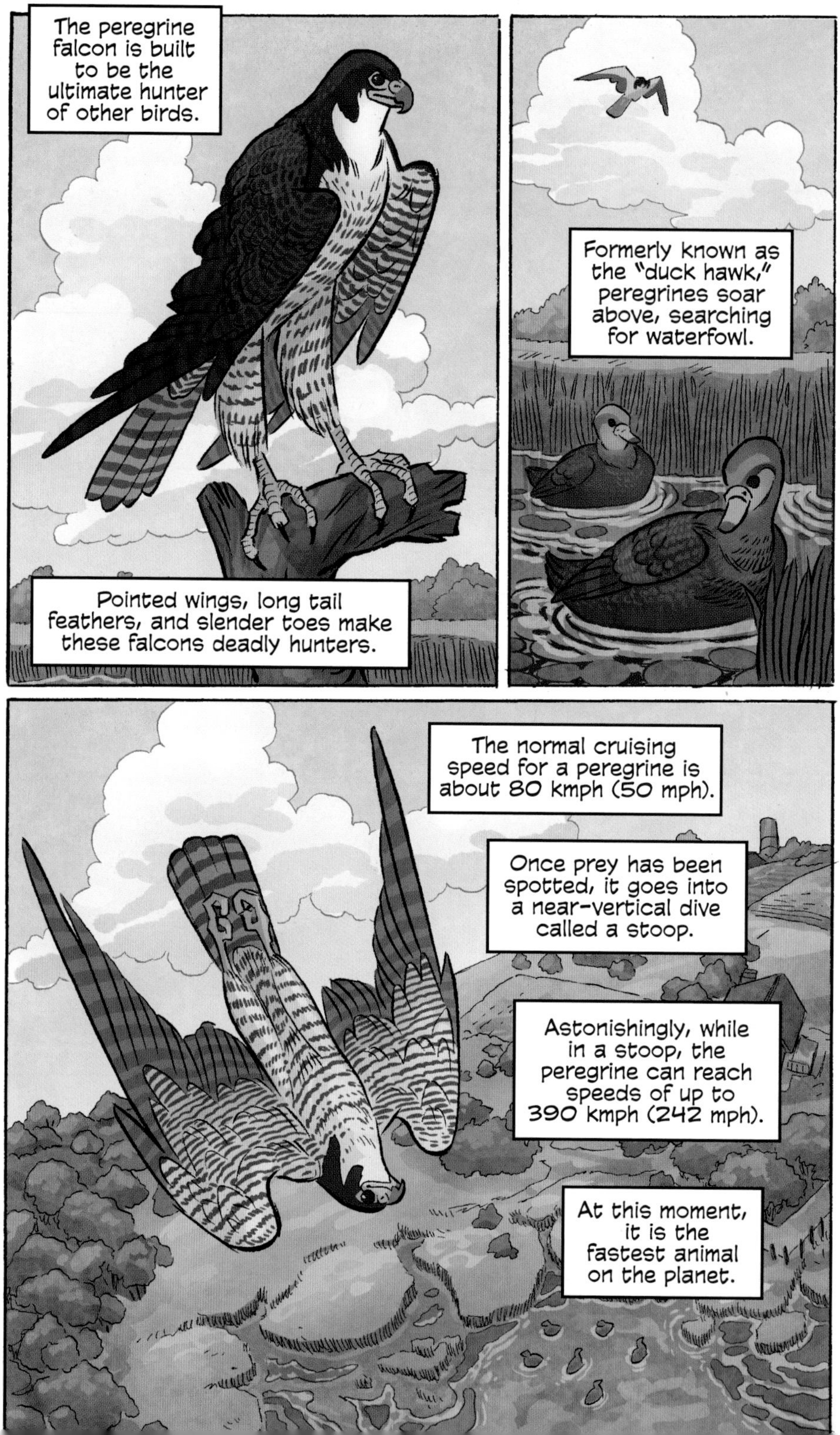
The peregrine falcon is built to be the ultimate hunter of other birds.
Pointed wings, long tail feathers, and slender toes make these falcons deadly hunters.
Formerly known as the "duck hawk," peregrines soar above, searching for waterfowl.
The normal cruising speed for a peregrine is about 80 kmph (50 mph).
Once prey has been spotted, it goes into a near-vertical dive called a stoop.
Astonishingly, while in a stoop, the peregrine can reach speeds of up to 390 kmph (242 mph).
At this moment, it is the fastest animal on the planet.

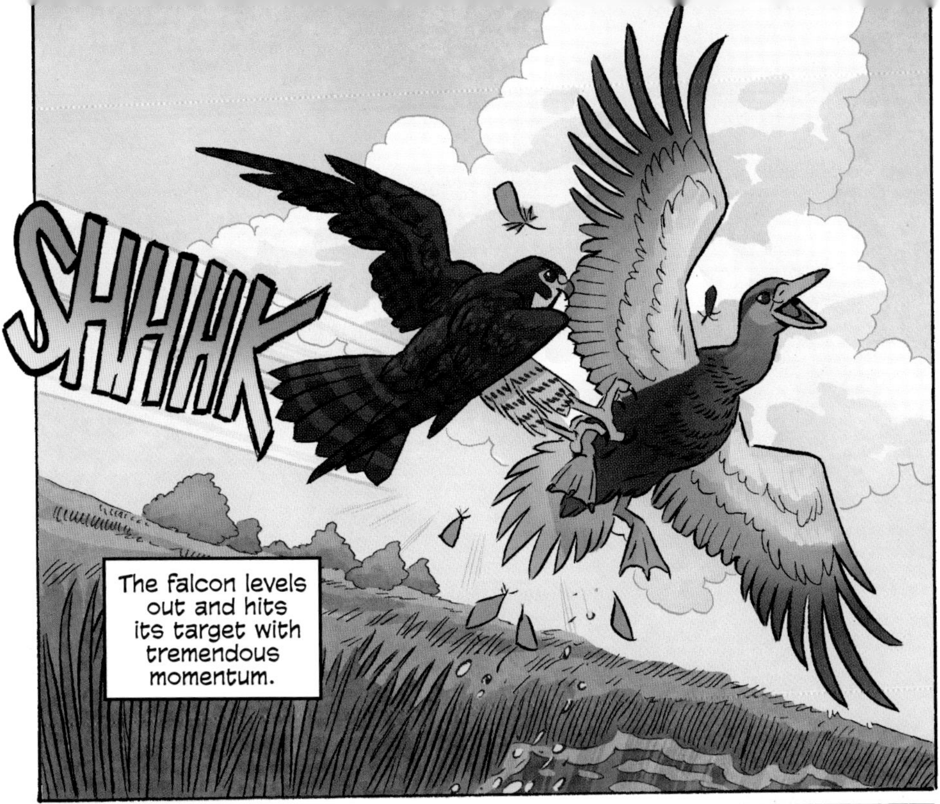
SHHHK
The falcon levels out and hits its target with tremendous momentum.

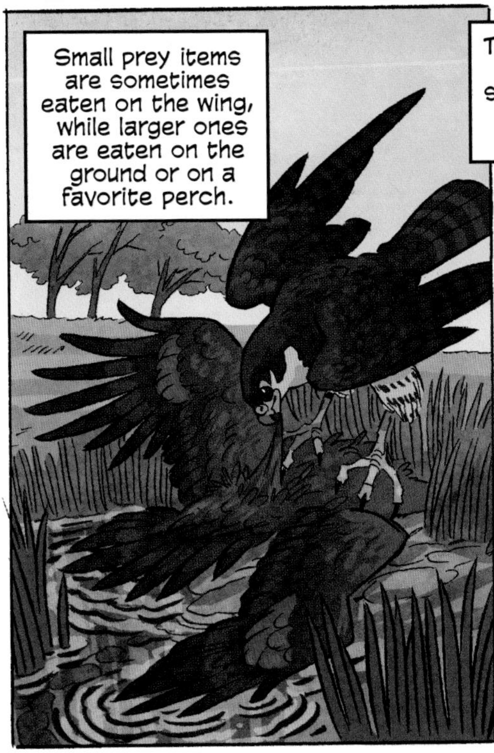
Small prey items are sometimes eaten on the wing, while larger ones are eaten on the ground or on a favorite perch.

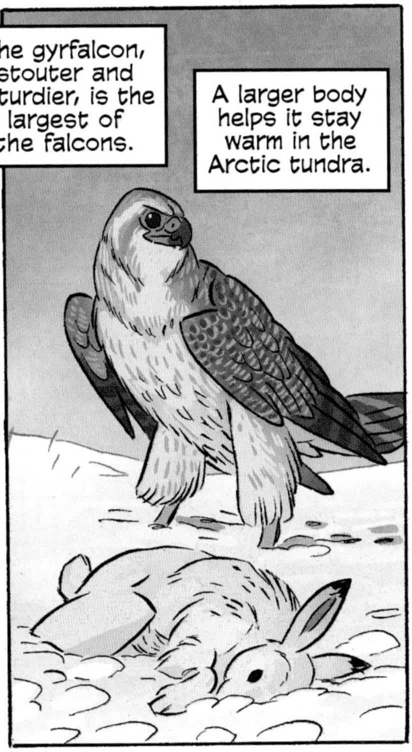
The gyrfalcon, stouter and sturdier, is the largest of the falcons.
A larger body helps it stay warm in the Arctic tundra.

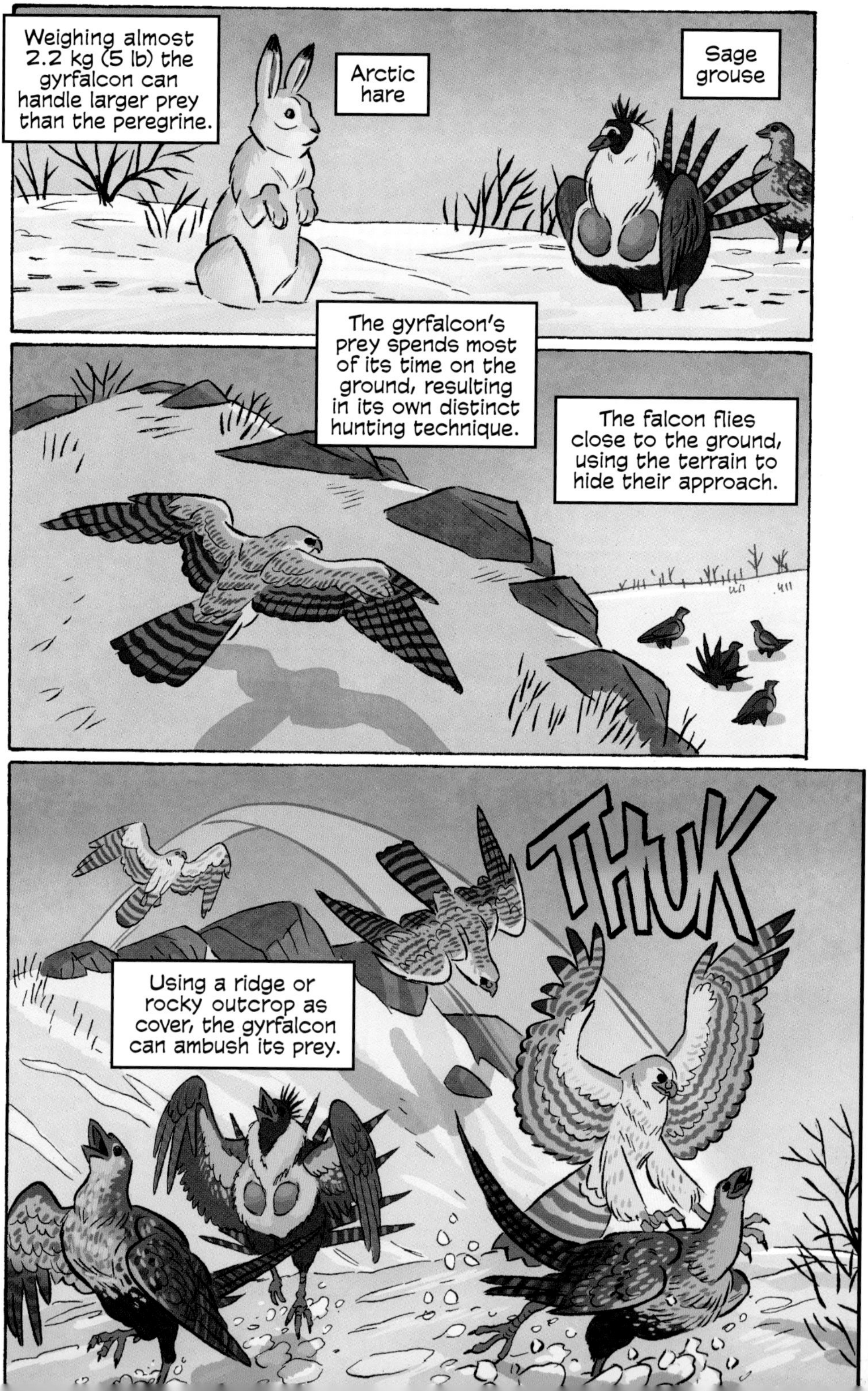
Weighing almost 2.2 kg (5 lb) the gyrfalcon can handle larger prey than the peregrine.
Arctic hare
Sage grouse
The gyrfalcon's prey spends most of its time on the ground, resulting in its own distinct hunting technique.
The falcon flies close to the ground, using the terrain to hide their approach.
THUK
Using a ridge or rocky outcrop as cover, the gyrfalcon can ambush its prey.

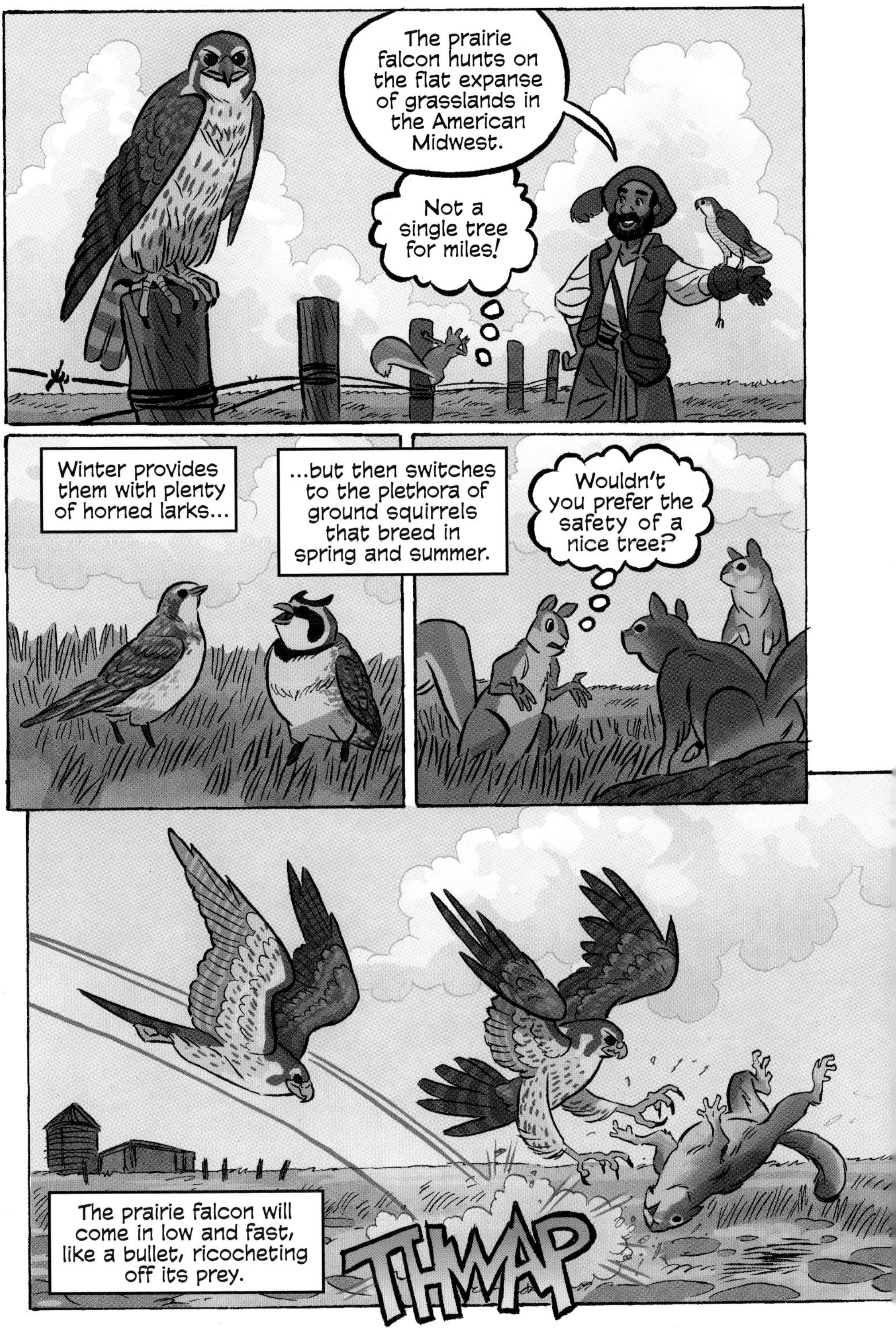
The prairie falcon hunts on the flat expanse of grasslands in the American Midwest.
Not a single tree for miles!
Winter provides them with plenty of horned larks...
...but then switches to the plethora of ground squirrels that breed in spring and summer.
Wouldn't you prefer the safety of a nice tree?
The prairie falcon will come in low and fast, like a bullet, ricocheting off its prey.
THWAP

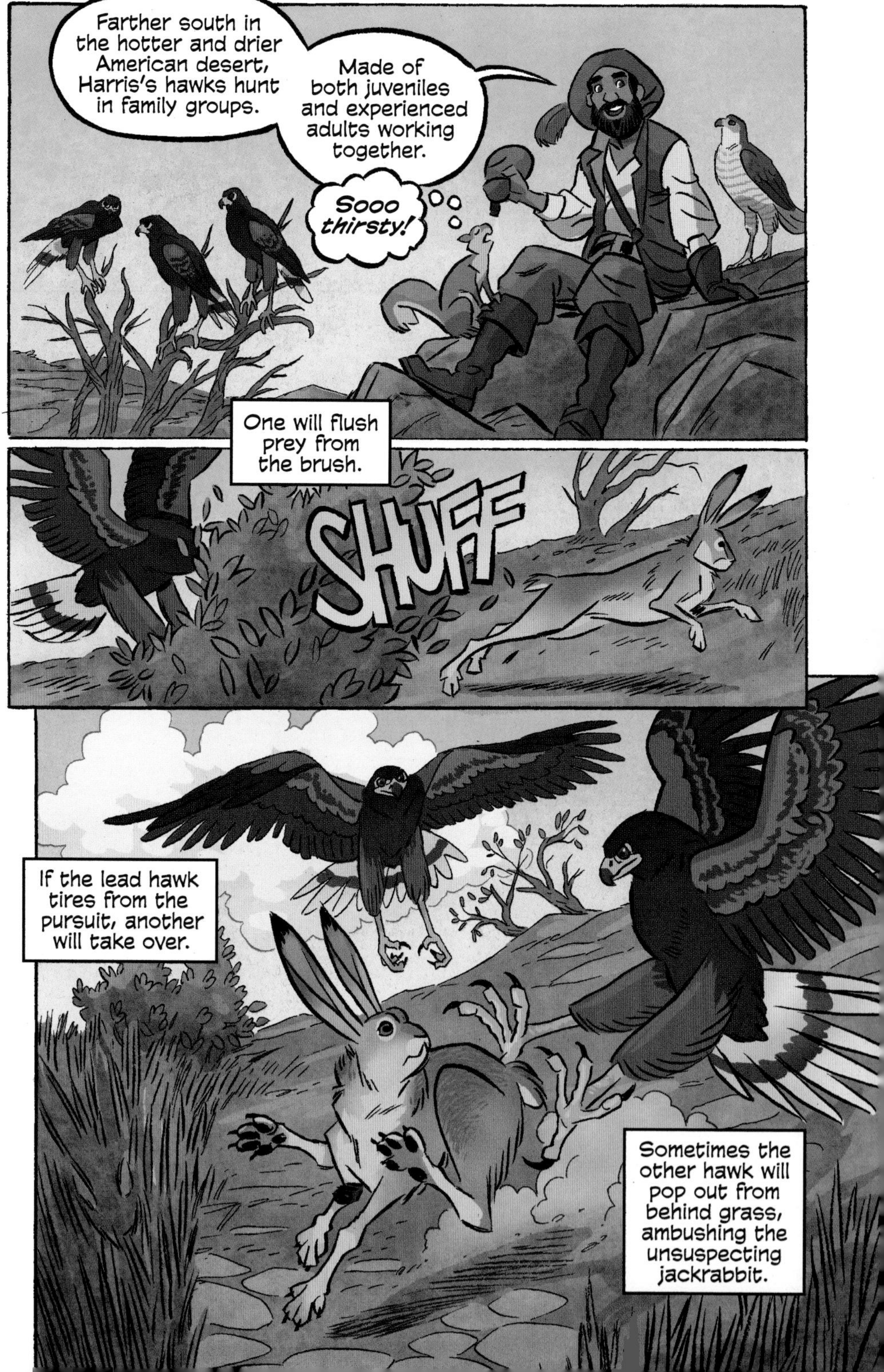
Farther south in the hotter and drier American desert, Harris's hawks hunt in family groups.
Made of both juveniles and experienced adults working together.
Sooo thirsty!
One will flush prey from the brush.
SHUFF
If the lead hawk tires from the pursuit, another will take over.
Sometimes the other hawk will pop out from behind grass, ambushing the unsuspecting jackrabbit.

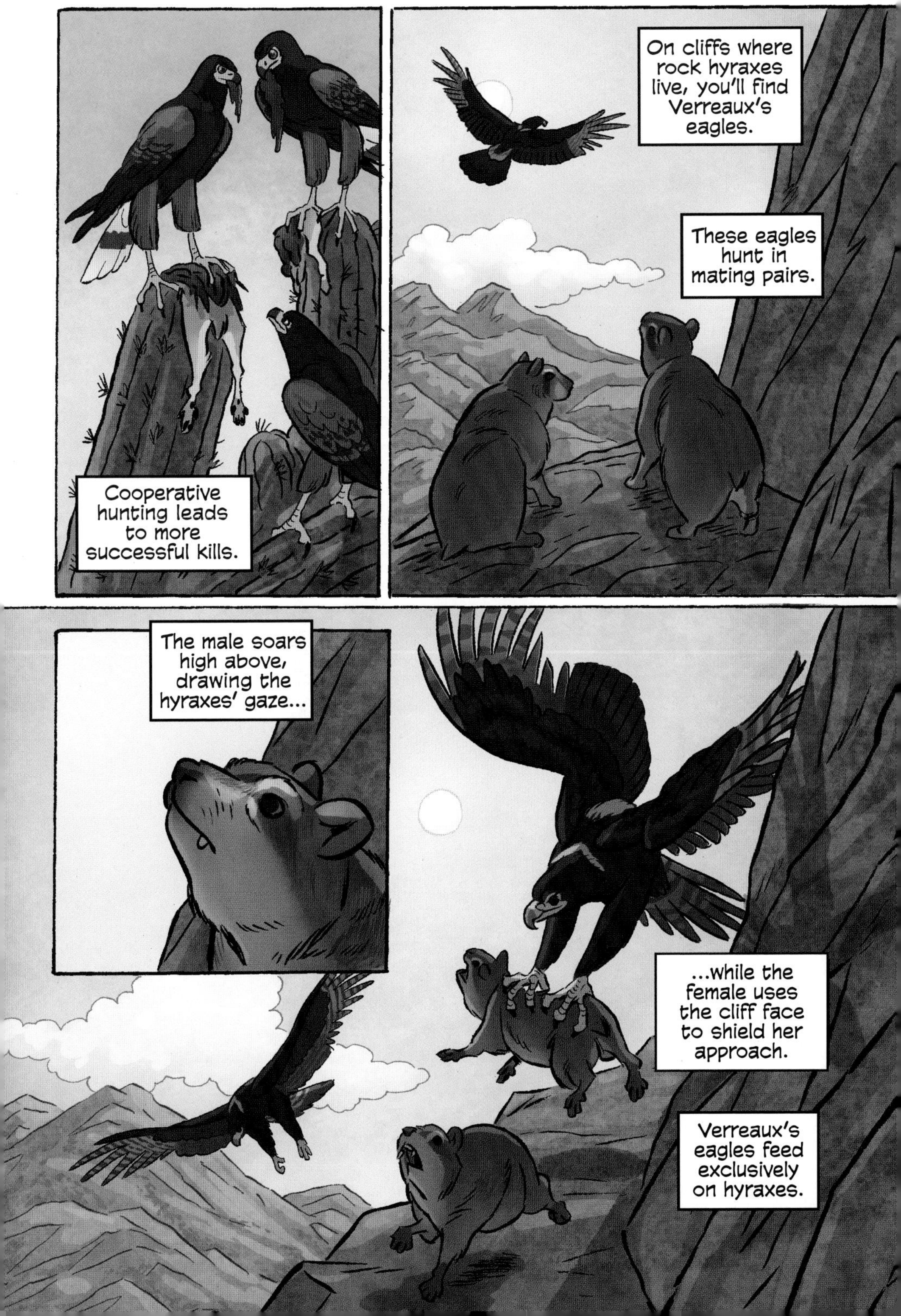
Cooperative hunting leads to more successful kills.
On cliffs where rock hyraxes live, you'll find Verreaux's eagles.
These eagles hunt in mating pairs.
The male soars high above, drawing the hyraxes' gaze...
...while the female uses the cliff face to shield her approach.
Verreaux's eagles feed exclusively on hyraxes.

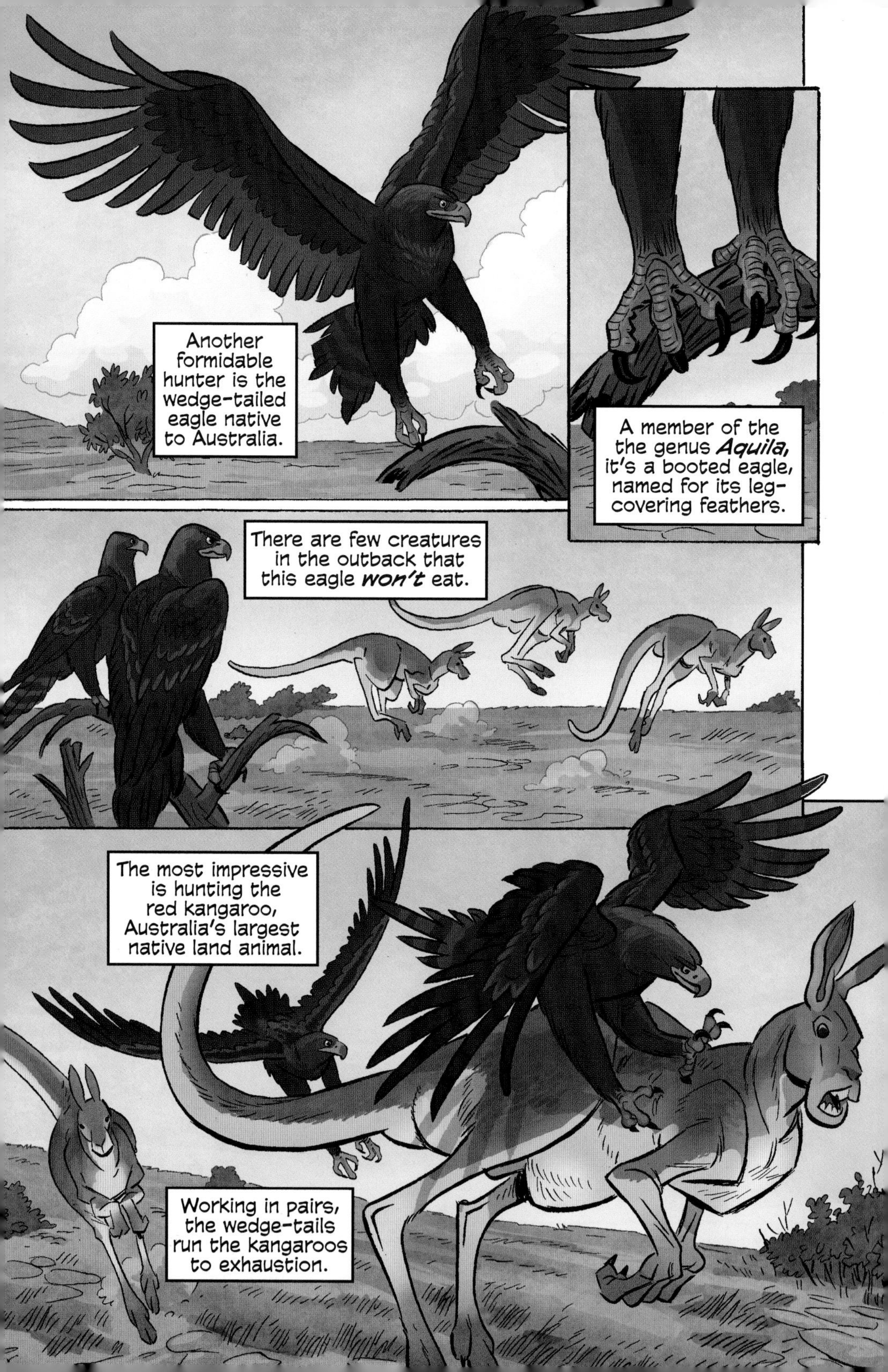
Another formidable hunter is the wedge-tailed eagle native to Australia.
A member of the the genus *Aquila,* it's a booted eagle, named for its leg-covering feathers.
There are few creatures in the outback that this eagle *won't* eat.
The most impressive is hunting the red kangaroo, Australia's largest native land animal.
Working in pairs, the wedge-tails run the kangaroos to exhaustion.

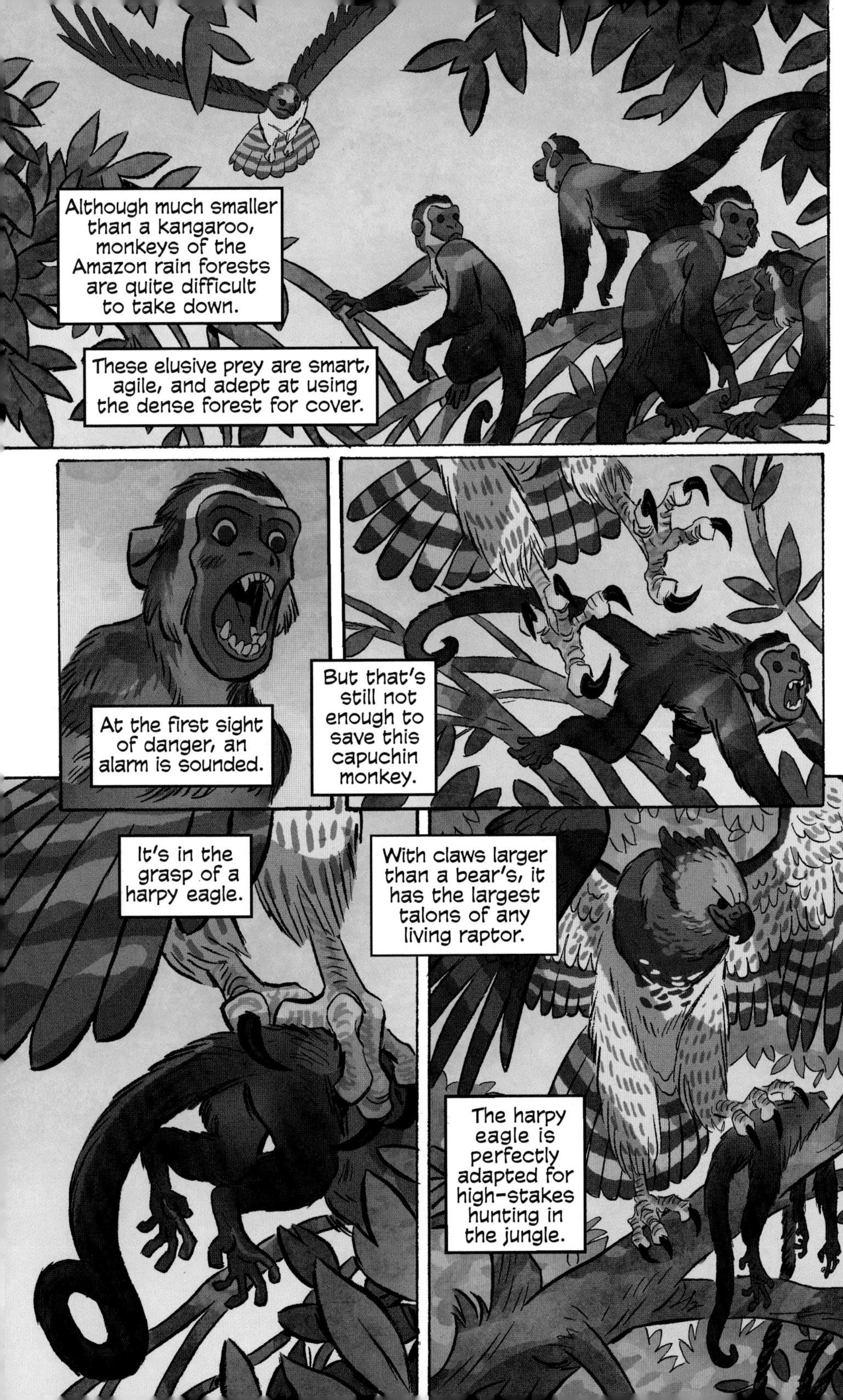
Although much smaller than a kangaroo, monkeys of the Amazon rain forests are quite difficult to take down.
These elusive prey are smart, agile, and adept at using the dense forest for cover.
At the first sight of danger, an alarm is sounded.
But that's still not enough to save this capuchin monkey.
It's in the grasp of a harpy eagle.
With claws larger than a bear's, it has the largest talons of any living raptor.
The harpy eagle is perfectly adapted for high-stakes hunting in the jungle.

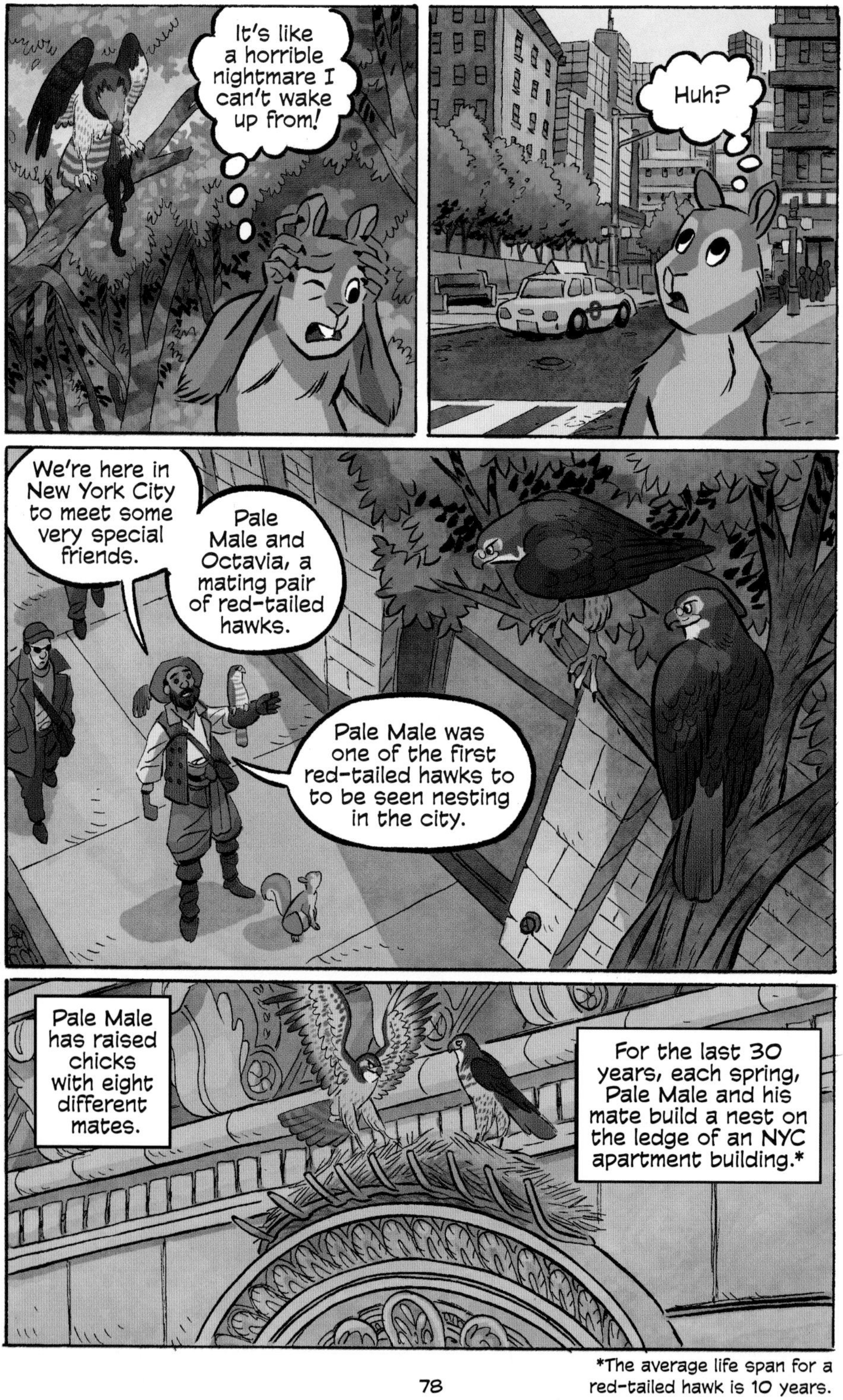
It's like a horrible nightmare I can't wake up from!
Huh?
We're here in New York City to meet some very special friends.
Pale Male and Octavia, a mating pair of red-tailed hawks.
Pale Male was one of the first red-tailed hawks to to be seen nesting in the city.
Pale Male has raised chicks with eight different mates.
For the last 30 years, each spring, Pale Male and his mate build a nest on the ledge of an NYC apartment building.*

*The average life span for a red-tailed hawk is 10 years.

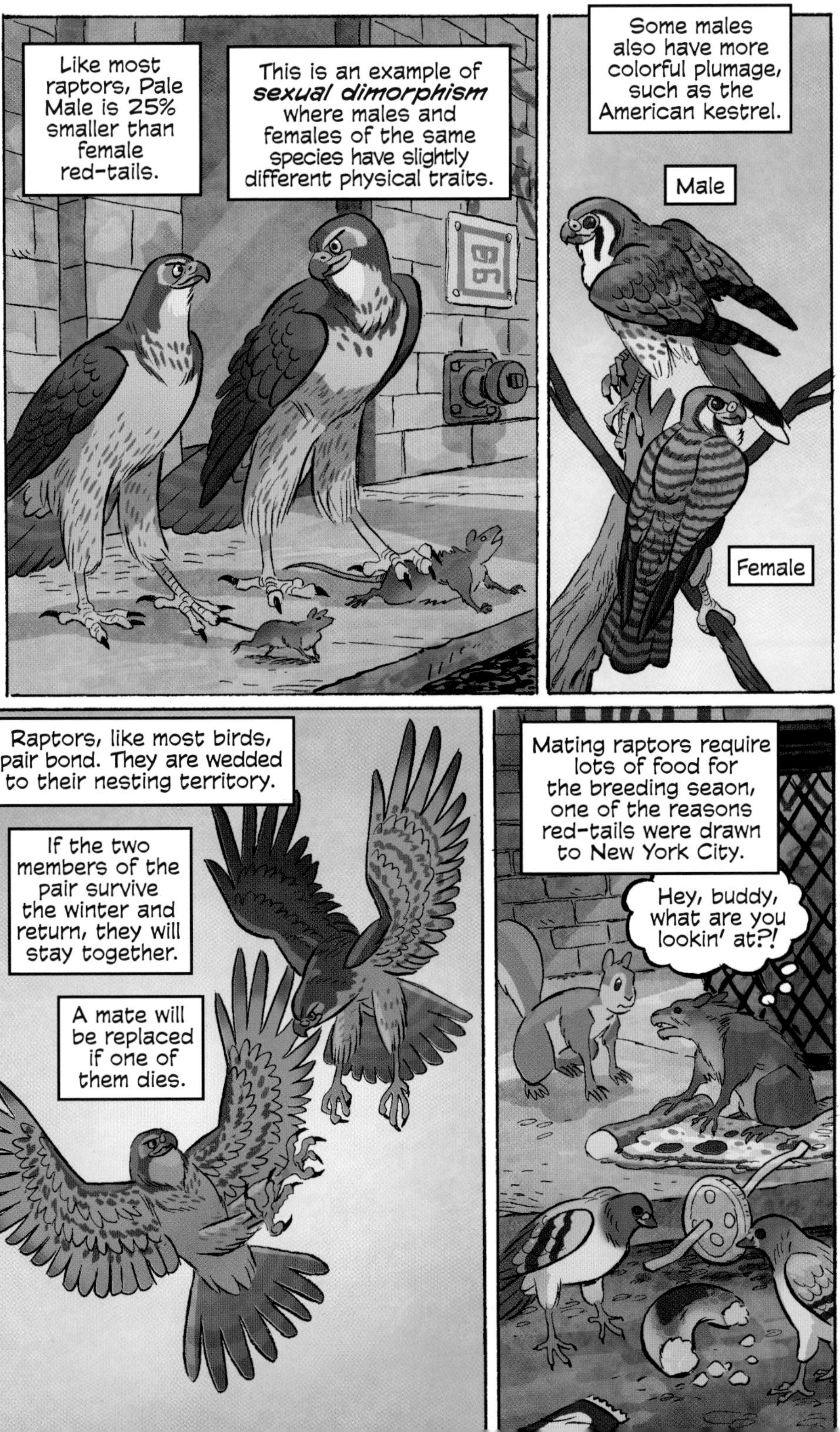
Like most raptors, Pale Male is 25% smaller than female red-tails.
This is an example of sexual dimorphism where males and females of the same species have slightly different physical traits.
Some males also have more colorful plumage, such as the American kestrel.
Male
Female
Raptors, like most birds, pair bond. They are wedded to their nesting territory.
If the two members of the pair survive the winter and return, they will stay together.
A mate will be replaced if one of them dies.
Mating raptors require lots of food for the breeding seaon, one of the reasons red-tails were drawn to New York City.
Hey, buddy, what are you lookin' at?!

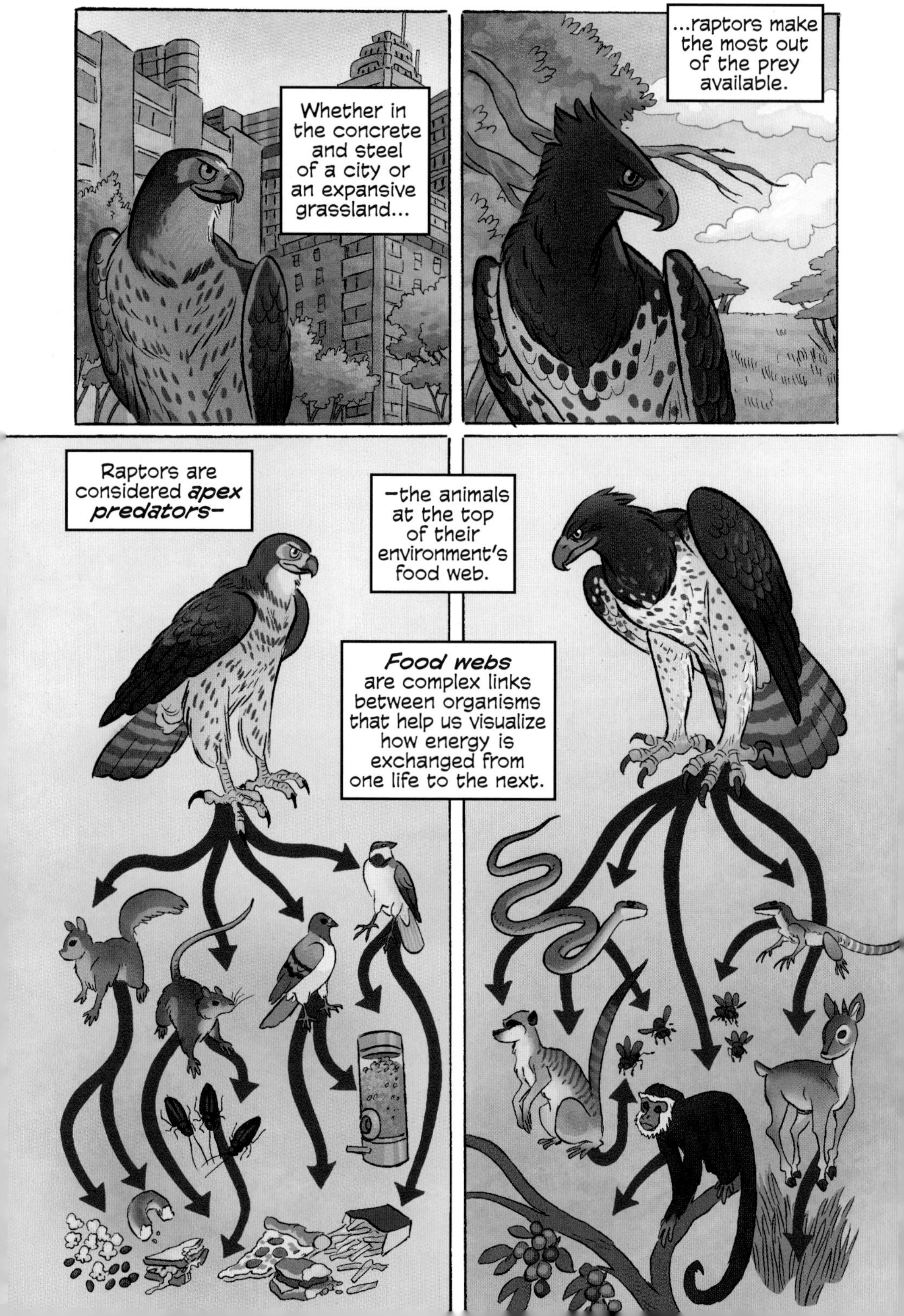
Whether in the concrete and steel of a city or an expansive grassland...
...raptors make the most out of the prey available.
Raptors are considered *apex predators*–
–the animals at the top of their environment's food web.
Food webs are complex links between organisms that help us visualize how energy is exchanged from one life to the next.

If winters are mild, some raptors will remain in the same habitat year-round.

But most birds of prey are forced to migrate to warmer climates where conditions are better for raising their young.

Why do I get the feeling this place isn't as nice as it seems?

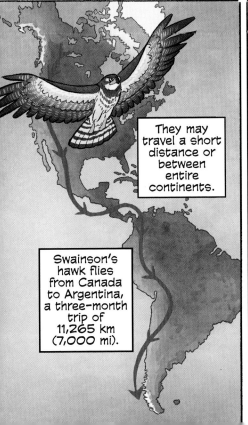

They may travel a short distance or between entire continents.

Swainson's hawk flies from Canada to Argentina, a three-month trip of 11,265 km (7,000 mi).

Migrating raptors follow the ridges of mountain ranges, using the updrafts created by wind deflected off the mountainsides being pushed upward.

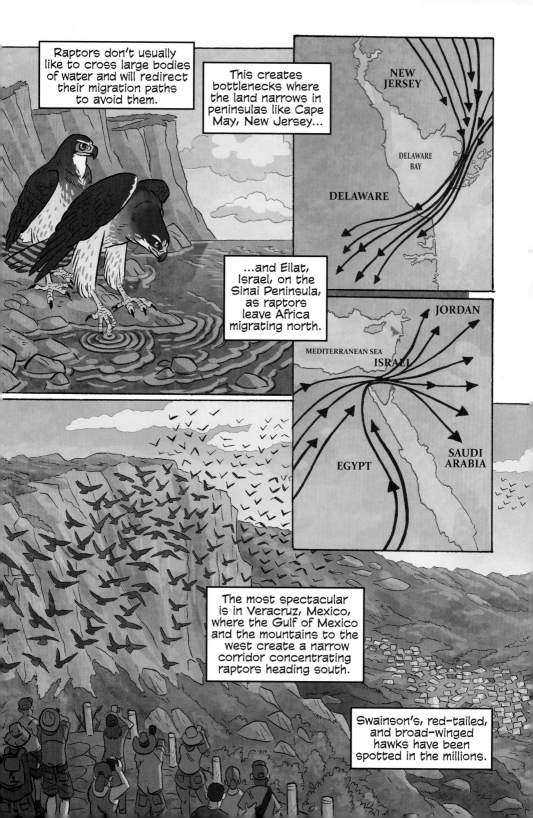

Raptors don't usually like to cross large bodies of water and will redirect their migration paths to avoid them.

This creates bottlenecks where the land narrows in peninsulas like Cape May, New Jersey...

NEW JERSEY

DELAWARE BAY

DELAWARE

...and Eilat, Israel, on the Sinai Peninsula, as raptors leave Africa migrating north.

JORDAN

MEDITERRANEAN SEA

ISRAEL

EGYPT

SAUDI ARABIA

The most spectacular is in Veracruz, Mexico, where the Gulf of Mexico and the mountains to the west create a narrow corridor concentrating raptors heading south.

Swainson's, red-tailed, and broad-winged hawks have been spotted in the millions.

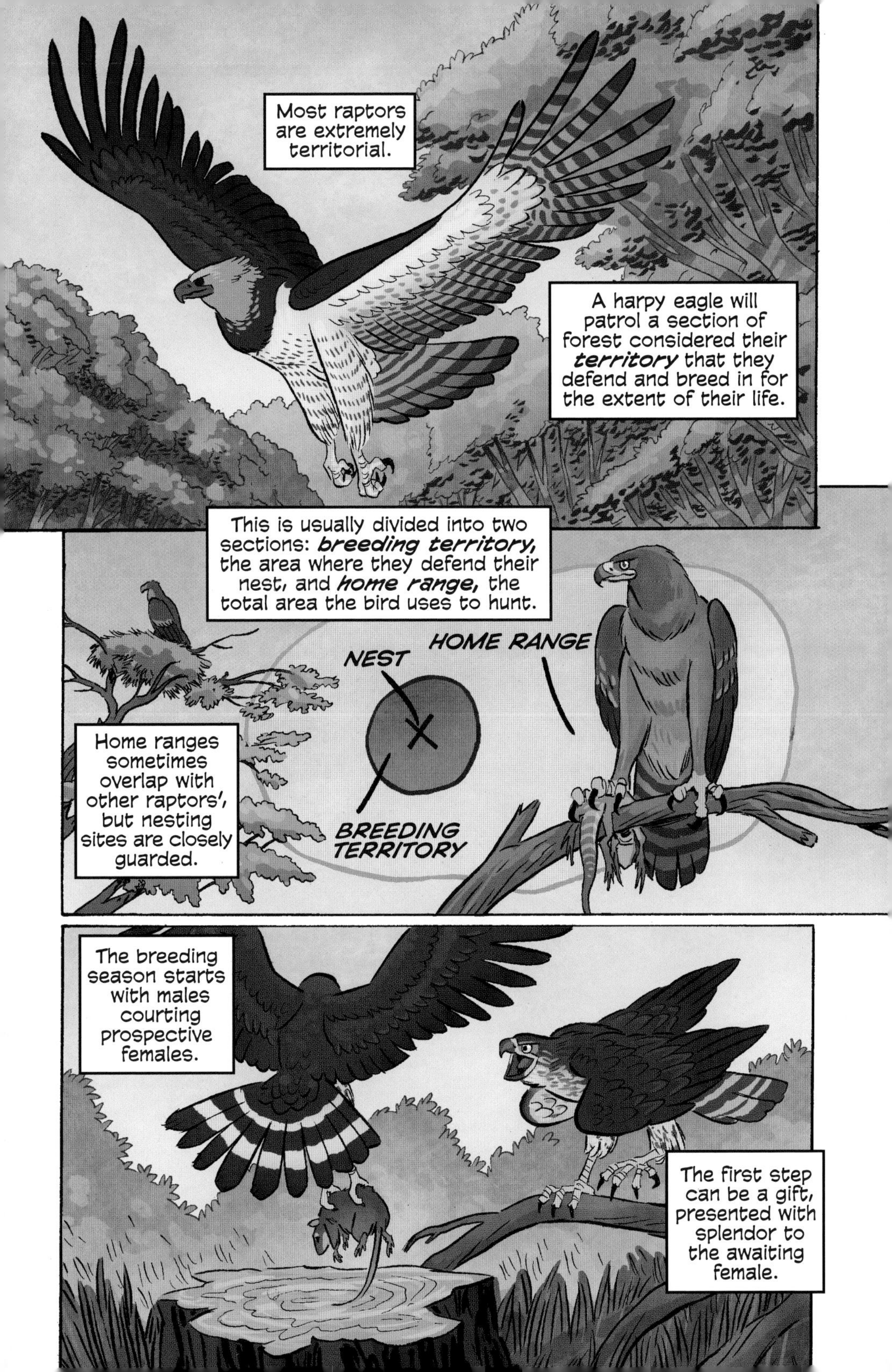
Most raptors are extremely territorial.
A harpy eagle will patrol a section of forest considered their *territory* that they defend and breed in for the extent of their life.
This is usually divided into two sections: *breeding territory,* the area where they defend their nest, and *home range,* the total area the bird uses to hunt.
HOME RANGE
NEST
BREEDING TERRITORY
Home ranges sometimes overlap with other raptors', but nesting sites are closely guarded.
The breeding season starts with males courting prospective females.
The first step can be a gift, presented with splendor to the awaiting female.

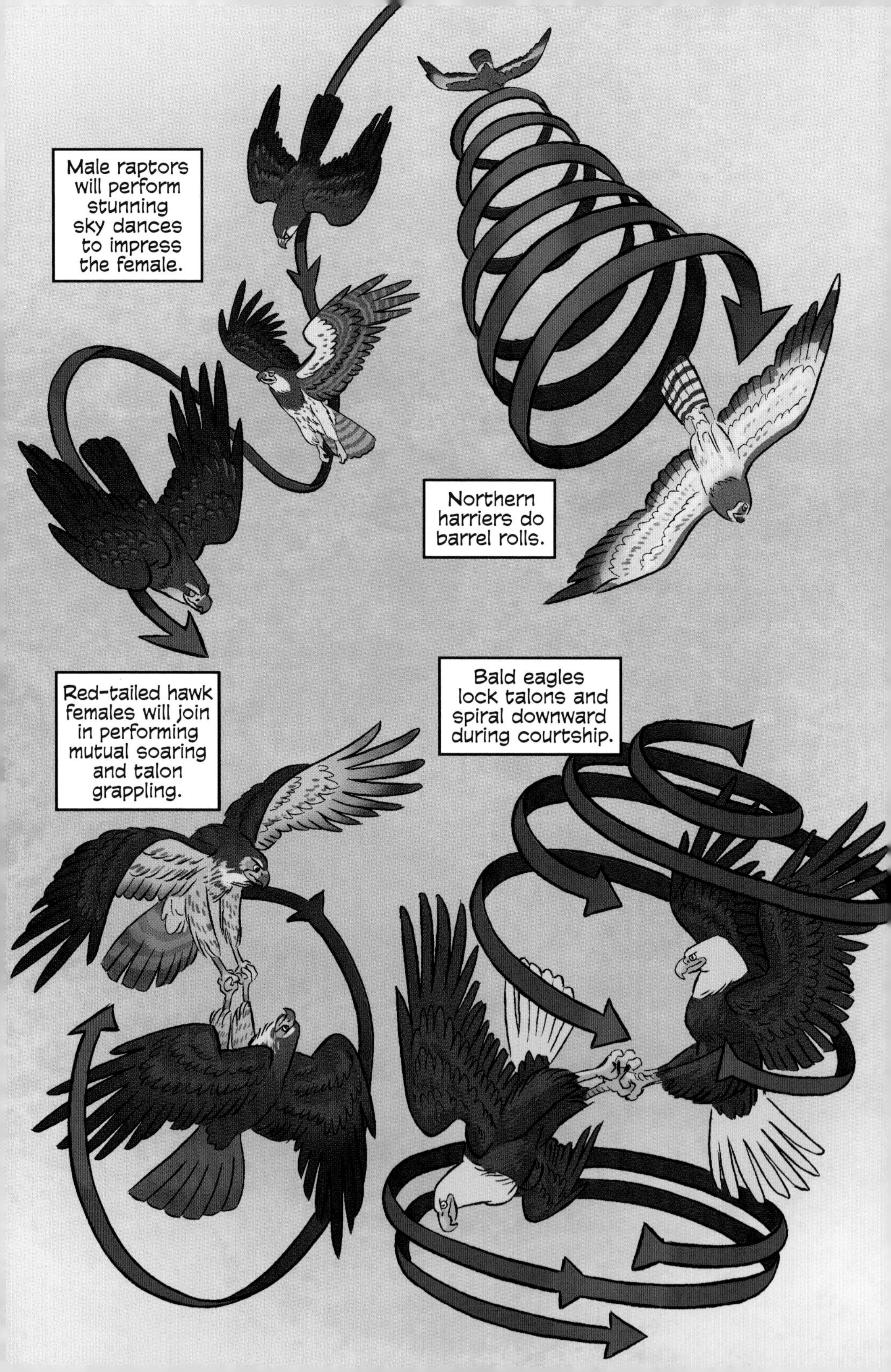
Male raptors will perform stunning sky dances to impress the female.
Northern harriers do barrel rolls.
Red-tailed hawk females will join in performing mutual soaring and talon grappling.
Bald eagles lock talons and spiral downward during courtship.

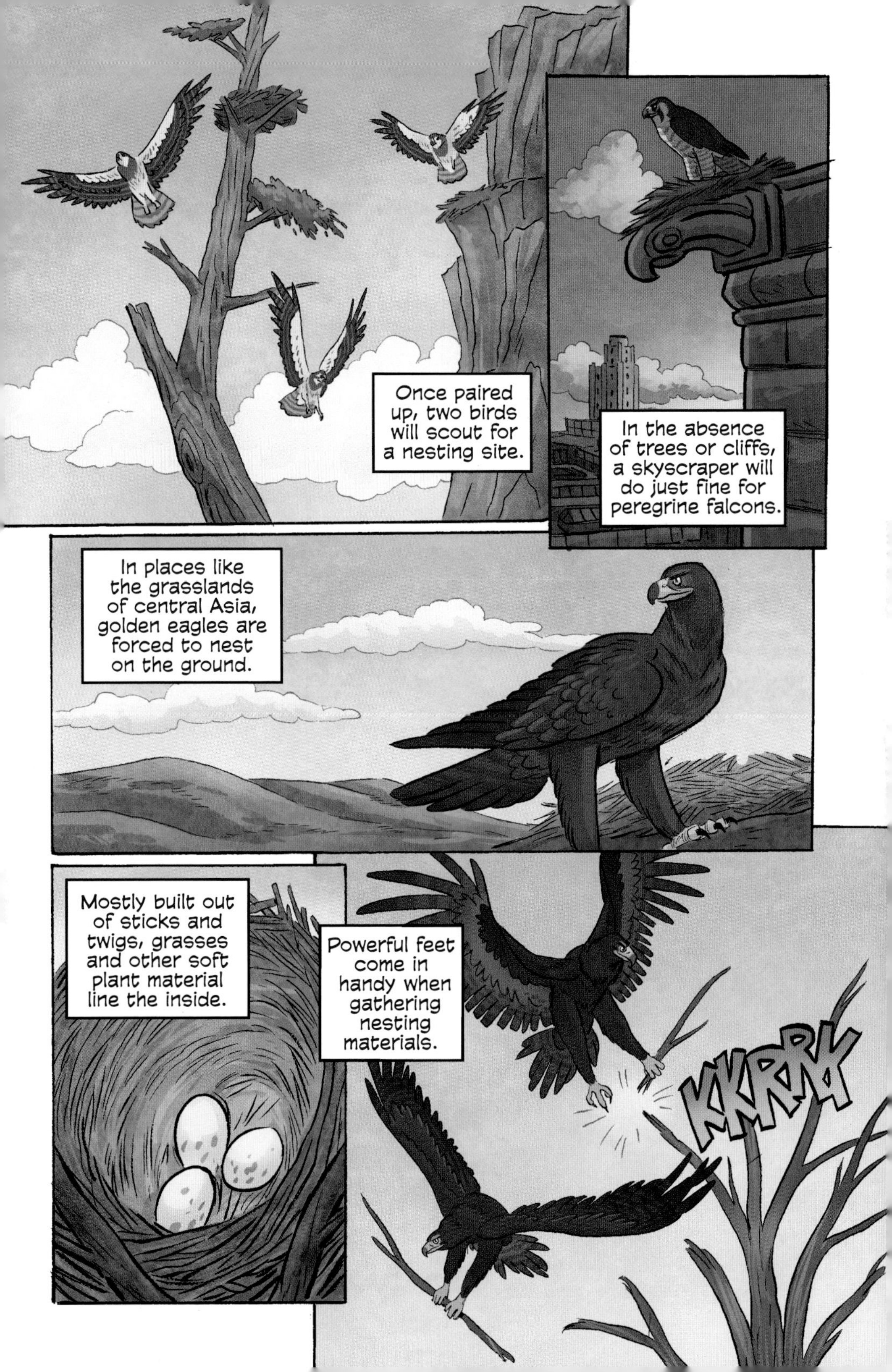
Once paired up, two birds will scout for a nesting site.
In the absence of trees or cliffs, a skyscraper will do just fine for peregrine falcons.
In places like the grasslands of central Asia, golden eagles are forced to nest on the ground.
Mostly built out of sticks and twigs, grasses and other soft plant material line the inside.
Powerful feet come in handy when gathering nesting materials.
KKRRK

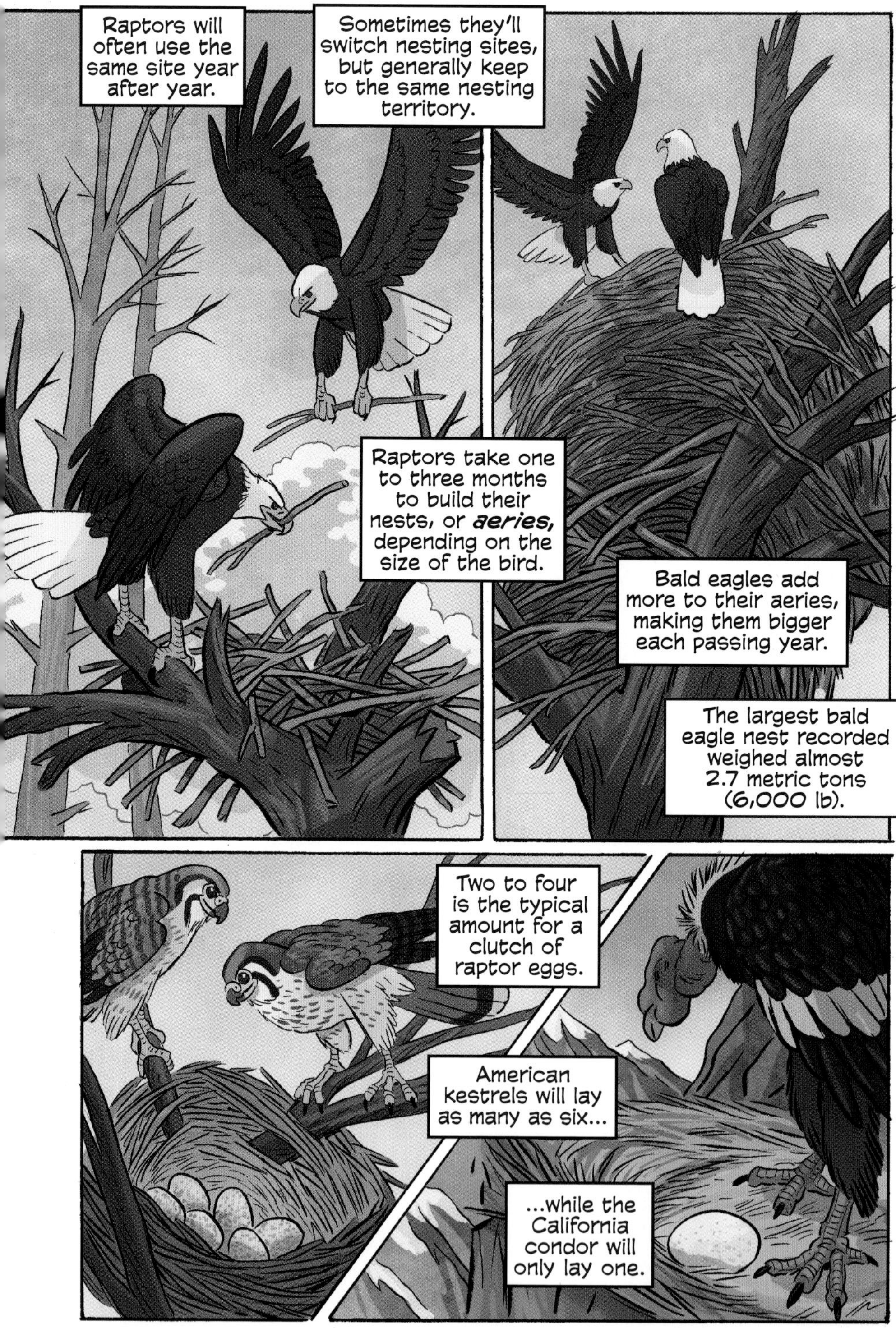
Raptors will often use the same site year after year.
Sometimes they'll switch nesting sites, but generally keep to the same nesting territory.
Raptors take one to three months to build their nests, or ***aeries,*** depending on the size of the bird.
Bald eagles add more to their aeries, making them bigger each passing year.
The largest bald eagle nest recorded weighed almost 2.7 metric tons (6,000 lb).
Two to four is the typical amount for a clutch of raptor eggs.
American kestrels will lay as many as six...
...while the California condor will only lay one.

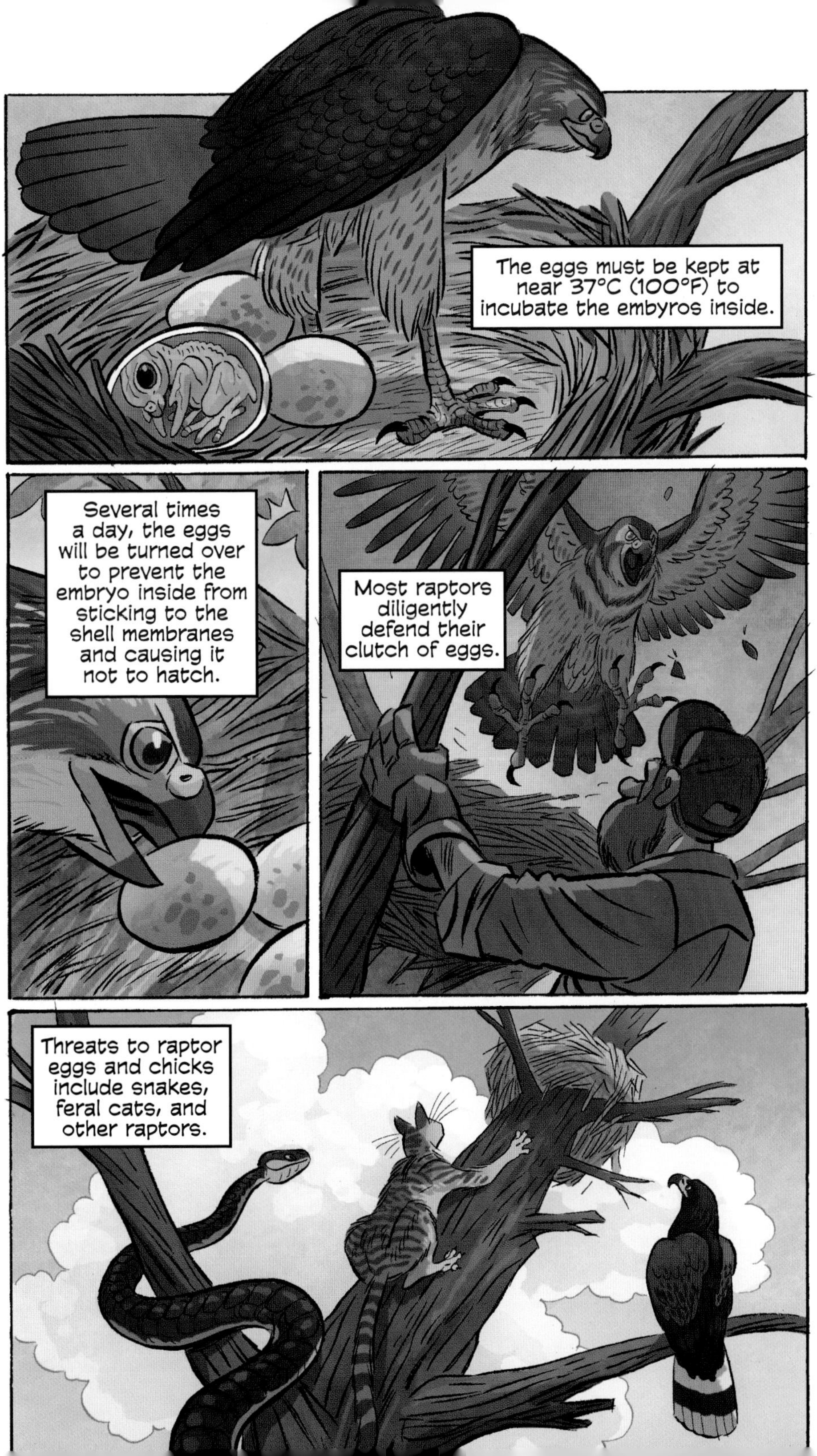
The eggs must be kept at near 37°C (100°F) to incubate the embyros inside.
Several times a day, the eggs will be turned over to prevent the embryo inside from sticking to the shell membranes and causing it not to hatch.
Most raptors diligently defend their clutch of eggs.
Threats to raptor eggs and chicks include snakes, feral cats, and other raptors.

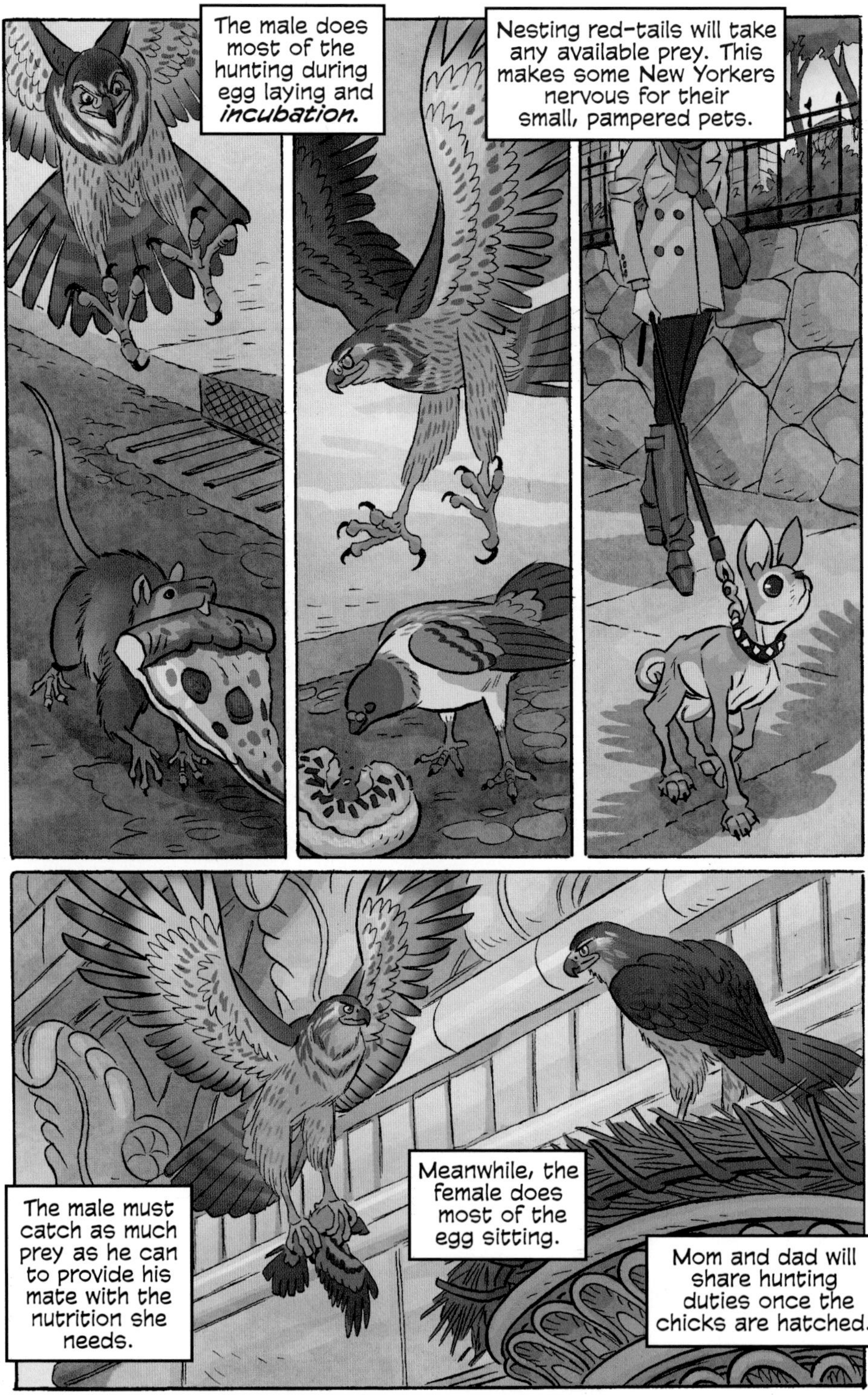
The male does most of the hunting during egg laying and *incubation*.
Nesting red-tails will take any available prey. This makes some New Yorkers nervous for their small, pampered pets.
The male must catch as much prey as he can to provide his mate with the nutrition she needs.
Meanwhile, the female does most of the egg sitting.
Mom and dad will share hunting duties once the chicks are hatched.

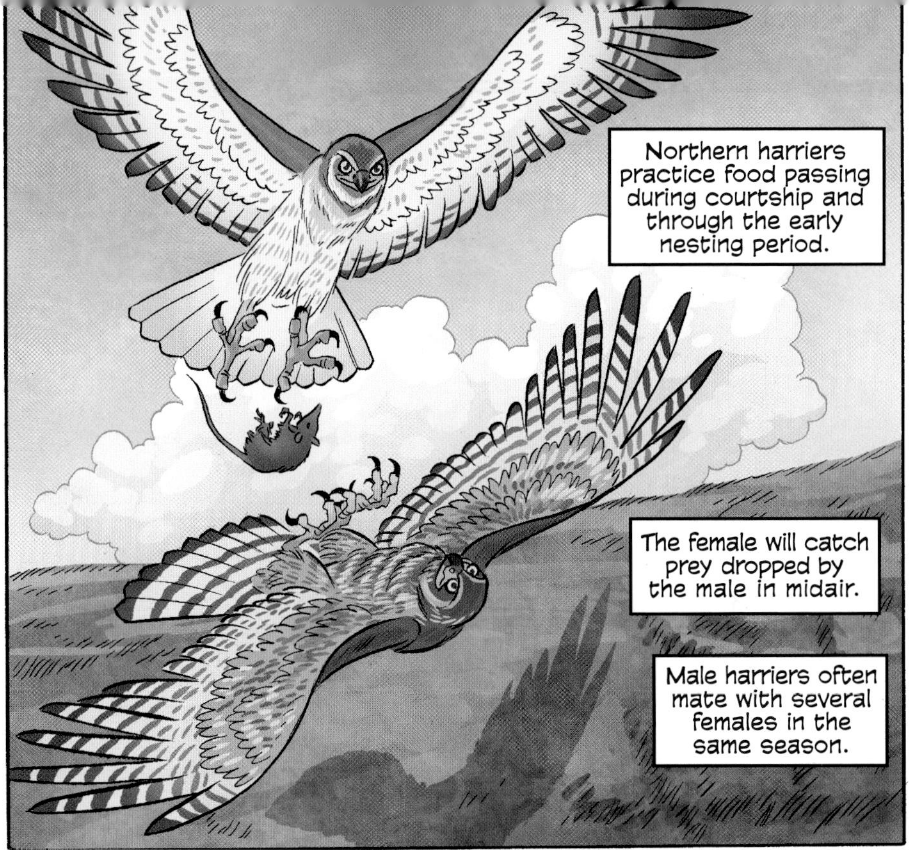
Northern harriers practice food passing during courtship and through the early nesting period.
The female will catch prey dropped by the male in midair.
Male harriers often mate with several females in the same season.

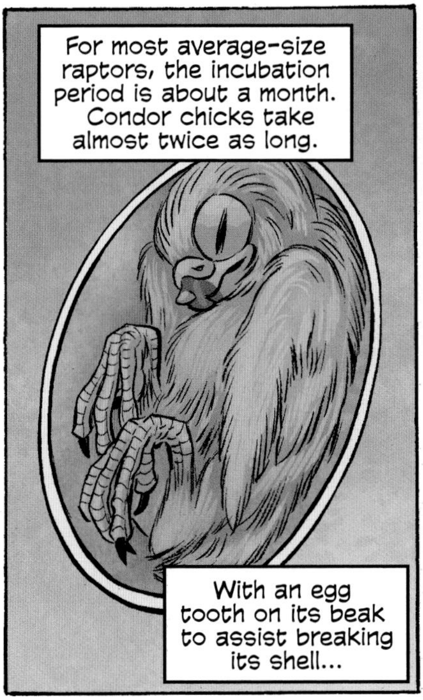
For most average-size raptors, the incubation period is about a month. Condor chicks take almost twice as long.
With an egg tooth on its beak to assist breaking its shell...

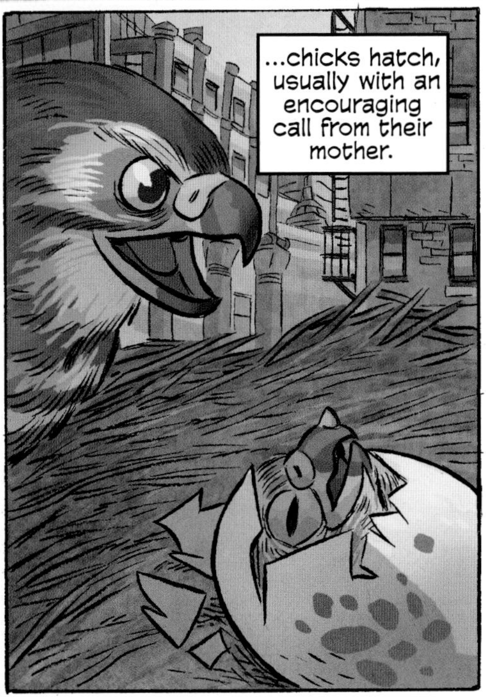
...chicks hatch, usually with an encouraging call from their mother.

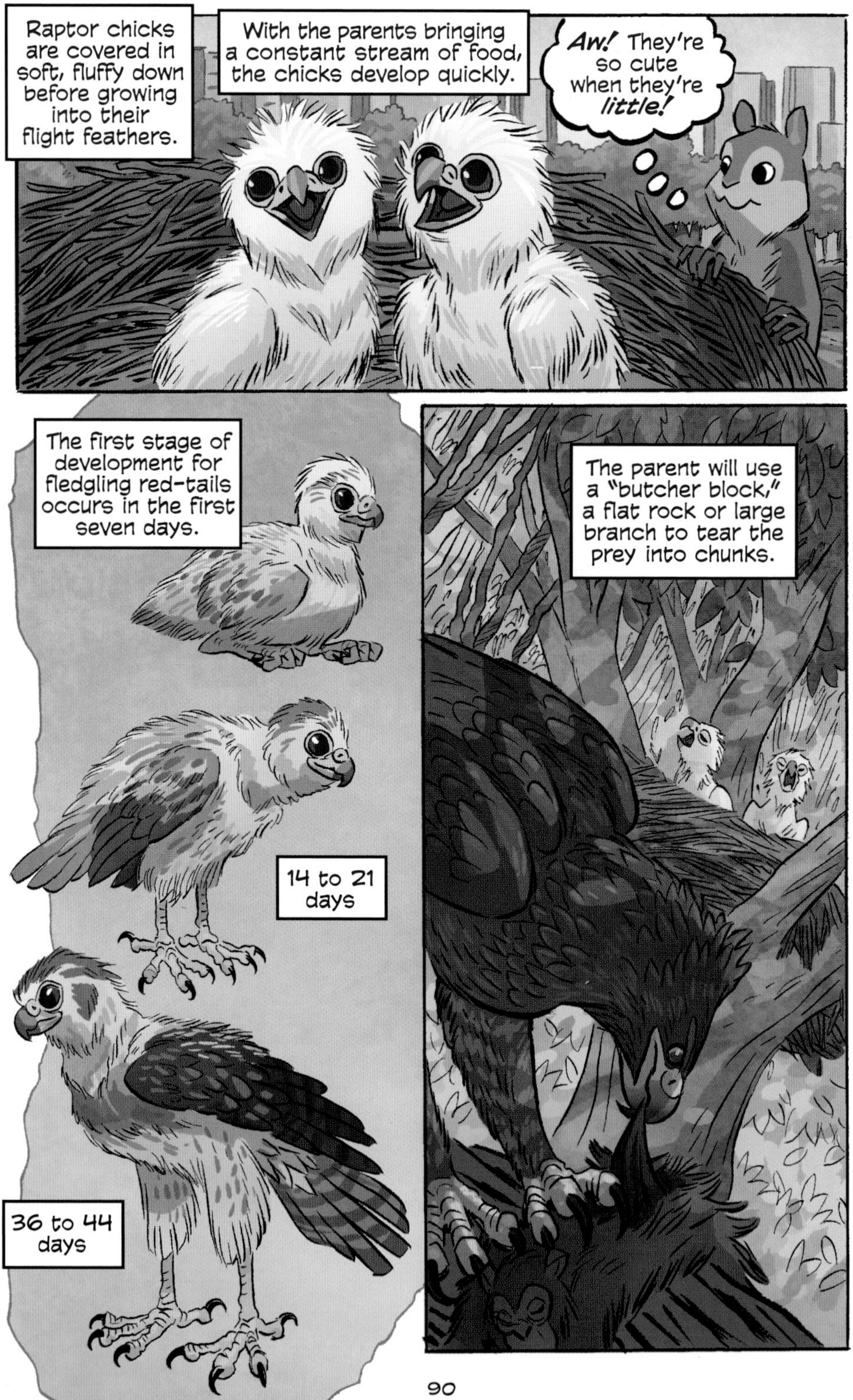
Raptor chicks are covered in soft, fluffy down before growing into their flight feathers.
With the parents bringing a constant stream of food, the chicks develop quickly.
Aw! They're so cute when they're *little!*
The first stage of development for fledgling red-tails occurs in the first seven days.
14 to 21 days
36 to 44 days
The parent will use a "butcher block," a flat rock or large branch to tear the prey into chunks.

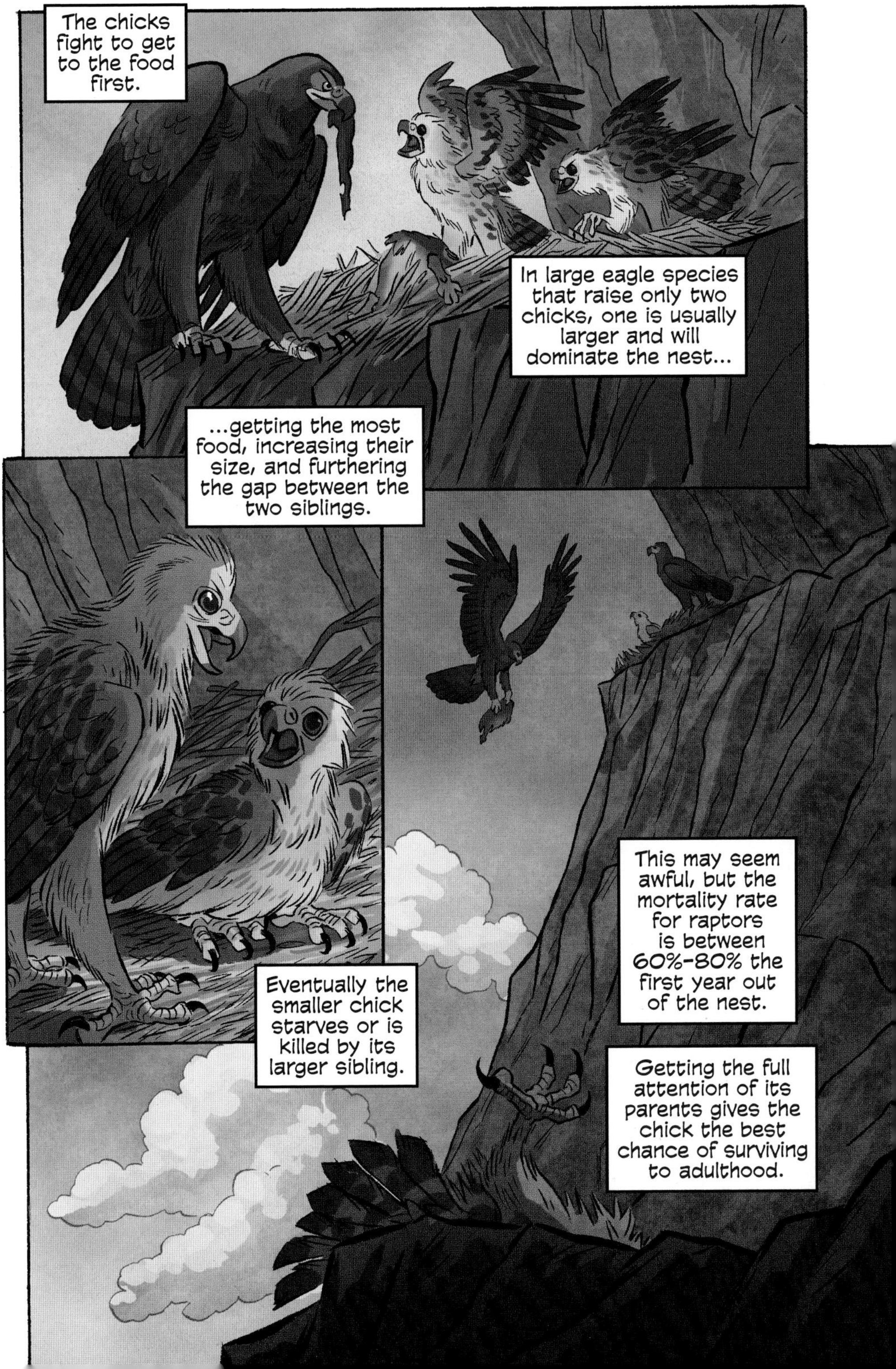
The chicks fight to get to the food first.
In large eagle species that raise only two chicks, one is usually larger and will dominate the nest...
...getting the most food, increasing their size, and furthering the gap between the two siblings.
Eventually the smaller chick starves or is killed by its larger sibling.
This may seem awful, but the mortality rate for raptors is between 60%-80% the first year out of the nest.
Getting the full attention of its parents gives the chick the best chance of surviving to adulthood.

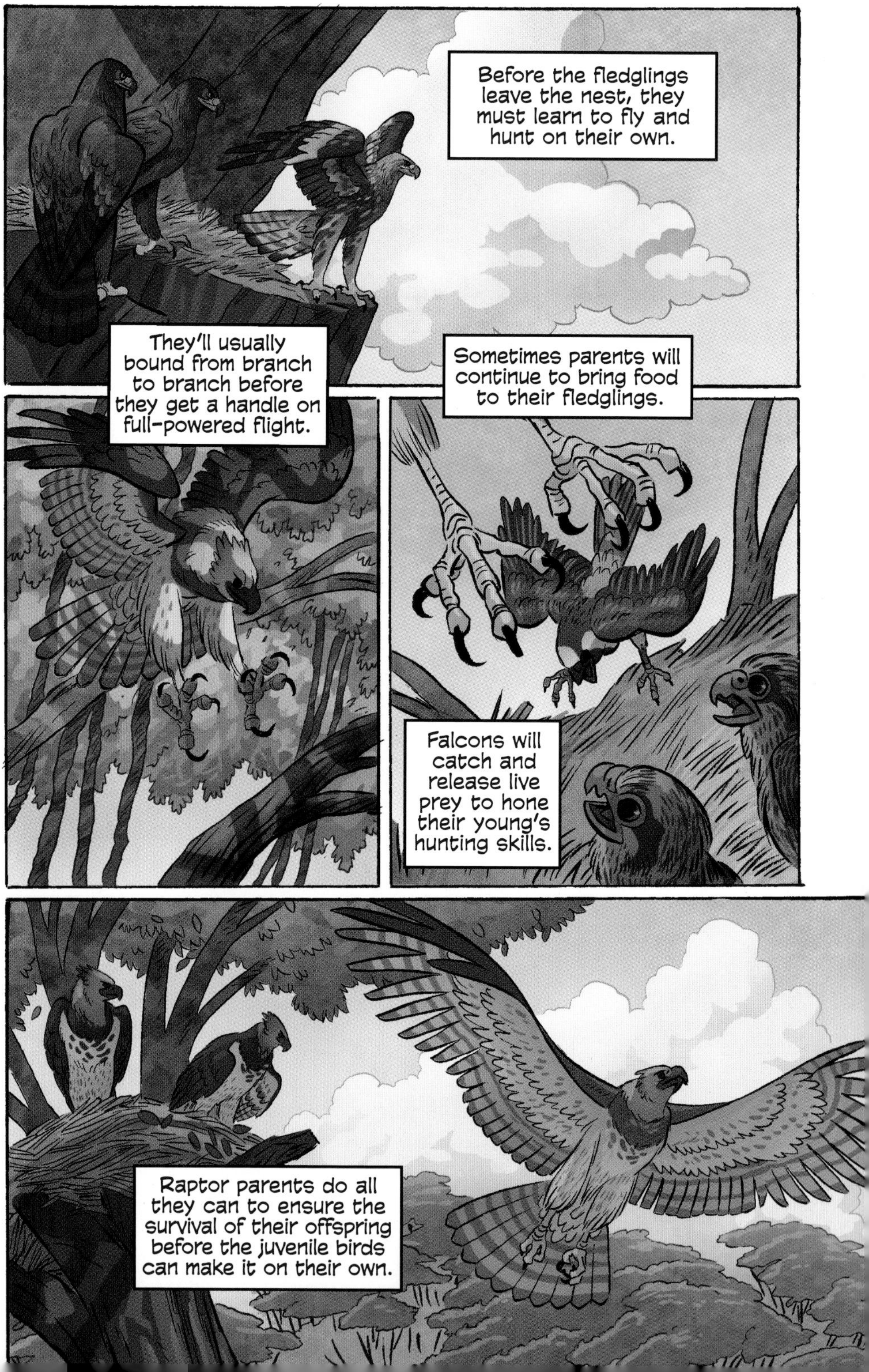
Before the fledglings leave the nest, they must learn to fly and hunt on their own.
They'll usually bound from branch to branch before they get a handle on full-powered flight.
Sometimes parents will continue to bring food to their fledglings.
Falcons will catch and release live prey to hone their young's hunting skills.
Raptor parents do all they can to ensure the survival of their offspring before the juvenile birds can make it on their own.

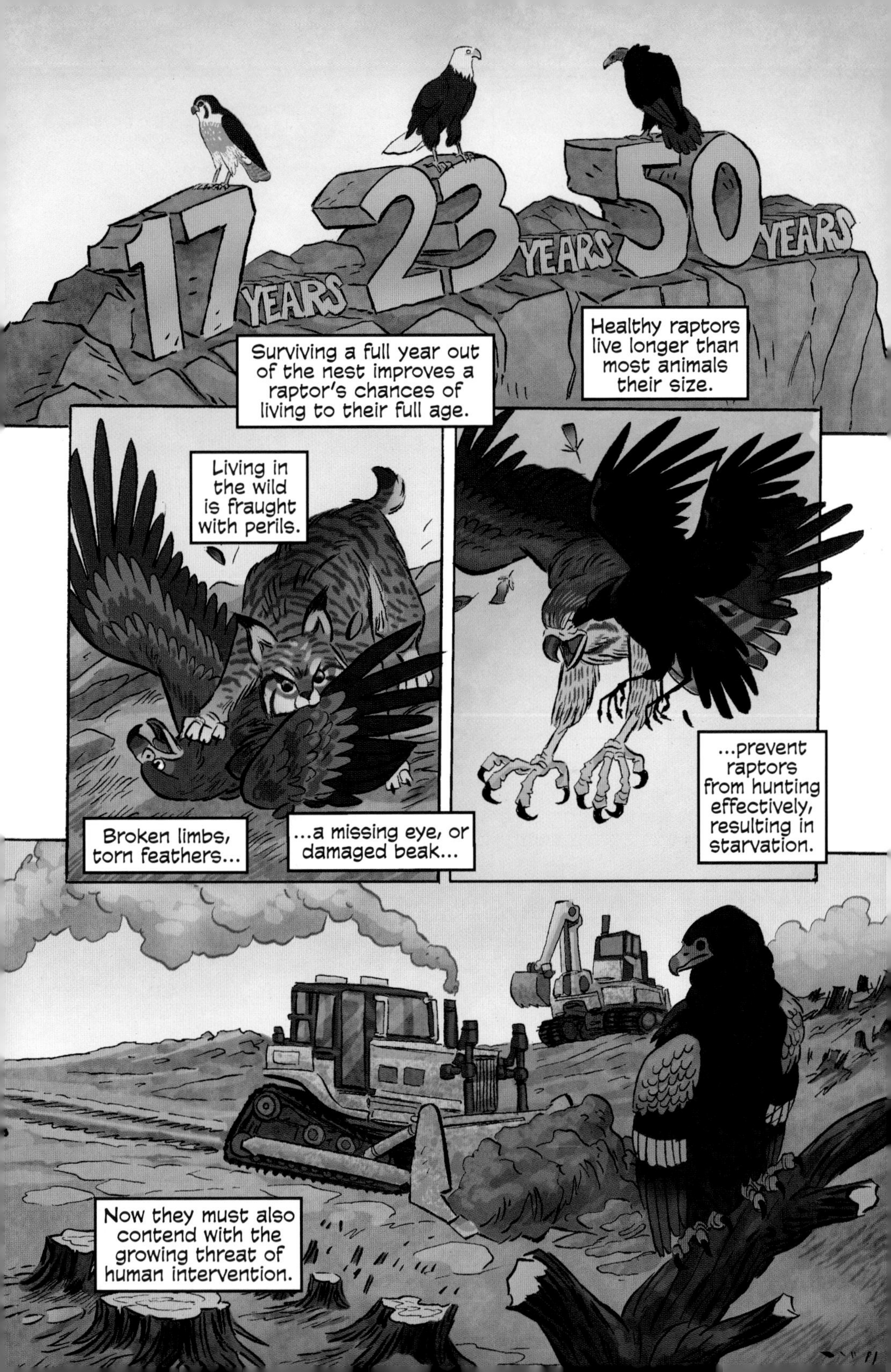
17 YEARS
23 YEARS
50 YEARS
Surviving a full year out of the nest improves a raptor's chances of living to their full age.
Healthy raptors live longer than most animals their size.
Living in the wild is fraught with perils.
Broken limbs, torn feathers...
...a missing eye, or damaged beak...
...prevent raptors from hunting effectively, resulting in starvation.
Now they must also contend with the growing threat of human intervention.

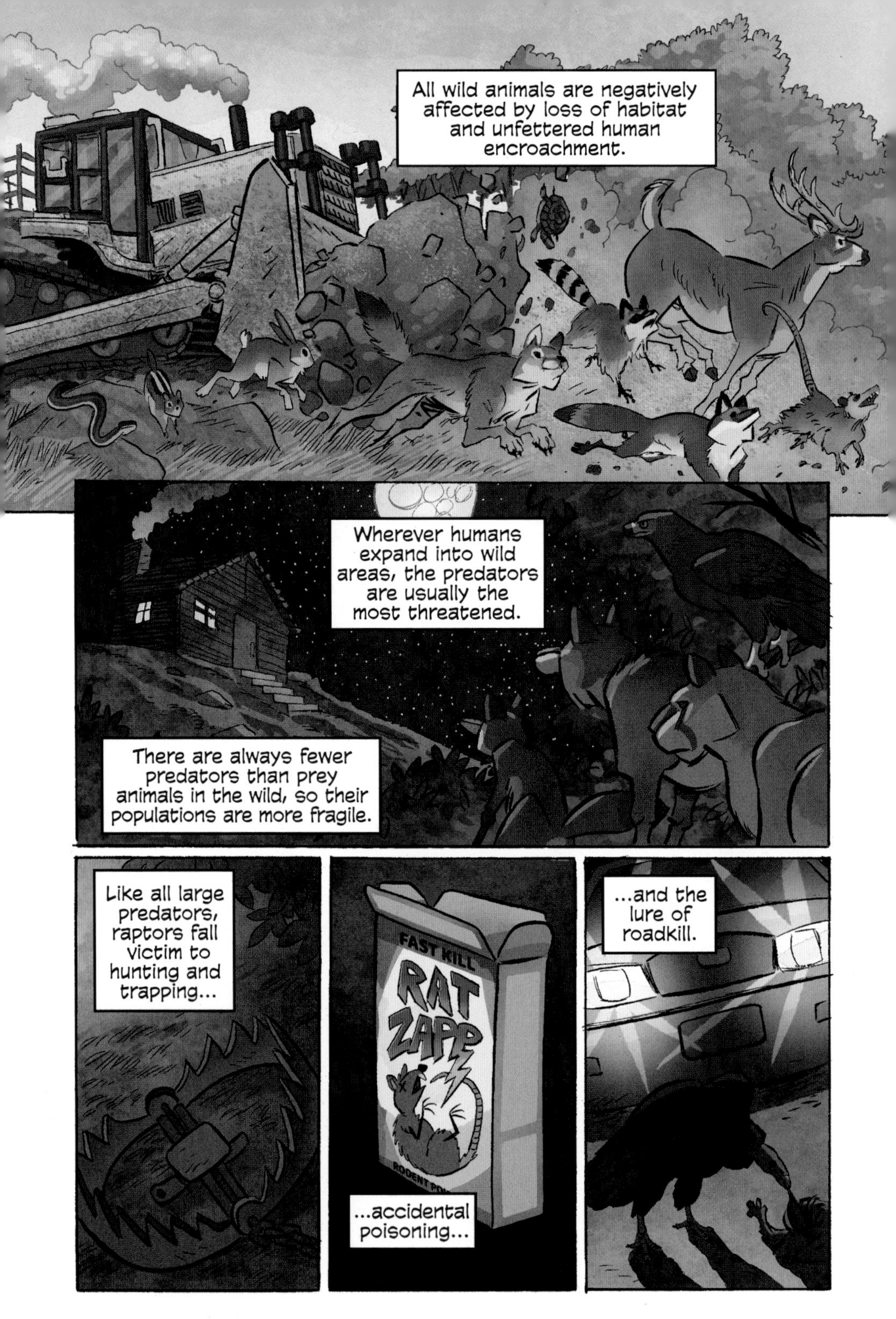
All wild animals are negatively affected by loss of habitat and unfettered human encroachment.
Wherever humans expand into wild areas, the predators are usually the most threatened.
There are always fewer predators than prey animals in the wild, so their populations are more fragile.
Like all large predators, raptors fall victim to hunting and trapping...
FAST KILL
RAT ZAPP
...accidental poisoning...
...and the lure of roadkill.

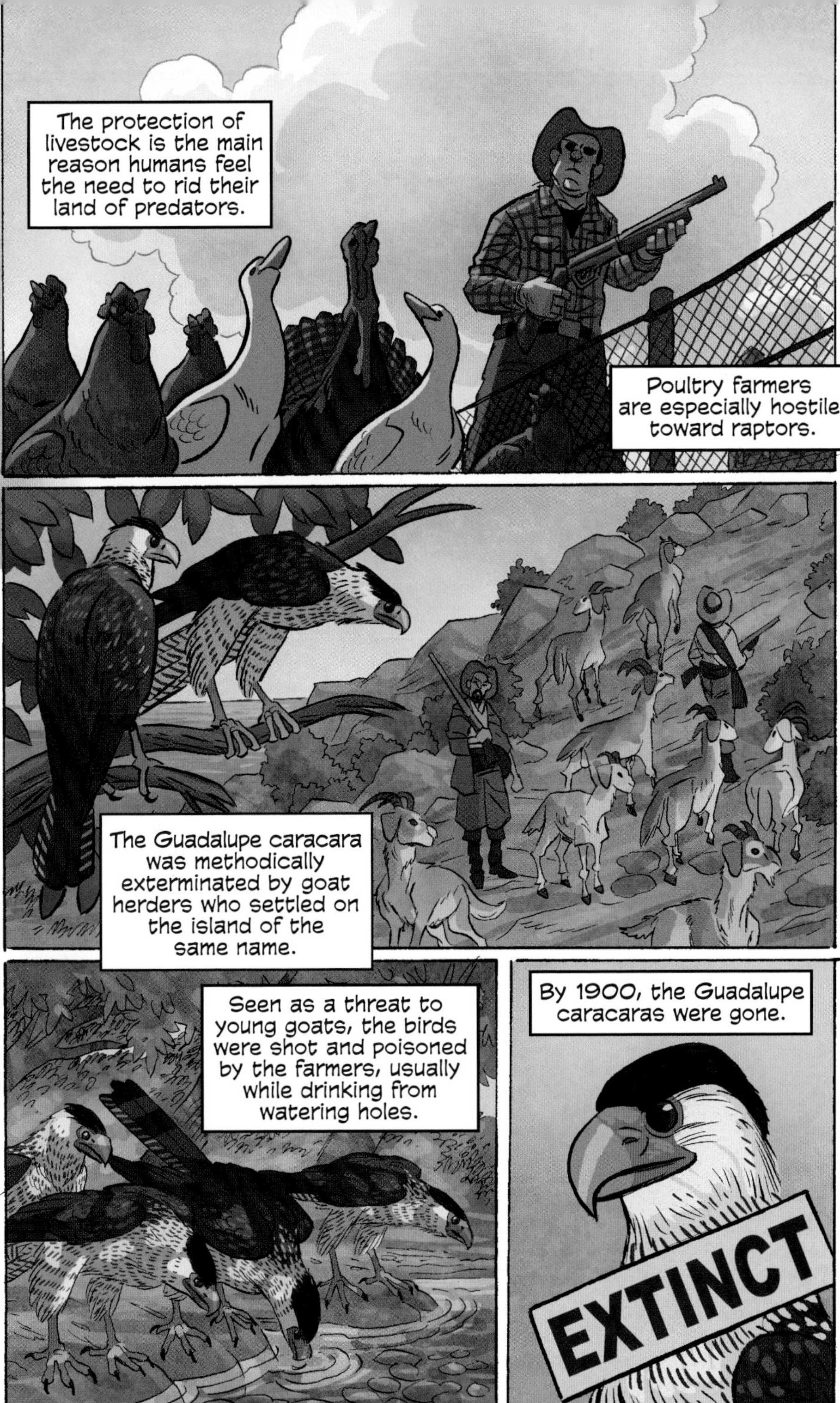
The protection of livestock is the main reason humans feel the need to rid their land of predators.
Poultry farmers are especially hostile toward raptors.
The Guadalupe caracara was methodically exterminated by goat herders who settled on the island of the same name.
Seen as a threat to young goats, the birds were shot and poisoned by the farmers, usually while drinking from watering holes.
By 1900, the Guadalupe caracaras were gone.
EXTINCT

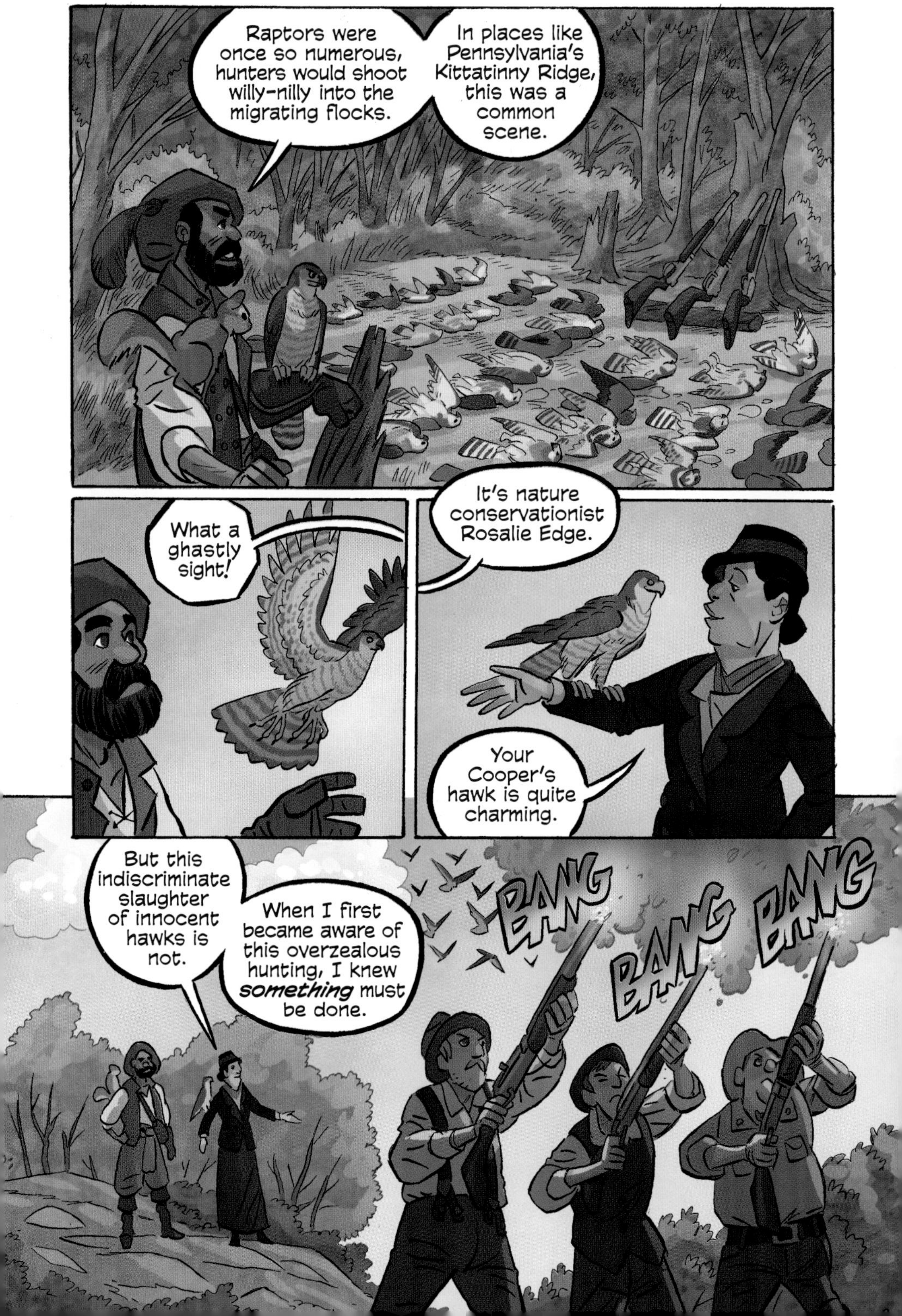
Raptors were once so numerous, hunters would shoot willy-nilly into the migrating flocks.
In places like Pennsylvania's Kittatinny Ridge, this was a common scene.
What a ghastly sight!
It's nature conservationist Rosalie Edge.
Your Cooper's hawk is quite charming.
But this indiscriminate slaughter of innocent hawks is not.
When I first became aware of this overzealous hunting, I knew *something* must be done.
BANG
BANG
BANG

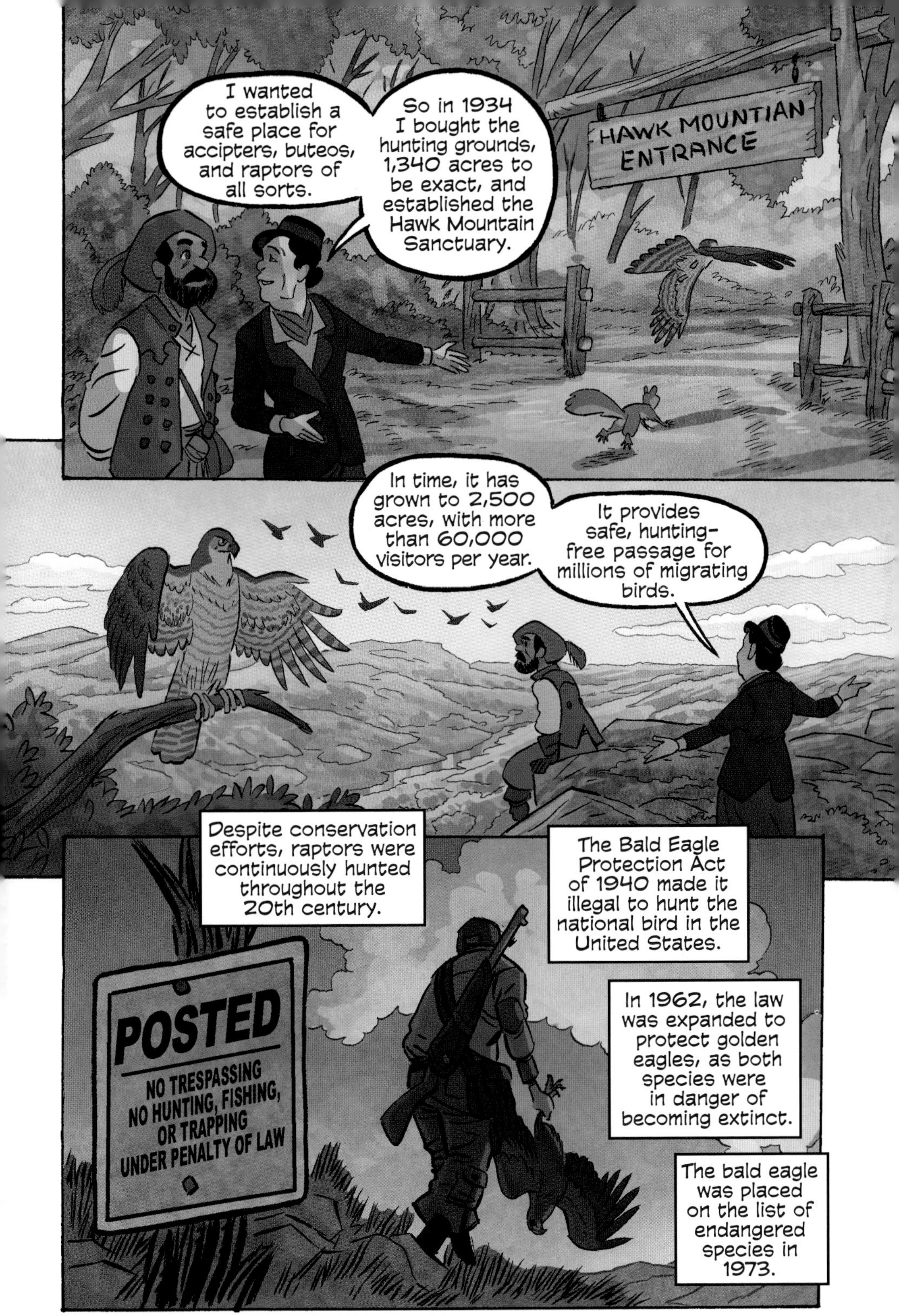
I wanted to establish a safe place for accipters, buteos, and raptors of all sorts.
So in 1934 I bought the hunting grounds, 1,340 acres to be exact, and established the Hawk Mountain Sanctuary.
HAWK MOUNTIAN ENTRANCE
In time, it has grown to 2,500 acres, with more than 60,000 visitors per year.
It provides safe, hunting-free passage for millions of migrating birds.
Despite conservation efforts, raptors were continuously hunted throughout the 20th century.
The Bald Eagle Protection Act of 1940 made it illegal to hunt the national bird in the United States.
POSTED
NO TRESPASSING
NO HUNTING, FISHING,
OR TRAPPING
UNDER PENALTY OF LAW
In 1962, the law was expanded to protect golden eagles, as both species were in danger of becoming extinct.
The bald eagle was placed on the list of endangered species in 1973.

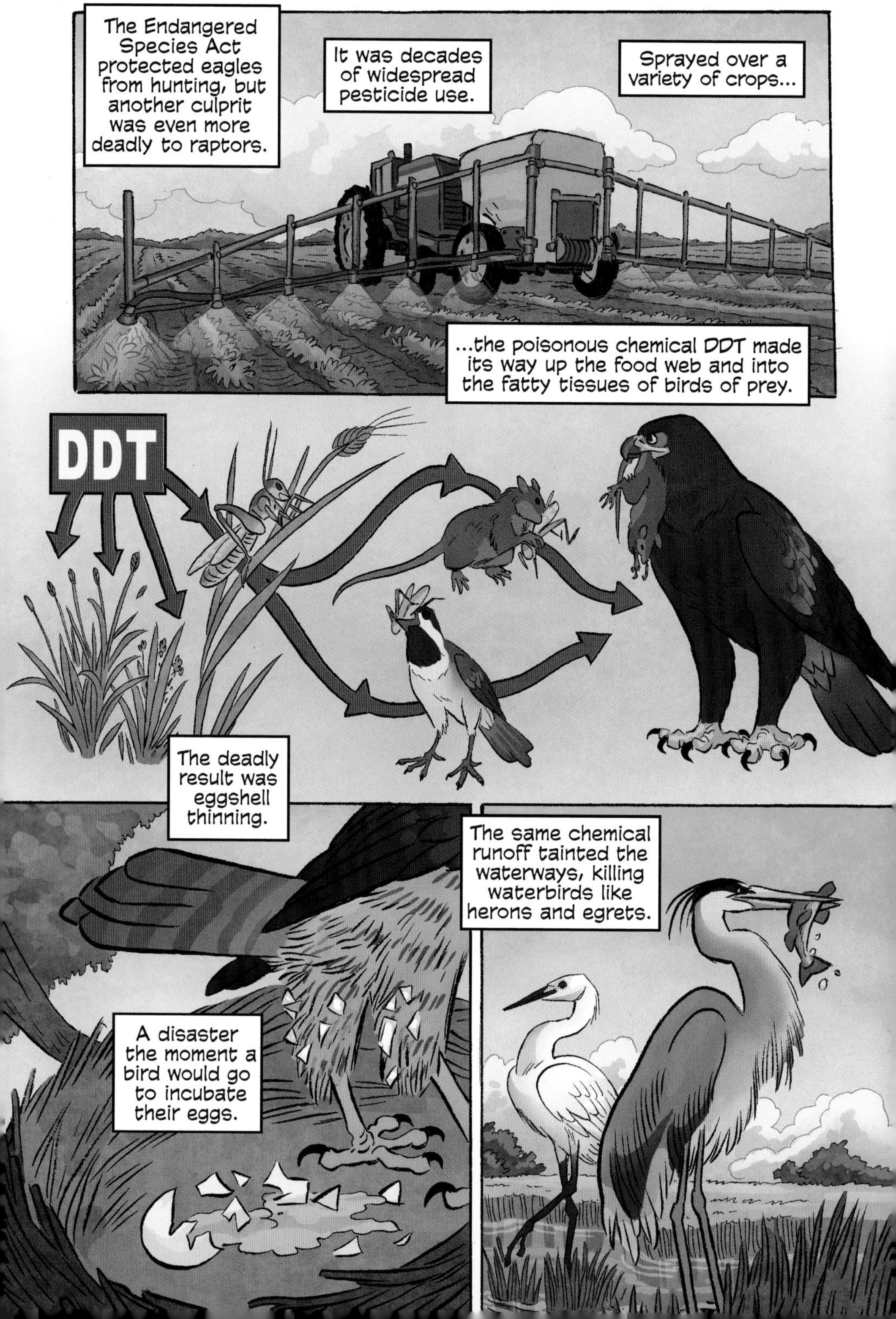
The Endangered Species Act protected eagles from hunting, but another culprit was even more deadly to raptors.
It was decades of widespread pesticide use.
Sprayed over a variety of crops...
...the poisonous chemical DDT made its way up the food web and into the fatty tissues of birds of prey.
DDT
The deadly result was eggshell thinning.
A disaster the moment a bird would go to incubate their eggs.
The same chemical runoff tainted the waterways, killing waterbirds like herons and egrets.

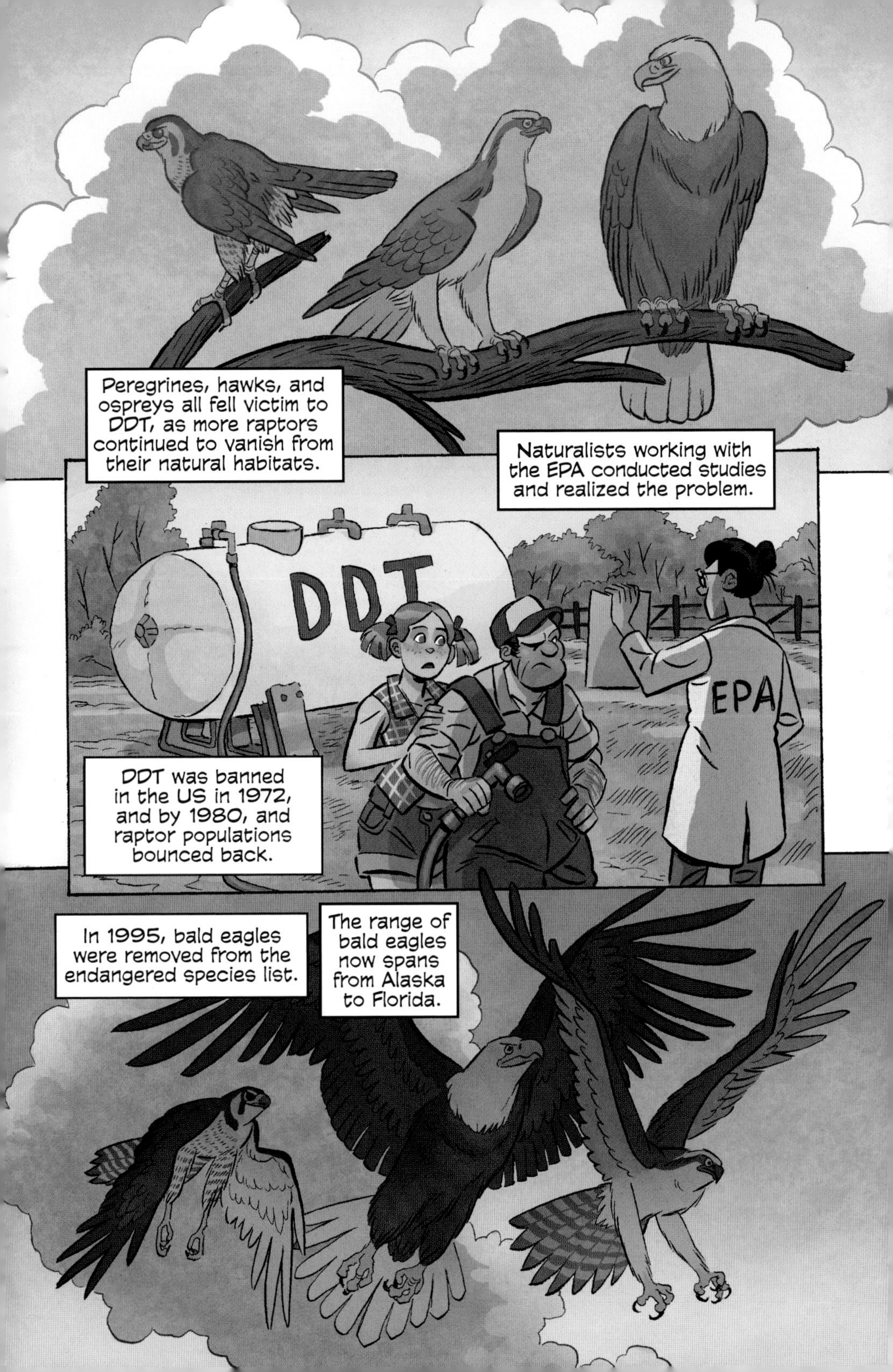
Peregrines, hawks, and ospreys all fell victim to DDT, as more raptors continued to vanish from their natural habitats.
Naturalists working with the EPA conducted studies and realized the problem.
DDT
EPA
DDT was banned in the US in 1972, and by 1980, and raptor populations bounced back.
In 1995, bald eagles were removed from the endangered species list.
The range of bald eagles now spans from Alaska to Florida.

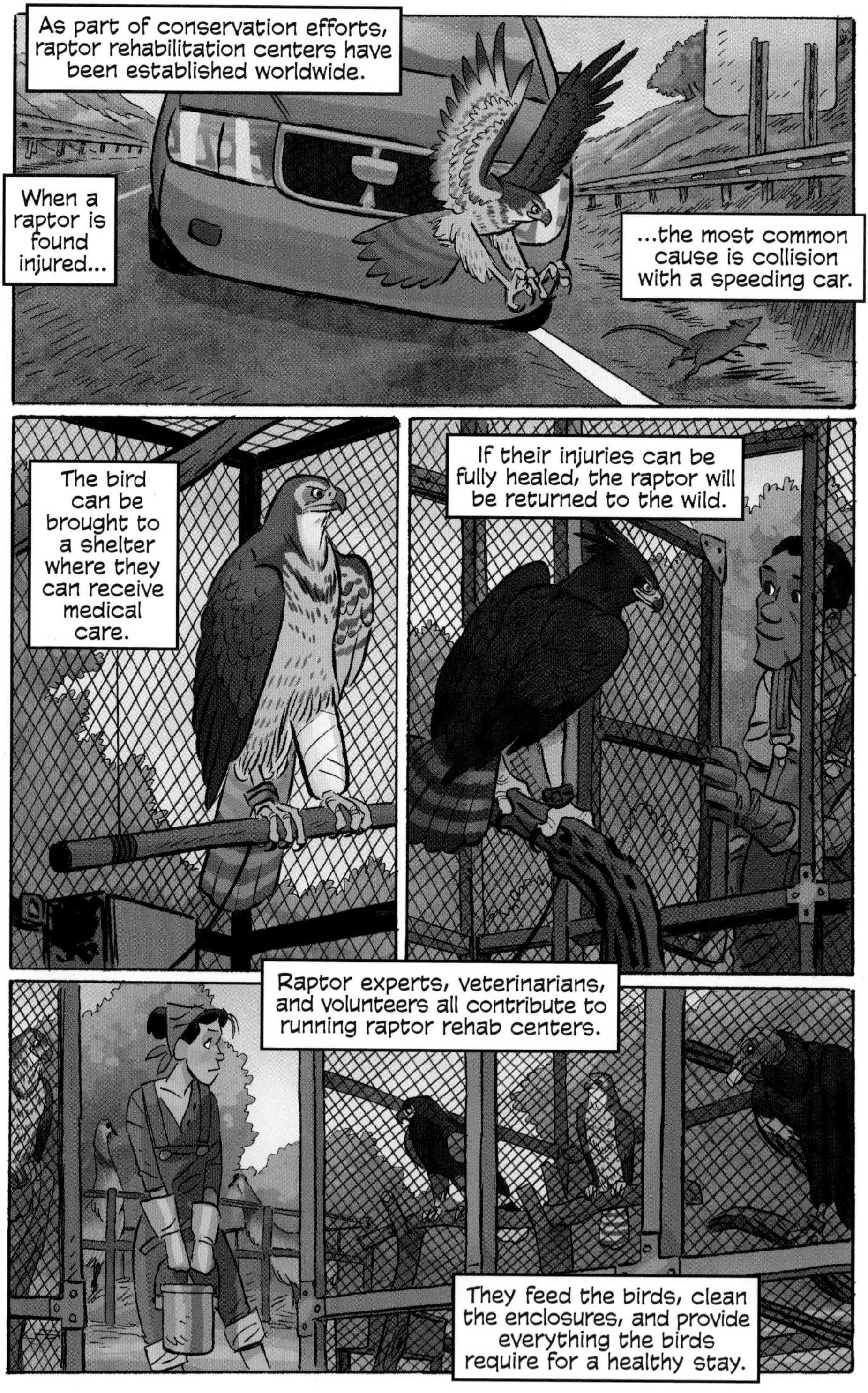
As part of conservation efforts, raptor rehabilitation centers have been established worldwide.
When a raptor is found injured...
...the most common cause is collision with a speeding car.
The bird can be brought to a shelter where they can receive medical care.
If their injuries can be fully healed, the raptor will be returned to the wild.
Raptor experts, veterinarians, and volunteers all contribute to running raptor rehab centers.
They feed the birds, clean the enclosures, and provide everything the birds require for a healthy stay.

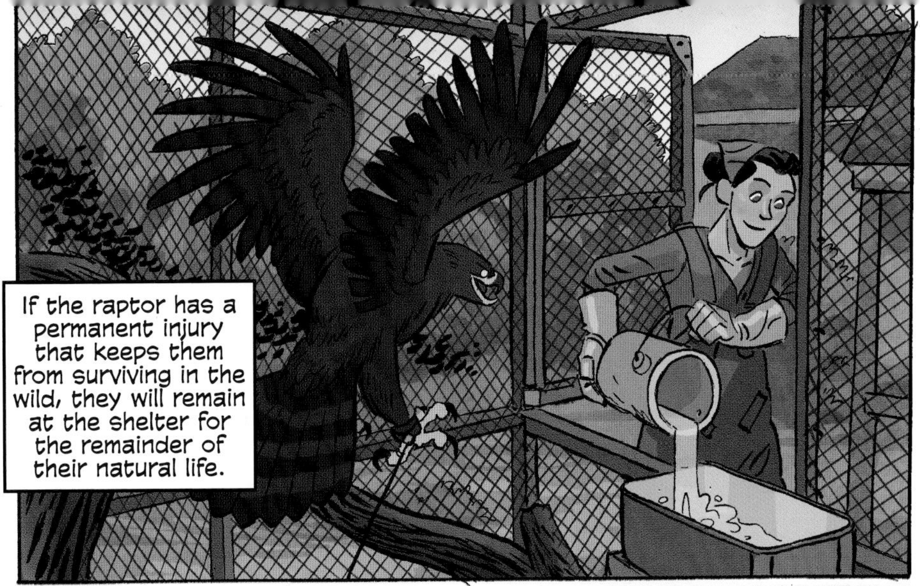
If the raptor has a permanent injury that keeps them from surviving in the wild, they will remain at the shelter for the remainder of their natural life.

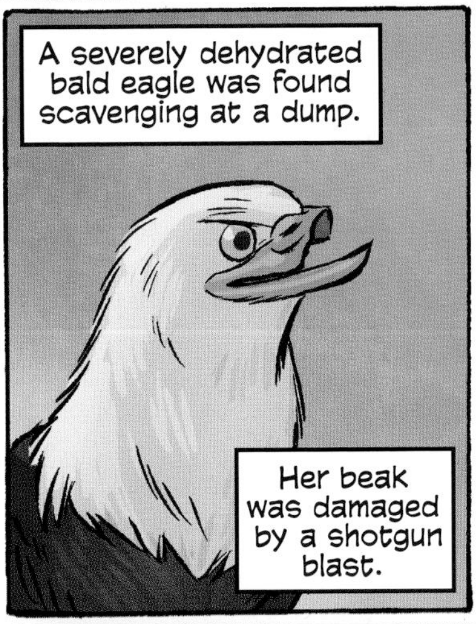
A severely dehydrated bald eagle was found scavenging at a dump.
Her beak was damaged by a shotgun blast.

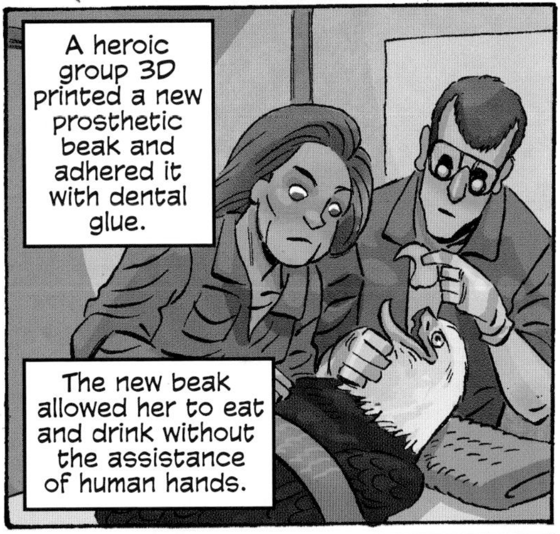
A heroic group 3D printed a new prosthetic beak and adhered it with dental glue.
The new beak allowed her to eat and drink without the assistance of human hands.

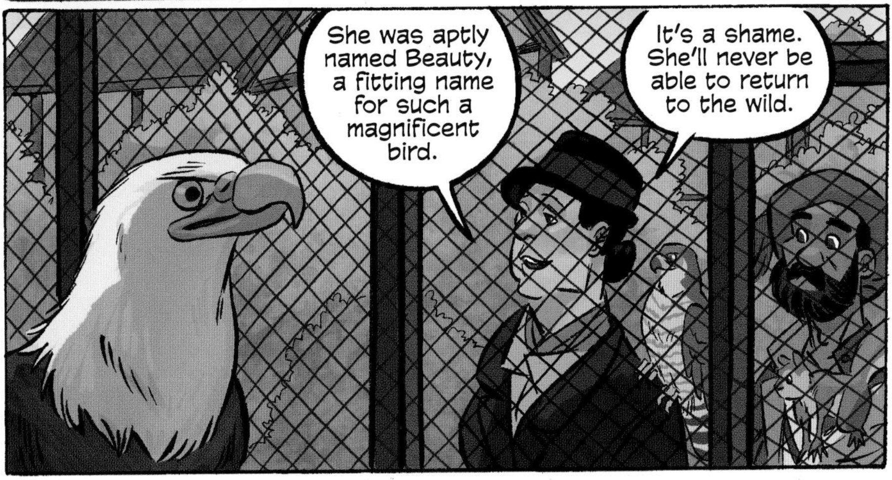
She was aptly named Beauty, a fitting name for such a magnificent bird.
It's a shame. She'll never be able to return to the wild.

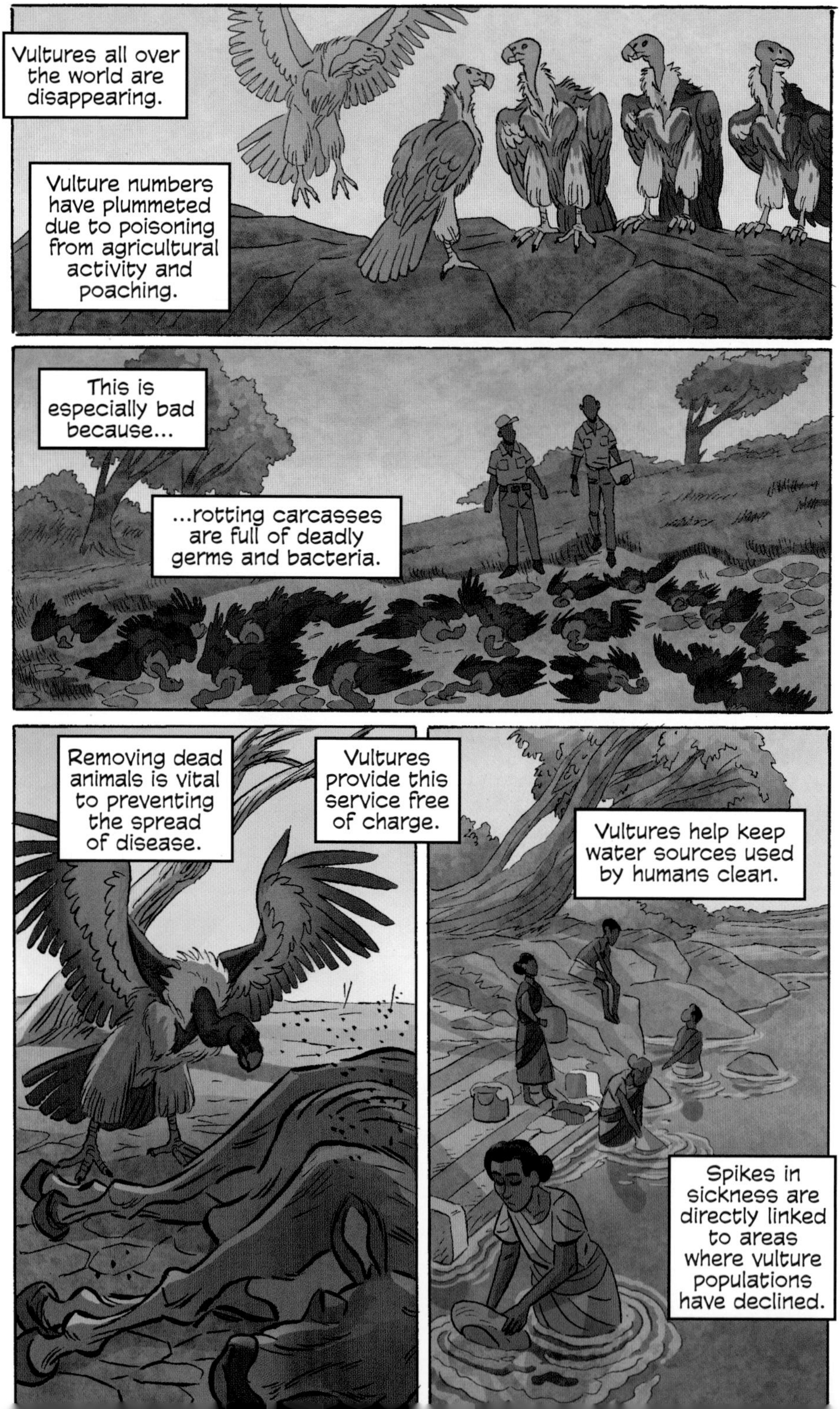
Vultures all over the world are disappearing.
Vulture numbers have plummeted due to poisoning from agricultural activity and poaching.
This is especially bad because...
...rotting carcasses are full of deadly germs and bacteria.
Removing dead animals is vital to preventing the spread of disease.
Vultures provide this service free of charge.
Vultures help keep water sources used by humans clean.
Spikes in sickness are directly linked to areas where vulture populations have declined.

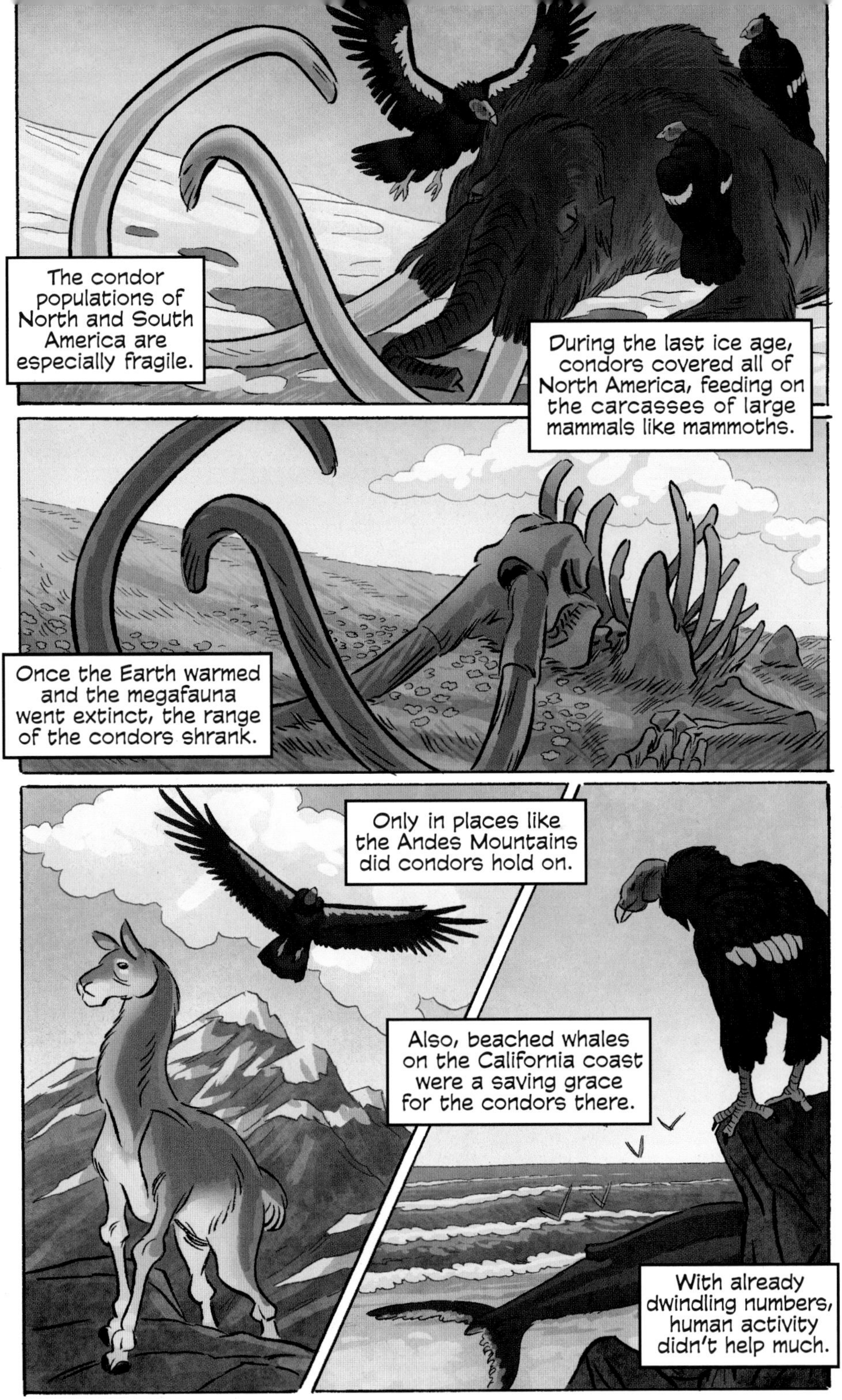
The condor populations of North and South America are especially fragile.
During the last ice age, condors covered all of North America, feeding on the carcasses of large mammals like mammoths.
Once the Earth warmed and the megafauna went extinct, the range of the condors shrank.
Only in places like the Andes Mountains did condors hold on.
Also, beached whales on the California coast were a saving grace for the condors there.
With already dwindling numbers, human activity didn't help much.

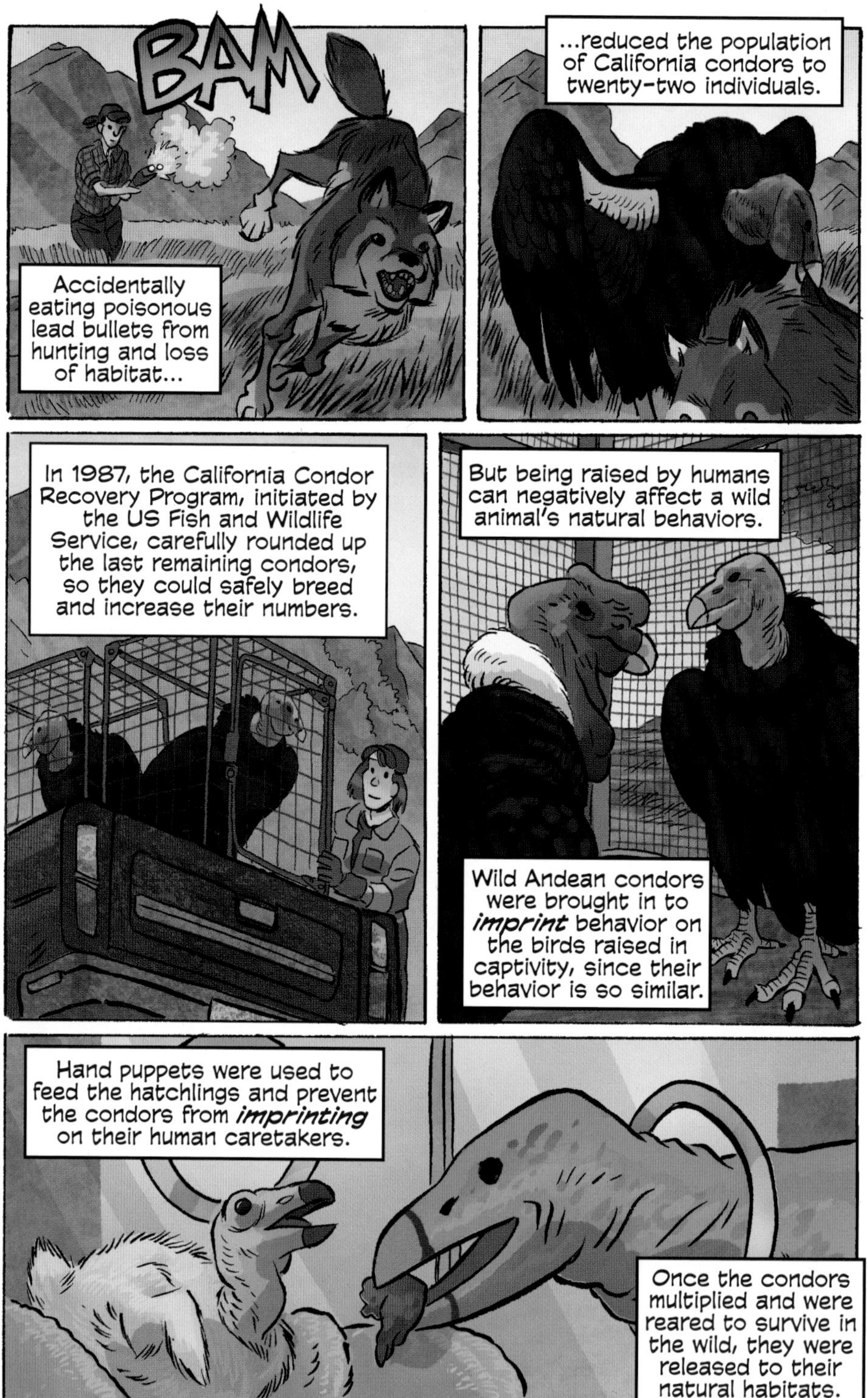
BAM
Accidentally eating poisonous lead bullets from hunting and loss of habitat...
...reduced the population of California condors to twenty-two individuals.
In 1987, the California Condor Recovery Program, initiated by the US Fish and Wildlife Service, carefully rounded up the last remaining condors, so they could safely breed and increase their numbers.
But being raised by humans can negatively affect a wild animal's natural behaviors.
Wild Andean condors were brought in to *imprint* behavior on the birds raised in captivity, since their behavior is so similar.
Hand puppets were used to feed the hatchlings and prevent the condors from *imprinting* on their human caretakers.
Once the condors multiplied and were reared to survive in the wild, they were released to their natural habitats.

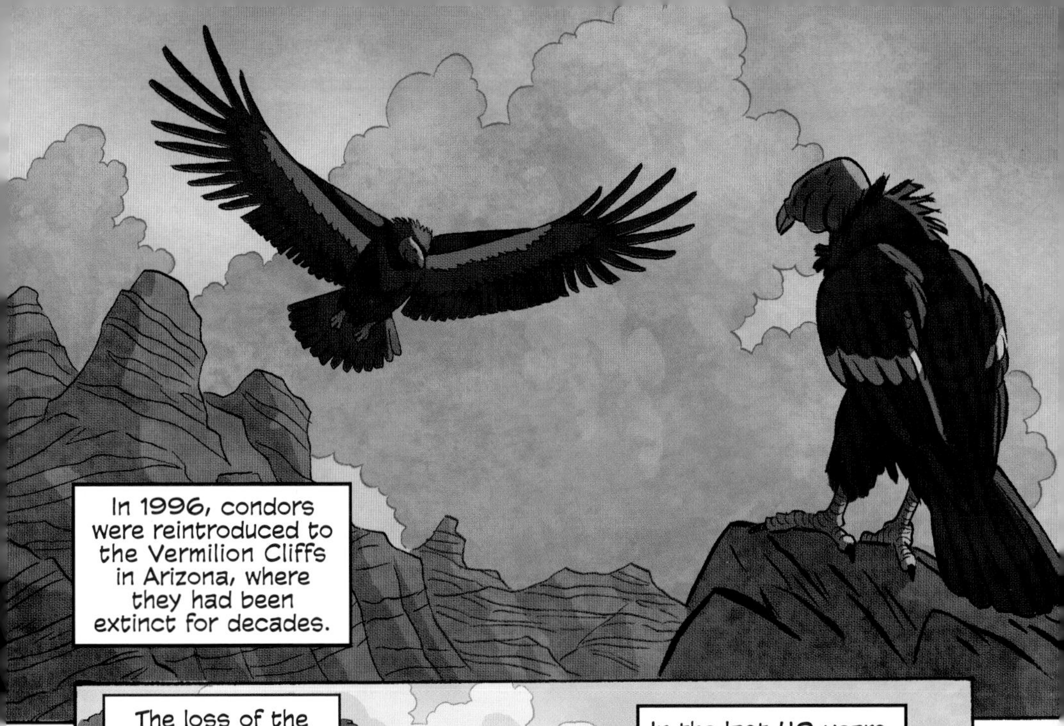
In 1996, condors were reintroduced to the Vermilion Cliffs in Arizona, where they had been extinct for decades.

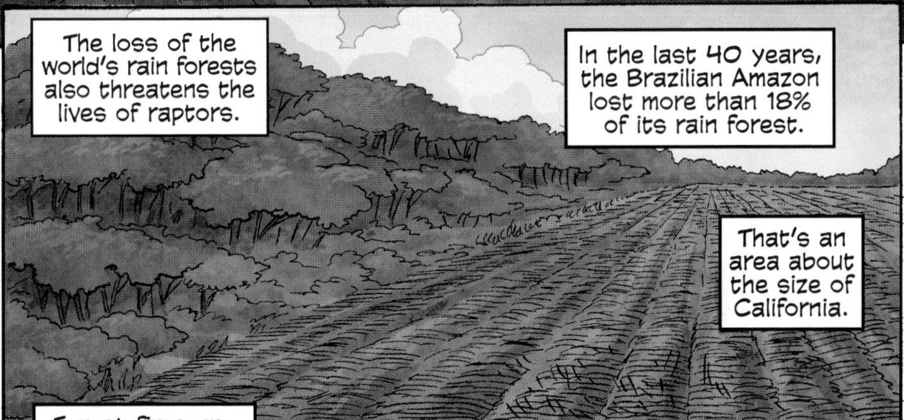
The loss of the world's rain forests also threatens the lives of raptors.
In the last 40 years, the Brazilian Amazon lost more than 18% of its rain forest.
That's an area about the size of California.

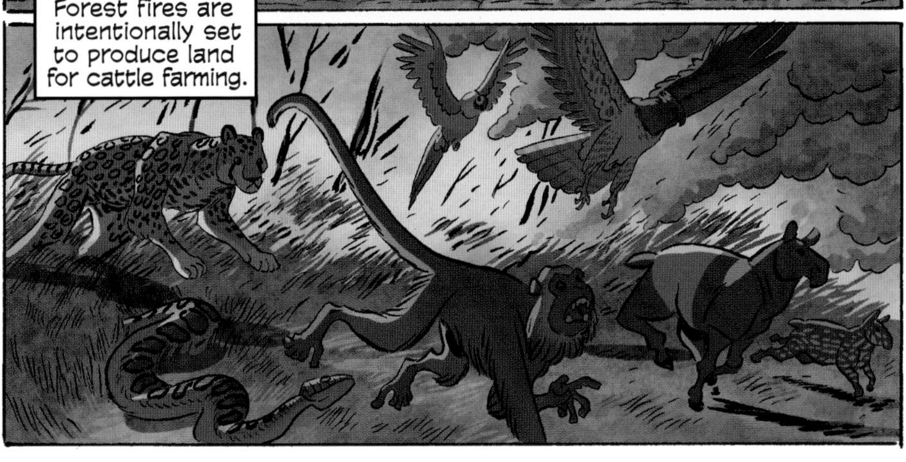
Forest fires are intentionally set to produce land for cattle farming.

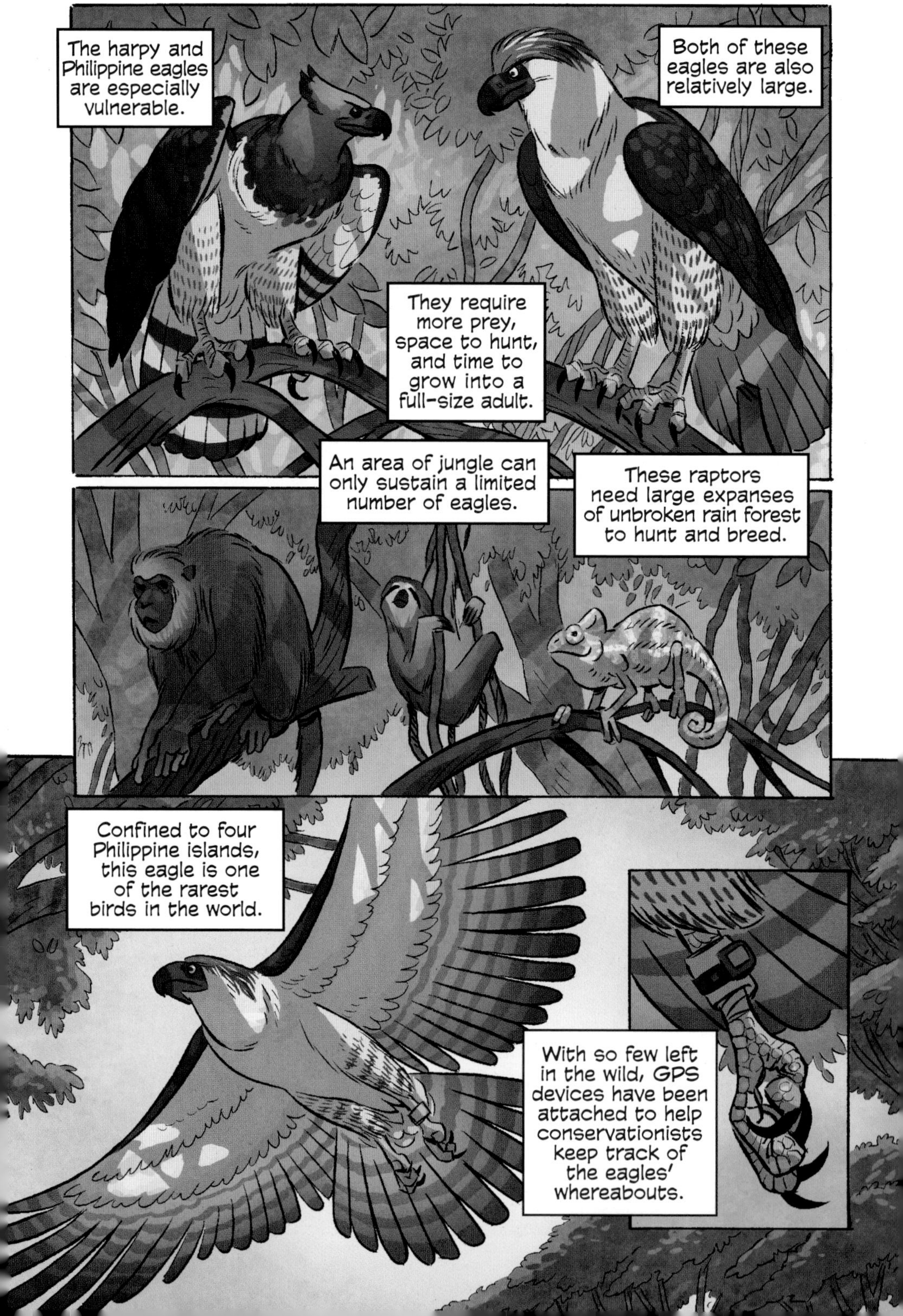
The harpy and Philippine eagles are especially vulnerable.
Both of these eagles are also relatively large.
They require more prey, space to hunt, and time to grow into a full-size adult.
An area of jungle can only sustain a limited number of eagles.
These raptors need large expanses of unbroken rain forest to hunt and breed.
Confined to four Philippine islands, this eagle is one of the rarest birds in the world.
With so few left in the wild, GPS devices have been attached to help conservationists keep track of the eagles' whereabouts.

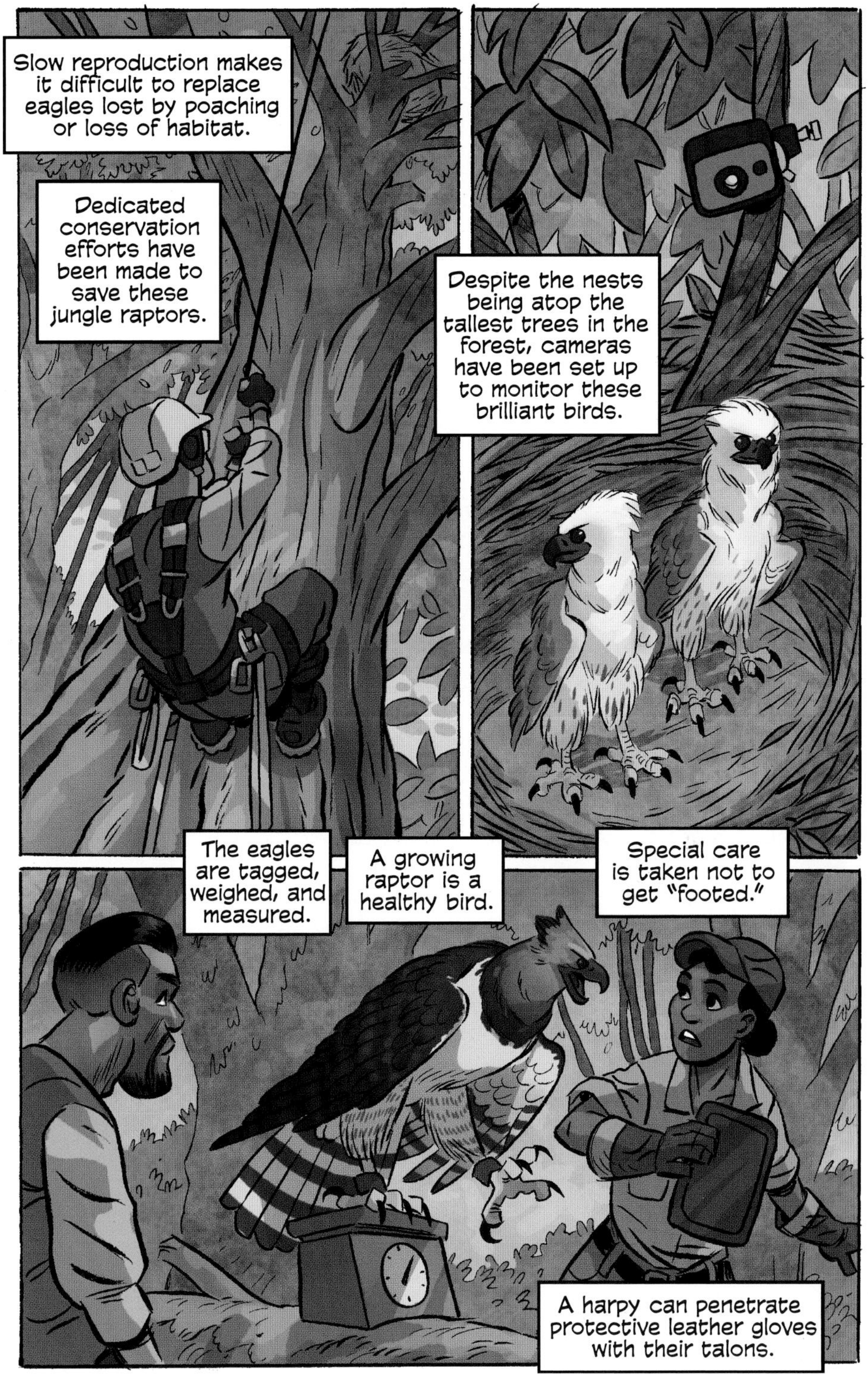
Slow reproduction makes it difficult to replace eagles lost by poaching or loss of habitat.
Dedicated conservation efforts have been made to save these jungle raptors.
Despite the nests being atop the tallest trees in the forest, cameras have been set up to monitor these brilliant birds.
The eagles are tagged, weighed, and measured.
A growing raptor is a healthy bird.
Special care is taken not to get "footed."
A harpy can penetrate protective leather gloves with their talons.

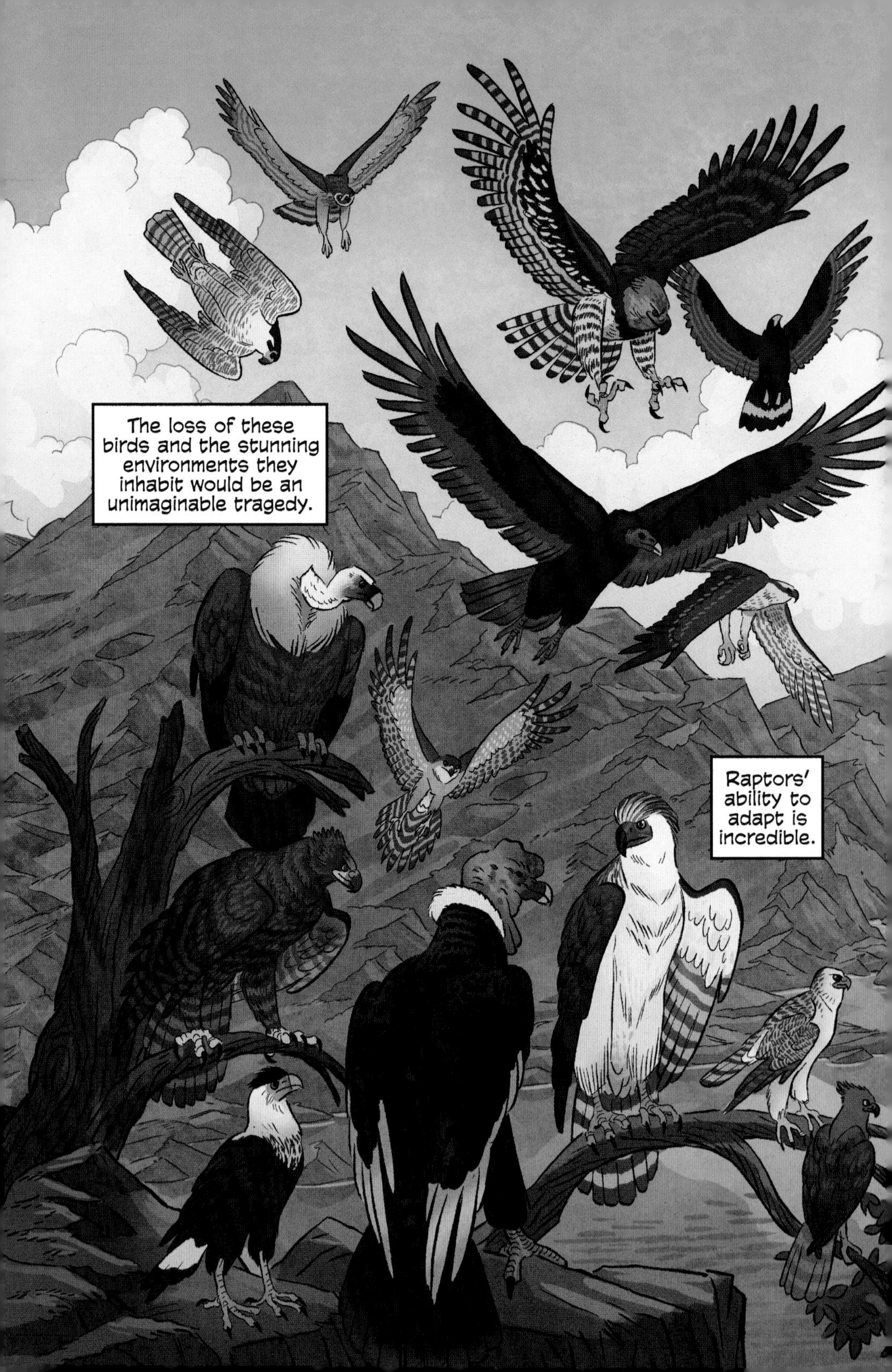
The loss of these birds and the stunning environments they inhabit would be an unimaginable tragedy.
Raptors' ability to adapt is incredible.

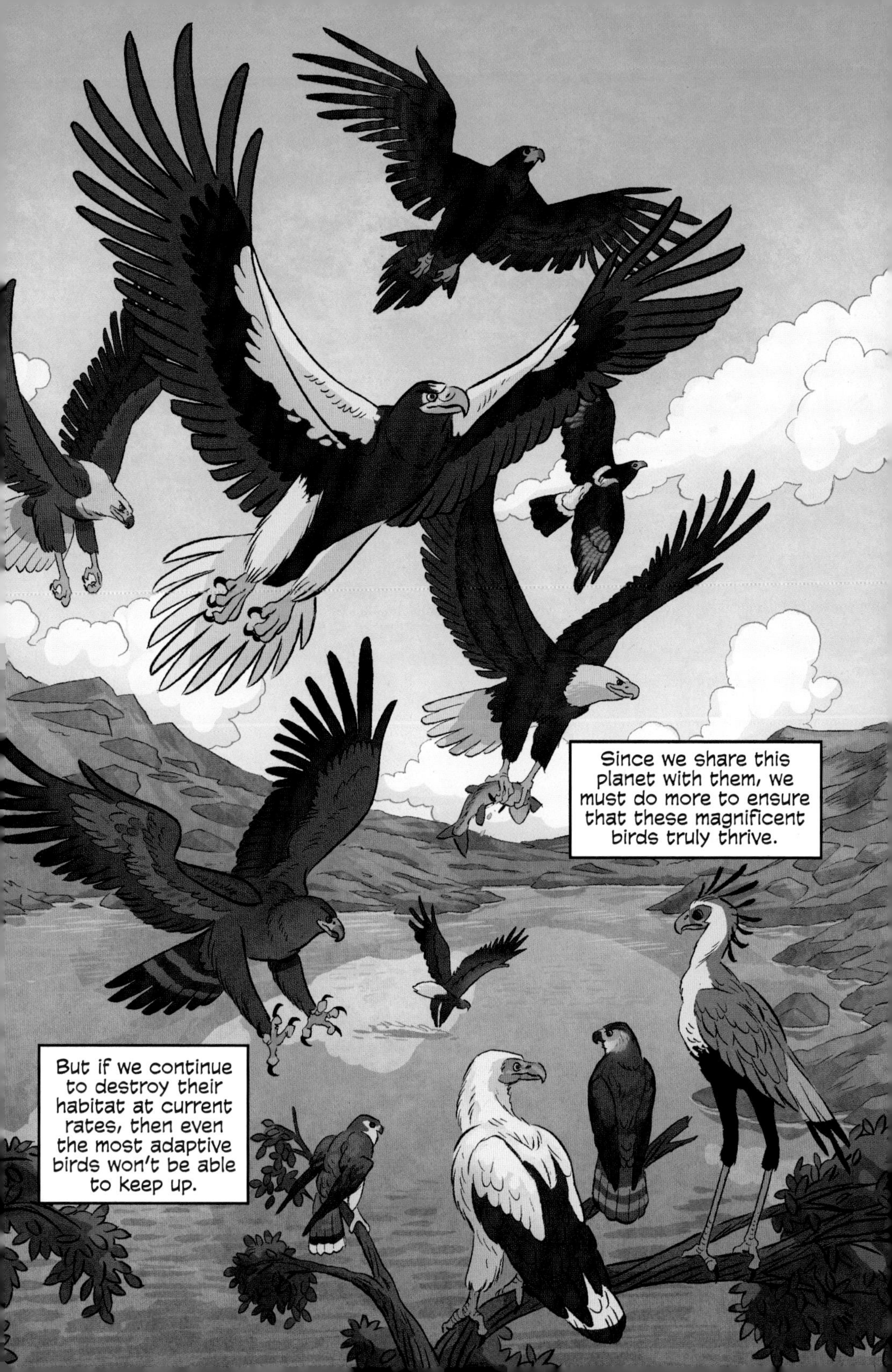
Since we share this planet with them, we must do more to ensure that these magnificent birds truly thrive.
But if we continue to destroy their habitat at current rates, then even the most adaptive birds won't be able to keep up.

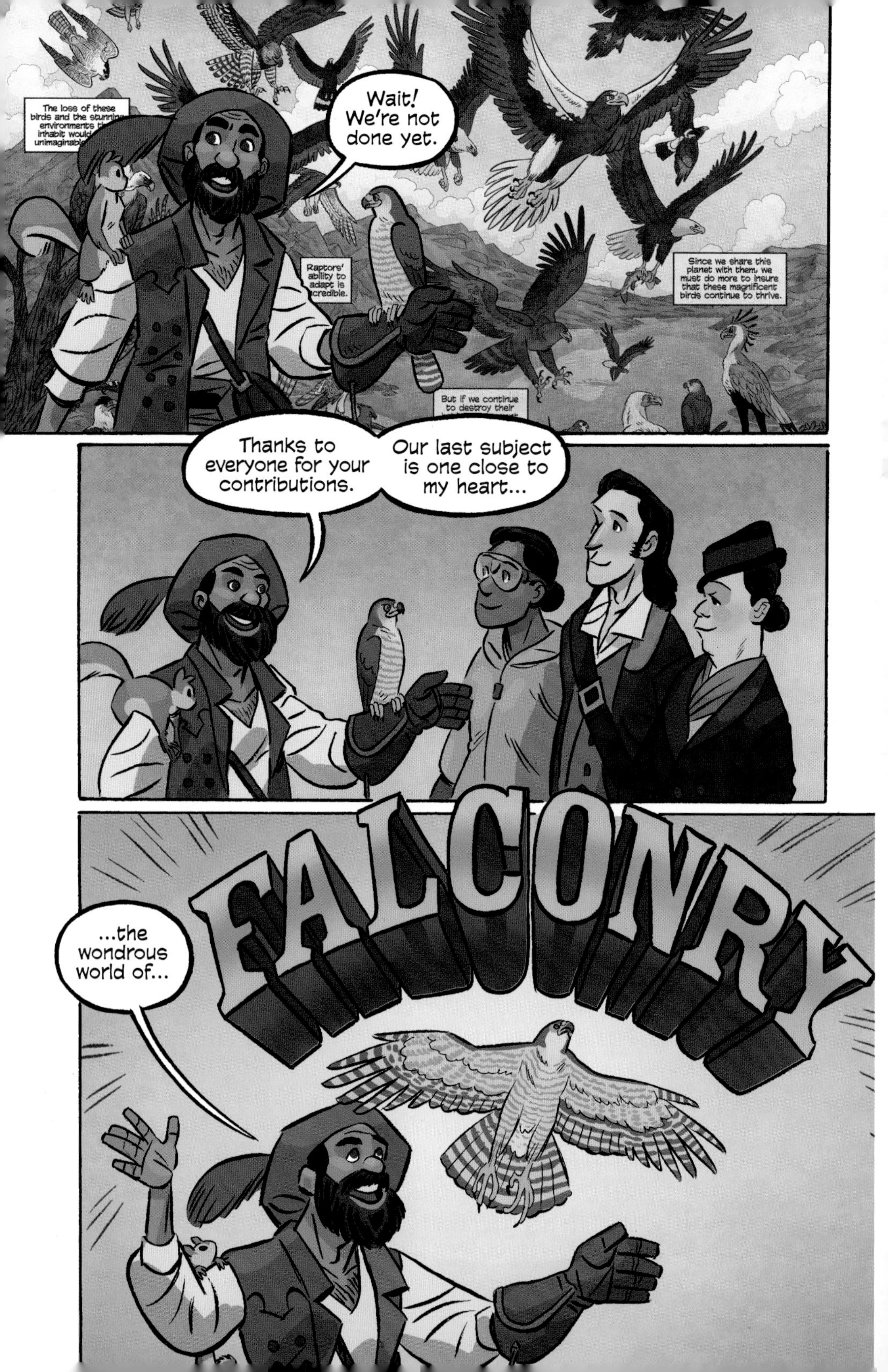

The loss of these birds and the stunnin environments t inhabit would unimaginabl
Wait! We're not done yet.
Raptors' ability to adapt is credible.
Since we share this planet with them, we must do more to insure that these magnificent birds continue to thrive.
But if we continue to destroy their
Thanks to everyone for your contributions.
Our last subject is one close to my heart...
...the wondrous world of...
FALCONRY

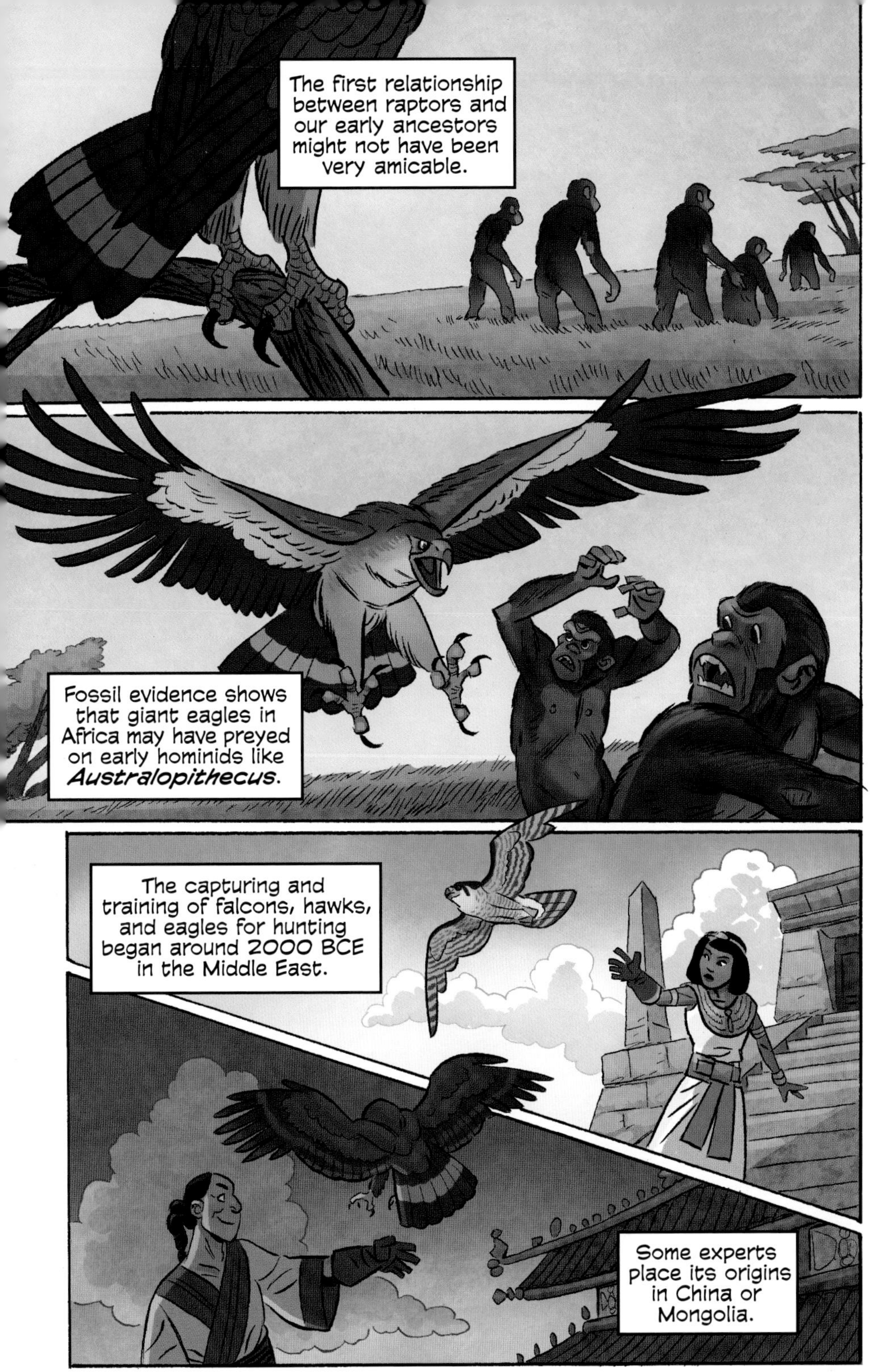
The first relationship between raptors and our early ancestors might not have been very amicable.
Fossil evidence shows that giant eagles in Africa may have preyed on early hominids like *Australopithecus*.
The capturing and training of falcons, hawks, and eagles for hunting began around 2000 BCE in the Middle East.
Some experts place its origins in China or Mongolia.

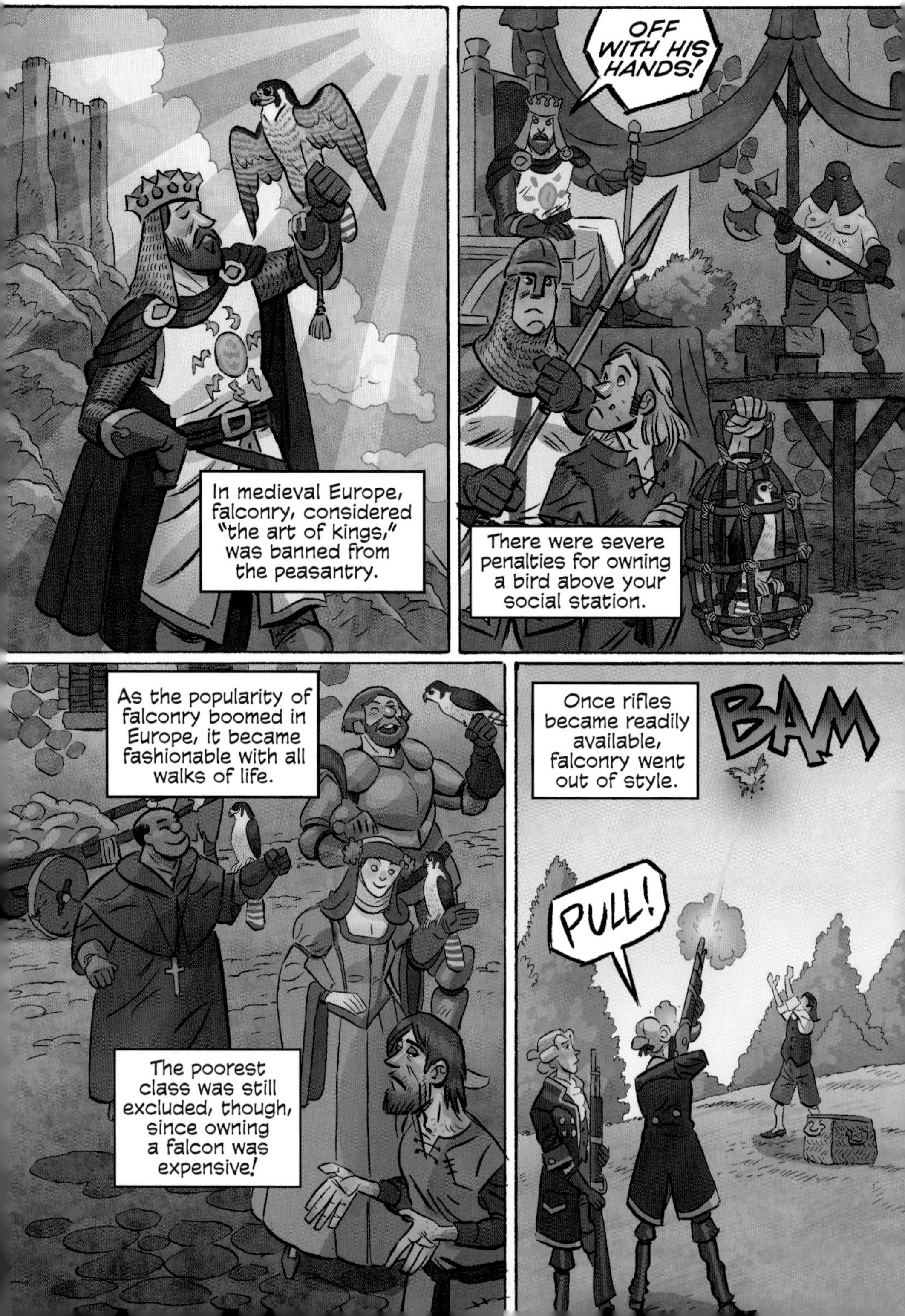
In medieval Europe, falconry, considered "the art of kings," was banned from the peasantry.
OFF WITH HIS HANDS!
There were severe penalties for owning a bird above your social station.
As the popularity of falconry boomed in Europe, it became fashionable with all walks of life.
The poorest class was still excluded, though, since owning a falcon was expensive!
Once rifles became readily available, falconry went out of style.
BAM
PULL!

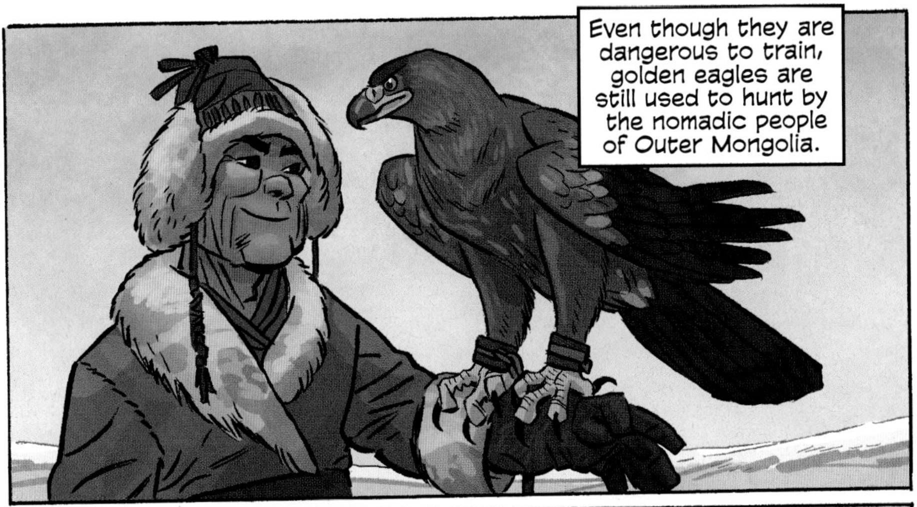
Even though they are dangerous to train, golden eagles are still used to hunt by the nomadic people of Outer Mongolia.

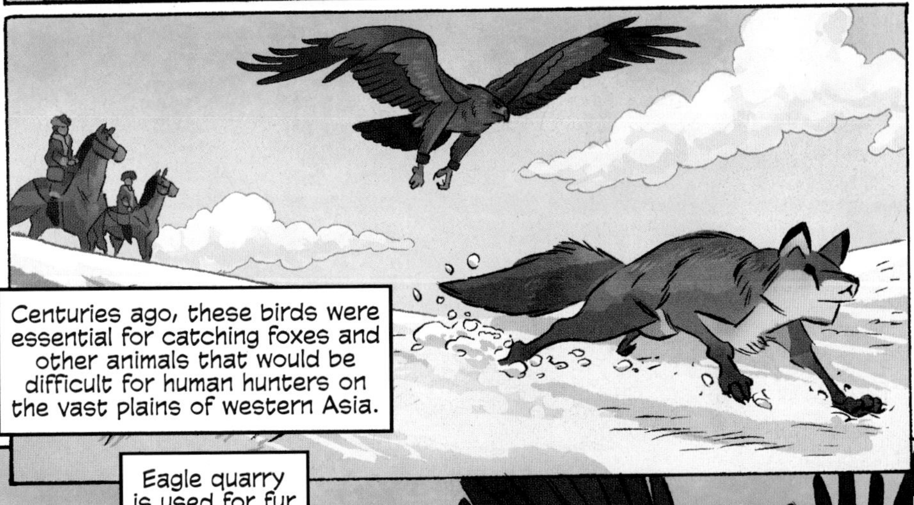
Centuries ago, these birds were essential for catching foxes and other animals that would be difficult for human hunters on the vast plains of western Asia.

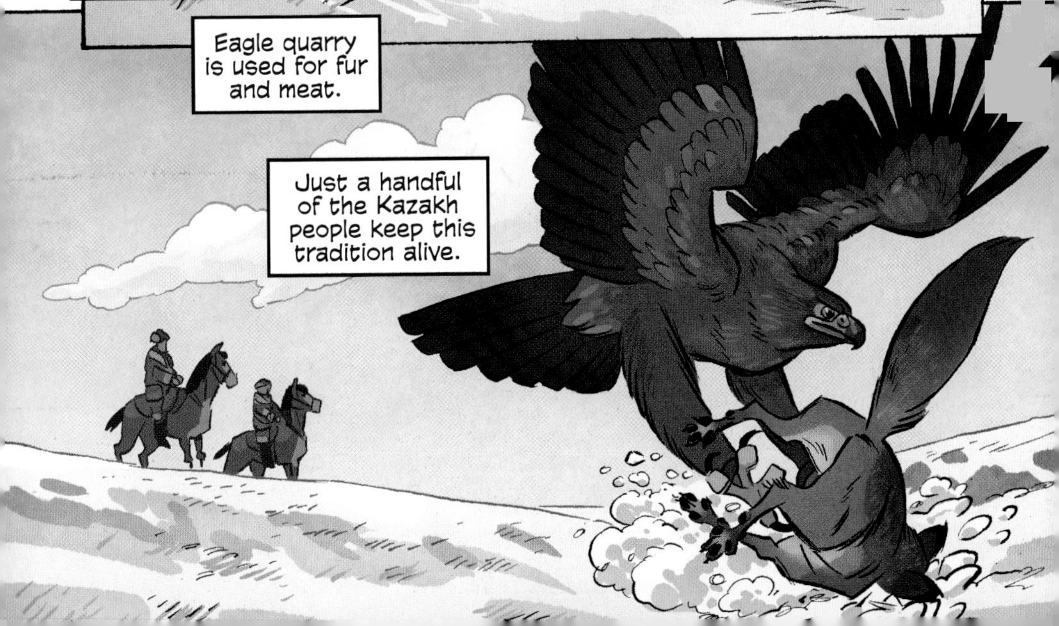
Eagle quarry is used for fur and meat.
Just a handful of the Kazakh people keep this tradition alive.

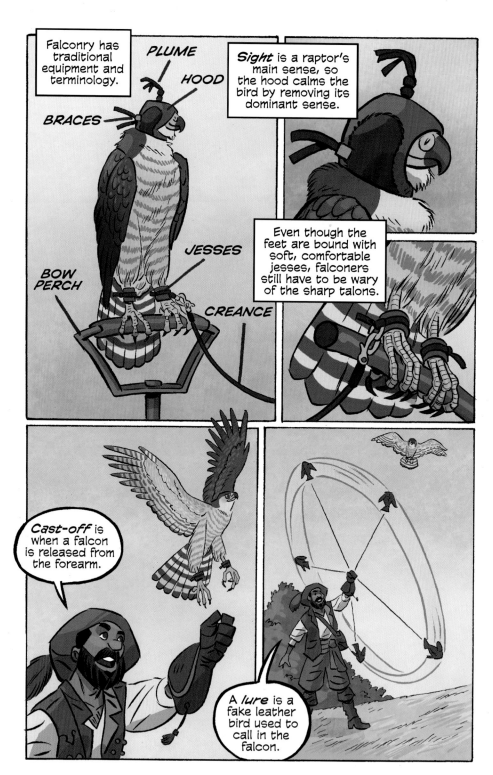

Falconry has traditional equipment and terminology.

PLUME

HOOD

BRACES

JESSES

BOW PERCH

CREANCE

Sight is a raptor's main sense, so the hood calms the bird by removing its dominant sense.

Even though the feet are bound with soft, comfortable jesses, falconers still have to be wary of the sharp talons.

Cast-off is when a falcon is released from the forearm.

A *lure* is a fake leather bird used to call in the falcon.

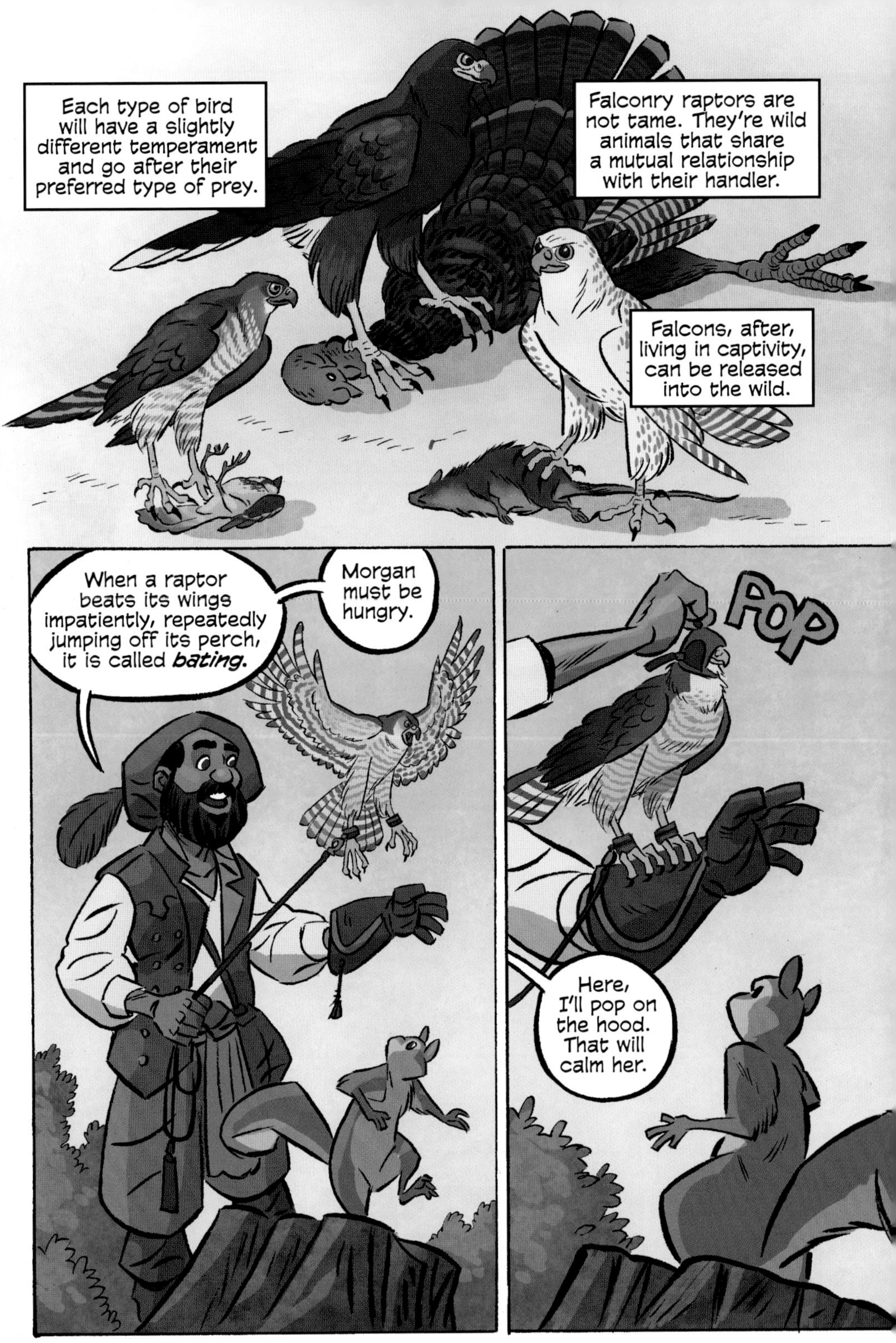
Each type of bird will have a slightly different temperament and go after their preferred type of prey.
Falconry raptors are not tame. They're wild animals that share a mutual relationship with their handler.
Falcons, after, living in captivity, can be released into the wild.
When a raptor beats its wings impatiently, repeatedly jumping off its perch, it is called *bating*.
Morgan must be hungry.
POP
Here, I'll pop on the hood. That will calm her.

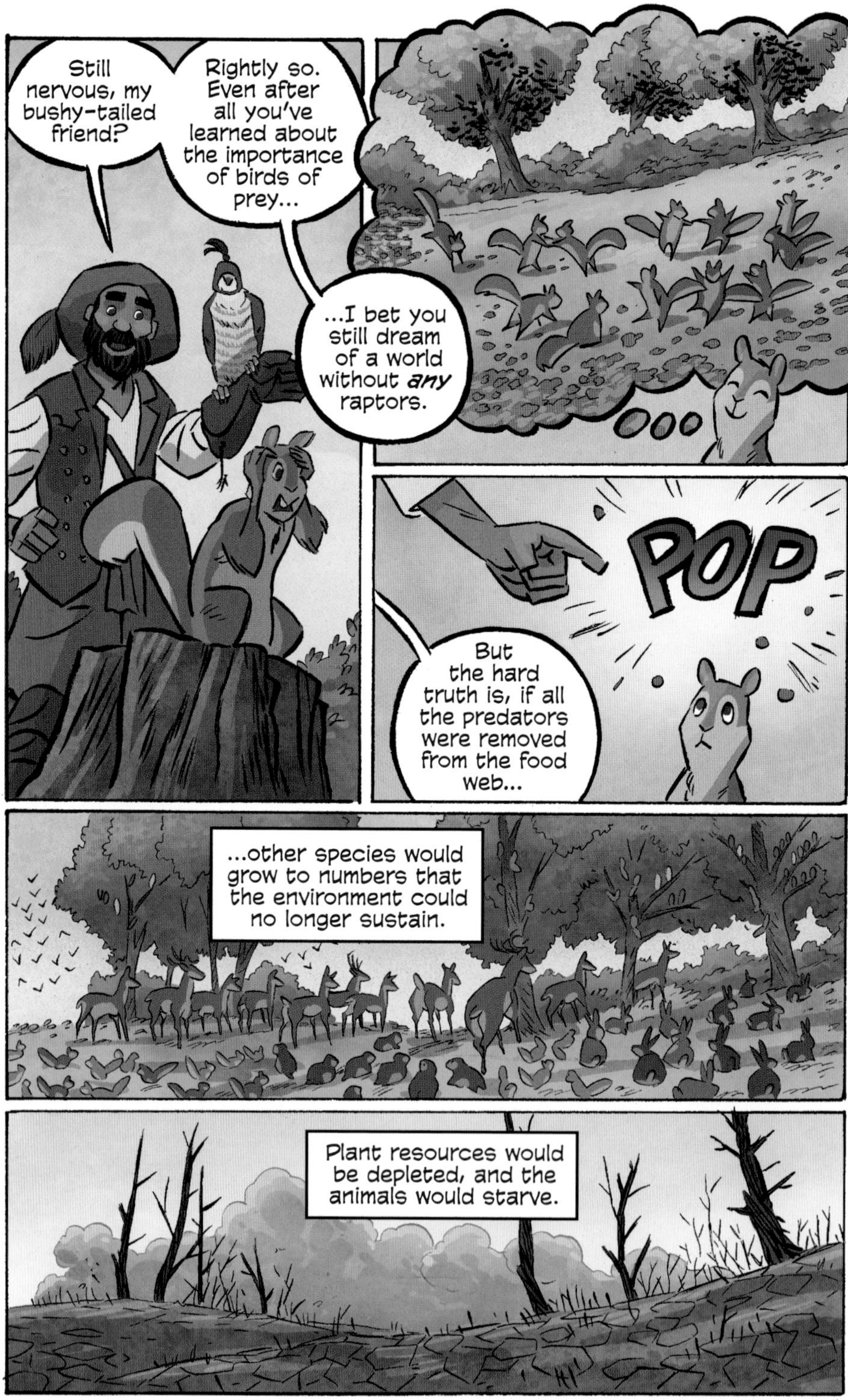

Still nervous, my bushy-tailed friend?
Rightly so. Even after all you've learned about the importance of birds of prey...
...I bet you still dream of a world without *any* raptors.
OOO
POP
But the hard truth is, if all the predators were removed from the food web...
...other species would grow to numbers that the environment could no longer sustain.
Plant resources would be depleted, and the animals would starve.

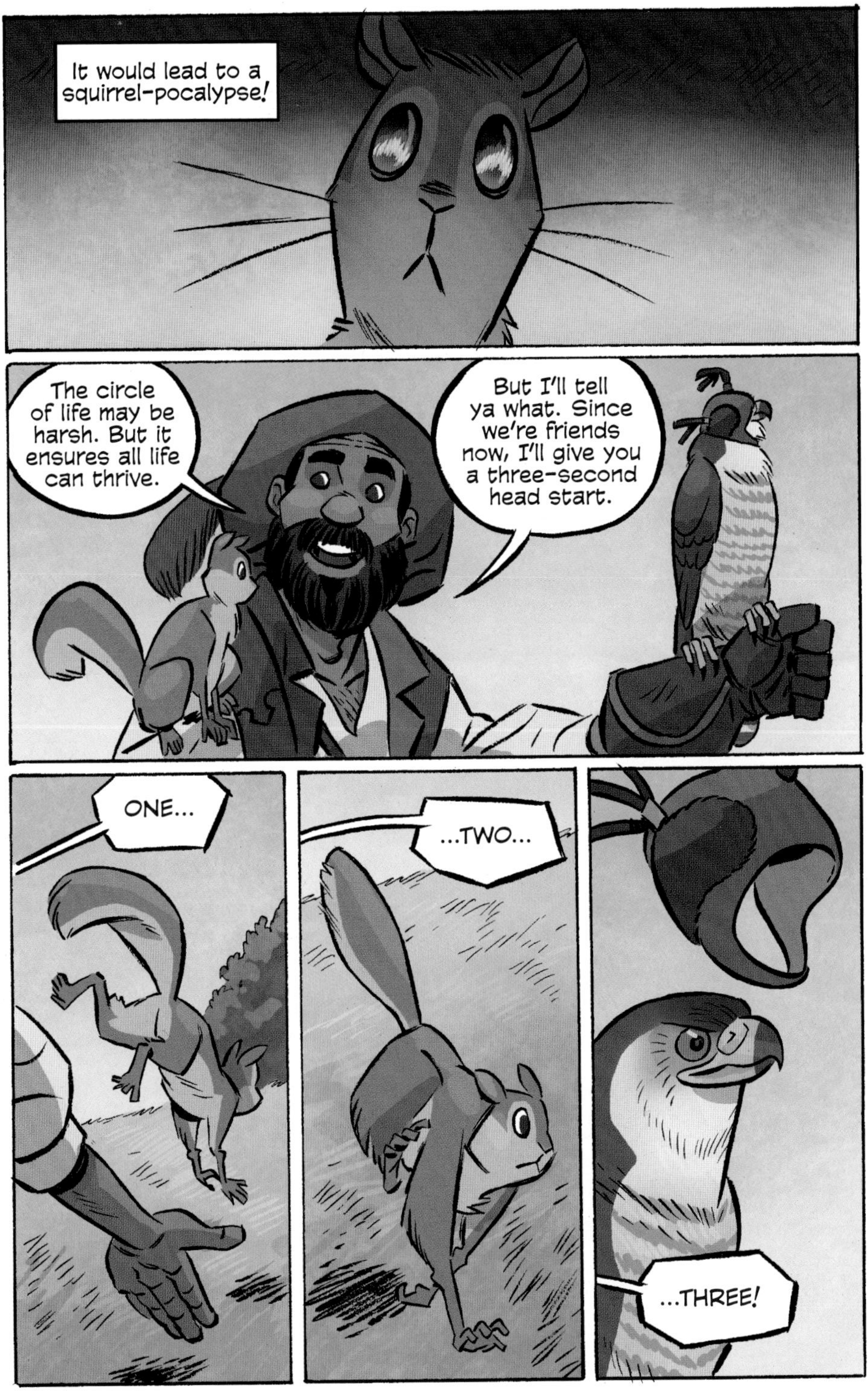
It would lead to a squirrel-pocalypse!
The circle of life may be harsh. But it ensures all life can thrive.
But I'll tell ya what. Since we're friends now, I'll give you a three-second head start.
ONE...
...TWO...
...THREE!

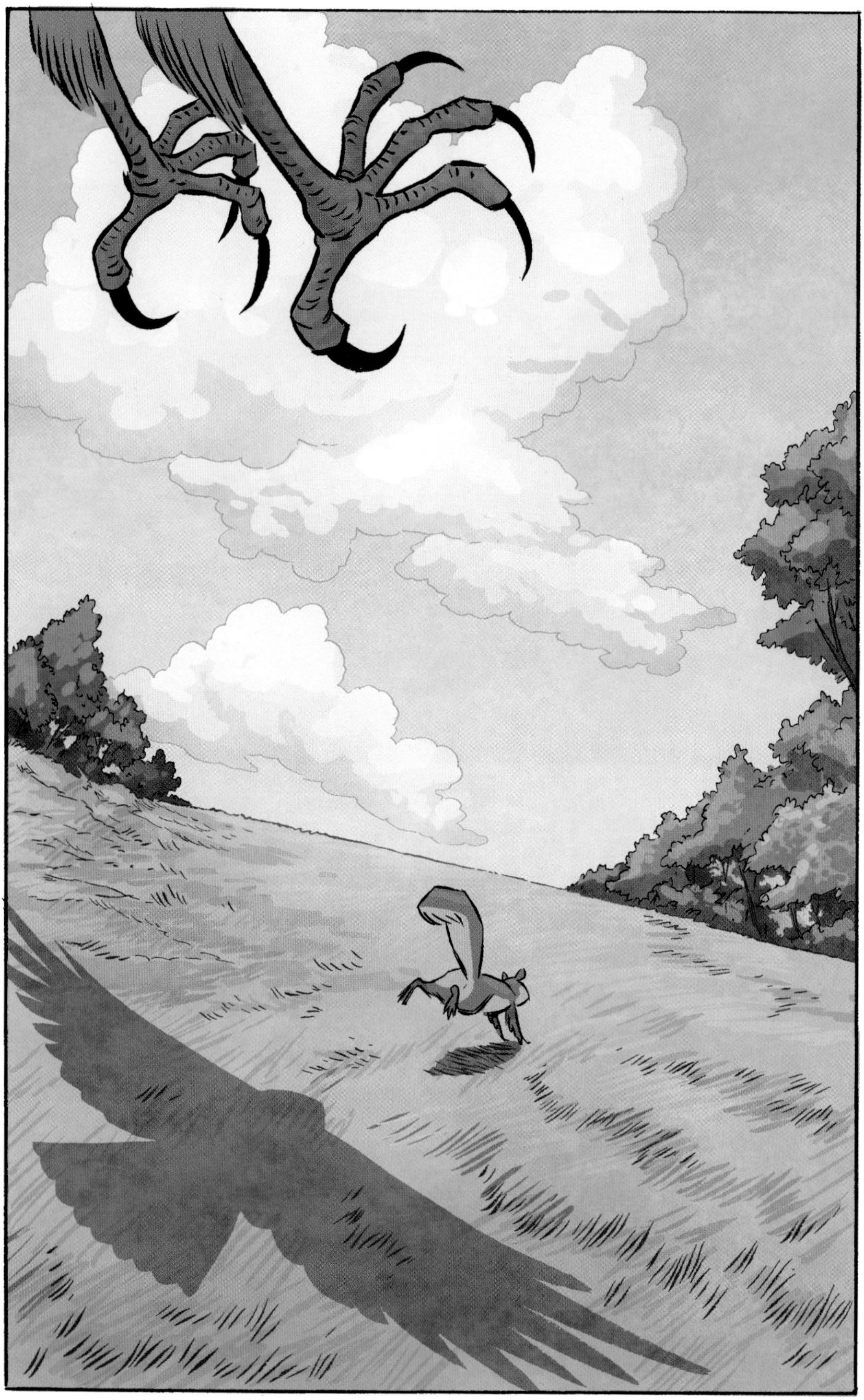

—GLOSSARY—

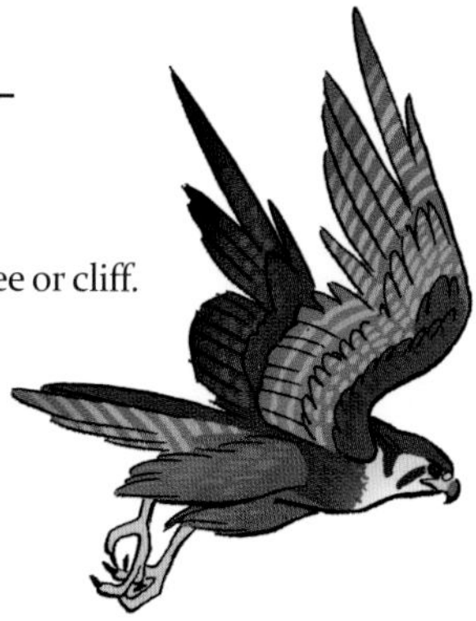

Aerie
The nest of a large bird of prey, often built on a high tree or cliff.

Apex predator
Top of the food chain; nothing else eats it.

Baffle
A structure used to change the flow of air or water.

Bating
The action of a bird attempting to fly from a perch or the fist while attached by a leash.

Bernoulli's law
An increase in the speed of a fluid occurs simultaneously with a decrease in static pressure or a decrease in the fluid's potential energy.

Carrion
The decaying flesh of dead animals; also known as a carcass.

Cere
A waxy fleshy covering at the base of the upper beak in some birds.

Convergent evolution
The process whereby organisms not closely genetically related, independently evolve similar traits as a result of having to adapt to similar environments or ecological niches.

Creance
A long, fine cord attached to a hawk's leash to prevent escape during training.

Dichlorodiphenyltrichloroethane (DDT)
This synthetic organic compound is used as an insecticide. Like other chlorinated aromatic hydrocarbons, DDT often breaks down into dichlorodiphenyldichloroethylene (DDE) and other derivatives that persist in the environment and can cause direct harm to animals at the head of the food chain.

Diurnal
Animals that are active chiefly in the daytime.

Ectotherm
An animal that is dependent on external sources of body heat; cold-blooded.

Endotherm
An animal that is dependent on or capable of the internal generation of heat; warm-blooded.

Environmental Protection Agency (EPA)
An independent executive agency of the United States federal government tasked with environmental protection matters.

Filaments
A slender, threadlike object or fiber, especially one found in animal or plant structures.

Fledgling
A young bird that has its feathers and is learning to fly.

Follicle
A small organ found just under the skin often used to house the hair or feathers of certain animals.

Imprinting
Learning process that takes place early in the life of birds and other social animals. Imprinting establishes behavior patterns such as recognition of and attraction to an animal's own kind or a substitute caregiver.

Jesses
Thin straps, traditionally made from leather, used to tether a hawk or falcon in falconry.

Keratin
A protein, less prone to scratching or tearing than other types of cells, often used as a protective coating on animals.

Mandible
The upper or lower jaw of an animal.

Migration
Movement from one region to another based on season or environmental changes.

Molt
To shed old feathers, hair, skin, or shell, to make way for the new growth of an animal.

Newton's Third Law
For every action (force) in nature, there is an equal and opposite reaction.

Nictitating membrane
A whitish or translucent membrane that forms an inner eyelid in birds, reptiles, and some mammals. It can be drawn across the eye to protect it from dust and keep it moist.

—GLOSSARY CONTINUED—

Ornithology
The scientific study of birds.

Pectoralis
A thick, fan-shaped muscle, situated at the chest of a bird.

Photoreceptors
A structure in a living organism, especially a sensory cell or sense organ, that responds to light falling on it.

Semi-zygodactyl
Having an arrangement of toes where the outer toe can be switched to face either forward or backward by the bird. Seen in ospreys and owls.

Sexual dimorphism
Distinct difference in size or appearance between the sexes of an animal.

Spicules
Any of various small spine-shaped anatomical structures occurring in organisms.

Stoop
The downward swoop or dive of a bird of prey.

Supraorbital ridge
A ridge of bone just above the eyes on the skull of certain animals.

Taxonomy
The branch of science concerned with classification of all living things.

Tendons
A flexible but inelastic cord of strong fibrous collagen tissue attaching a muscle to a bone.

Thermal
A column of rising air in the lower altitudes of Earth's atmosphere.

Tundra
A vast, flat, treeless Arctic region of Europe, Asia, and North America in which the subsoil is permanently frozen.

Vertebrae
One of the small bones that make up the spine.